Microsoft®
MCSE
Readiness Review

Exam 70-067
Microsoft Windows NT®
Server 4.0

Microsoft Press

PUBLISHED BY
Microsoft Press
A Division of Microsoft Corporation
One Microsoft Way
Redmond, Washington 98052-6399

Library of Congress Cataloging-in-Publication Data
MCSE Readiness Review—Exam 70-067: Microsoft Windows NT Server 4.0 /
 Ethan Wilansky.
      p. cm.
   Includes index.
   ISBN 0-7356-0538-6
   1. Electronic data processing personnel--Certification.
   2. Microsoft software--Examinations--Study guides.   3. Microsoft
Windows NT Server.   I. Microsoft Corporation.
QA76.3.M33254   1998
005.4'4769--dc21
                                                   98-39271
                                                      CIP

Printed and bound in the United States of America.

   3 4 5 6 7 8 9   MLML   4 3 2 1 0 9

Distributed in Canada by ITP Nelson, a division of Thomson Canada Limited.

A CIP catalogue record for this book is available from the British Library.

Microsoft Press books are available through booksellers and distributors worldwide. For further information about international editions, contact your local Microsoft Corporation office or contact Microsoft Press International directly at fax (425) 936-7329. Visit our Web site at mspress.microsoft.com.

Program Manager: Jeff Madden
Project Editor: Michael Bolinger

Contents

Welcome to Microsoft Windows NT Server 4.0

Welcome to *MCSE Readiness Review—Exam 70-067: Microsoft Windows NT Server 4.0*. The Readiness Review series gives you a focused, timesaving way to identify the information you need to know to pass the Microsoft Certified Professional (MCP) exams. The series combines a realistic electronic assessment with a review book to help you become familiar with the types of questions you will encounter on the MCP exam. By reviewing the objectives and sample questions, you can focus on the specific skills that you need to improve before taking the exam.

This book helps you evaluate your readiness for the MCP Exam 70-067: Implementing and Supporting Microsoft Windows NT Server 4.0. When you pass this exam, you earn core credit toward the Microsoft Certified Systems Engineer (MCSE) certification or the Microsoft Certified Systems Engineer + Internet certification.

Note You can find a complete list of MCP exams and their related objectives on the Microsoft Certified Professional Web site at http://www.microsoft.com/mcp.

The Readiness Review series lets you identify any areas in which you may need additional training. To help you get the training you need to successfully pass the certification exams, Microsoft Press publishes a complete line of self-paced training kits and other study materials. For comprehensive information about the topics covered in the Implementing and Supporting Microsoft Windows NT Server 4.0 exam, you might want to see the corresponding training kits—*Microsoft Windows NT Technical Support Training* kit and the *Microsoft Windows NT Network Administration Training* kit.

Before You Begin

This MCSE Readiness Review consists of two main parts: the Readiness Review electronic assessment on the accompanying compact disc, and this Readiness Review book.

The Readiness Review Components

The electronic assessment is a practice certification exam that helps you evaluate your skills. It provides instant scoring feedback, so you can determine areas in which additional study may be helpful before you take the certification exam. Although your score on the electronic assessment does not necessarily indicate what your score will be on the certification exam, it does give you the opportunity to answer questions that are similar to those on the actual certification exam.

The Readiness Review book is organized by the exam's objectives. Each chapter of the book pertains to one of the six primary groups of objectives on the actual exam, called the *Objective Domains*. Each Objective Domain lists the tested skills that you need to master to adequately answer the exam questions. Because the certification exams focus on real-world skills, the tested skills lists provide suggested practices that emphasize the practical application of the exam objectives.

Within each Objective Domain you will find the related objectives that are covered on the exam. Each objective provides you with the following:

- Key terms you must know in order to understand the objective, which can help you answer the objective's questions correctly.

- Several sample exam questions with the correct answers. The answers are accompanied by discussions as to why each answer is correct or incorrect. (These questions match the questions you find on the electronic assessment.)

- Suggestions for further reading or additional resources to help you understand the objective and increase your ability to perform the task or skills specified by the objective.

You use the electronic assessment to determine the exam objectives that you need to study, and then use the Readiness Review book to learn more about those particular objectives and discover additional study materials to supplement your knowledge. You can also use the Readiness Review book to research the answers to specific sample test questions. Keep in mind that to pass the exam, you should understand not only the answer to the question, but also the concepts on which the correct answer is based.

MCP Exam Prerequisites

No exams or classes are required before you take the Implementing and Supporting Microsoft Windows NT Server 4.0 exam. However, in addition to the Windows NT configuration and support skills tested by the exam, you should have a working knowledge of the operation and support of hardware and software in standalone computers. This knowledge should include:

- Using an operating system with a graphical user interface, such as Microsoft Windows 95, Microsoft Windows 98, or Microsoft Windows NT 4.0.

- Using major networking components, including clients, servers, network adapter cards, drivers, protocols, and network operating systems.

- Installing hardware, such as memory, communication peripherals, and disk drives.

- Supporting networks and end users.

Note After you have used the Readiness Review and determined that you are ready for the exam, see the "Test Registration and Fees" section in the Appendix for information on scheduling for the exam. You can schedule exams up to six weeks in advance, or as late as one working day before the exam date.

Know the Products

Microsoft's certification program relies on exams that measure your ability to perform a specific job function or set of tasks. Microsoft develops the exams by analyzing the tasks performed by people who are currently performing the job function to be tested. Therefore, the specific knowledge, skills, and abilities relating to the job are reflected in each certification exam.

Because the certification exams are based on real-world tasks, you need to gain hands-on experience with the applicable technology in order to master the exam. You might consider hands-on experience in an organizational environment to be a prerequisite for passing an MCP exam, or pursue MCSE training on Microsoft products. Many of the questions relate directly to Microsoft products or technology, so use opportunities at your organization or home to practice using the relevant tools.

Using the MCSE Readiness Review

Although you can use the Readiness Review in a number of ways, you might start your studies by taking the electronic assessment as a pretest. After completing the exam, review your results for each Objective Domain and focus your studies first on the Objective Domains where you received the lowest scores. The electronic assessment allows you to print your results, and a printed report of how you fared can be useful when reviewing the exam material in this book.

After you have taken the Readiness Review electronic assessment, use the Readiness Review book to learn more about the Objective Domains that you find difficult and to find listings of appropriate study materials that may supplement your knowledge. By reviewing why the answers are correct or incorrect, you can determine if you made a simple comprehension error or if you need to study the objective topics more.

Alternatively, you can use the Learn Now feature of the electronic assessment to review your answer to each question. This feature provides you with the correct answer and a reference to the *Microsoft Windows NT Technical Support Training* kit (purchased separately) or other resources. If you use this method, and you need additional information to understand an answer, you can also reference the question in the Readiness Review book.

You can also use the Readiness Review book to focus on the exact objectives that you need to master. Each objective in the book contains several questions that help you determine if you understand the information related to that particular skill. The book is also designed for you to try to answer each question before turning the page to look up the correct answer.

The best method to prepare for the MCP exam is to use the Readiness Review book in conjunction with the electronic assessment and other study material. Lots of study and lots of practice combined with a lot of real-world experience can help you fully prepare for the MCP exam.

Understanding the Readiness Review Conventions

Before you start using the Readiness Review, it is important that you understand the terms and conventions used in the electronic assessment and book.

Question Numbering System

The Readiness Review electronic assessment and book contain reference numbers for each question. Understanding the numbering format will help you use the Readiness Review more effectively. When Microsoft creates the exams, the questions are grouped by job skills called *Objectives*. These Objectives are then organized by sections known as Objective Domains. Each question can be identified by the Objective Domain and Objective it covers. The question numbers follow this format:

Test Number.Objective Domain.Objective.Question Number

For example, question number 70-067.02.01.003 means this is question three (3) for Objective one (1) in Objective Domain two (2) of the Implementing and Supporting Microsoft Windows NT Server 4.0 exam (70-067). Refer to the "Exam Objectives Summary" section later in this introduction to locate the numbers associated with particular objectives. Each question is numbered based on its presentation in the printed book. You can use this numbering system to reference questions on the electronic assessment or in the Readiness Review book. Even though the questions in the book are organized by objective, you will see questions in random order during the electronic assessment and actual certification exam.

Notational Conventions

- Characters or commands that you type appear in **bold** type.

- Variable information is *italicized*. *Italic* is also used to identify new terms and book titles.

- Acronyms appear in FULL CAPITALS.

Notes

Notes appear throughout the book.

- Notes marked **Note** contain supplementary or needed information.

- Notes marked **Caution** contain warnings regarding potential information loss or system error.

Icons

The following table describes the icons that are used throughout this book.

Icon	Description
	References a book resource that contains more information pertinent to the discussed subject.
	References a compact disc resource that contains more information pertinent to the discussed subject.
	References a Microsoft Press Training kit or Resource Kit that contains more information pertinent to the discussed subject.
	References a Web site that contains more information pertinent to the discussed subject.

Using the Readiness Review Electronic Assessment

The Readiness Review electronic assessment is designed to provide you with an experience that simulates that of the actual MCP exam. The electronic assessment material mirrors the type and nature of the questions you will see on the certification exam. Furthermore, the electronic assessment format approximates the certification exam format and includes additional features to help you prepare for the real examination.

Each iteration of the electronic assessment consists of 60 questions covering all the objectives for the Implementing and Supporting Microsoft Windows NT Server 4.0 exam. (The actual certification exams generally consist of 50 to 70 questions.) Just like a real certification exam, you see questions from the objectives in random order during the practice test. Similar to the certification exam, the electronic assessment allows you to mark questions and review them after you finish the test.

To increase its value as a study aid, you can take the electronic assessment multiple times. Each time you are presented with a different set of questions in a revised order; however, some questions may be repeated from exams you may have taken earlier.

If you have used one of the certification exam preparation tests available from Microsoft, then the Readiness Review electronic assessment should look familiar. The difference is that the electronic assessment covers more questions, and it provides you with the ability to learn as you take the exam.

Installing and Running the Electronic Assessment Software

Before you begin using the electronic assessment, you need to install the software. You need a computer with the following minimum configuration:

- 486 or higher Intel-based processor (486 must be running in Enhanced Mode).

- Microsoft Windows 95 or later (including Windows NT).

- 4 MB of RAM.

- 15 MB of available disk space.

- CD-ROM drive

- Mouse or other pointing device (recommended).

▶ **To install the electronic assessment**

1. Insert the Readiness Review compact disc into your CD-ROM drive.

2. From the root directory of the compact disc, open the Assess folder and double-click the Setup.exe file.

   A dialog box appears indicating you will install the MCSE Readiness Review test.

3. Click Next.

The Select Destination Directory dialog box appears showing a default installation directory (named C:\MP067, where C: is the name assigned to your hard disk).

4. Either accept the default or change the installation directory if needed, and then click Next.

The electronic assessment software installs.

Note These procedures describe using the electronic assessment on a Windows 95, Windows 98, or Windows NT 4.0–based computer.

▶ **To start the electronic assessment**

1. From the Start menu, point to Programs, point to MCSE Readiness Review, and then click (70-067) Windows NT Server 4.0.

The electronic assessment program starts.

2. Click Start Test, or from the main menu, double-click the test name.

Information about the MCSE Readiness Review series appears.

3. Click Start Test.

Taking the Electronic Assessment

The Readiness Review electronic assessment consists of 60 multiple-choice questions, and like the certification exam, you can skip, or mark, questions for later review. Each exam question contains a reference number that you can use to refer back to the Readiness Review book, and, if you want, you can pause and continue taking the exam at a later time. Before you end the electronic assessment you should make sure to answer all the questions. When the exam is graded, unanswered questions are counted as incorrect and will lower your score. Similarly, on the actual certification exam you should complete all questions or they will be counted as incorrect.

No trick questions appear on the exam. The correct answer will always be among the list of choices. Some questions may require more than one response, and this will be indicated in the question. A good strategy is to eliminate the most obvious incorrect answers first to make it easier for you to select the correct answer.

You have 75 minutes to complete the electronic assessment. During the exam you will see a timer indicating the amount of time you have remaining. This will help you to gauge the amount of time you should use to answer each question and to complete the exam. The amount of time you are given on the actual certification exam varies with each exam. Generally, certification exams take approximately 90 minutes to complete.

During the electronic assessment, you can find the answer to any question by clicking the Learn Now button as you review the question. You see the correct answer, and a reference to the applicable section of the Microsoft Press *Microsoft Windows NT Network Administration Training* kit, *Microsoft Windows NT Technical Support Training Kit,* or other resources, which can be purchased separately.

Ending and Grading the Electronic Assessment

By clicking the Grade Now button, you have the opportunity to review the questions you marked or left incomplete. This format is similar to the one used on the actual certification exam. When you are satisfied with your answers, click the Grade Test button. The electronic assessment is graded, and the software presents your section scores and total score.

Note You can always end a test without grading your electronic assessment by clicking the Quit Test button.

After your electronic assessment is graded, you can view a list of Microsoft Press references by clicking the Review Incorrect Answers button. You can then click OK to view the questions you have missed.

Interpreting the Electronic Assessment Results

The Section Scoring screen shows you the number of questions in each Objective Domain section, the number of questions you answered correctly, and a percentage grade for each section. You can use the Section Scoring screen to determine where to spend additional time studying. On the actual certification exam, the number of questions and passing score will depend on the exam you are taking. The electronic assessment records your score each time you grade an exam so you can track your progress over time.

▶   **To view your progress and exam records**

1. From the electronic assessment main menu, select File, then select History, and then choose View.

2. Click View History.

   Each attempt score and your total score appears.

3. Select an attempt, and then click View Details.

   The section score for each attempt appears. You can review the section score information to determine which Objective Domains you should study further. You can also use the scores to determine your progress as you continue to study and prepare for the real exam.

Ordering More Questions

Self Test Software offers practice tests to help you prepare for a variety of MCP certification exams. These practice tests contain hundreds of additional questions and are similar to the Readiness Review electronic assessment. For a fee, you can order exam practice tests for this exam and other Microsoft certification exams. Click on the To Order More Questions button on the electronic assessment main menu for more information.

Using the Readiness Review Book

You can use the Readiness Review book as a supplement to the Readiness Review electronic assessment, or as a standalone study aid. If you decide to use the book as a standalone study aid, review the Table of Contents or the list of objectives to find topics of interest or an appropriate starting point for you. To get the greatest benefit from the book, use the electronic assessment as a pretest to determine the Objective Domains where you should spend the most study time. Or, if you would like to research specific questions while taking the electronic assessment, you can use the question number located on the question screen to reference the question number in the Readiness Review book.

One way to determine areas where additional study may be helpful is to carefully review your individual section scores from the electronic assessment and note objective areas where your score could be improved. The section scores correlate to the Objective Domains listed in the Readiness Review book.

Reviewing the Objectives

Each Objective Domain in the book contains an introduction and a list of practice skills. Each list of practice skills describes suggested tasks you can perform to help you understand the objectives. Some of the tasks suggest reading additional material, while others are hands-on practices with software or hardware. You should pay particular attention to the hands-on suggestions, as the certification exam reflects real-world knowledge you can gain only by working with the software or technology. Increasing your real-world experience with the relevant products and technologies will greatly enhance your performance on the exam.

Once you have determined the objectives you would like to study, you can use the Table of Contents to locate the objectives in the Readiness Review book. When reviewing a specific objective, you should make sure you understand the purpose of the objective, and the skill or knowledge it is measuring on the certification exam. You can study each objective separately, but you may need to understand the concepts explained in other objectives.

Make sure you understand the key terms for each objective. You will need a thorough understanding of these terms to answer the objective's questions correctly. Key term definitions are located in the Glossary of this book.

Reviewing the Questions

Each odd-numbered page contains one or two questions, followed by the possible answers. After you review the question and select a probable answer, you can turn to the following page to determine if you answered the question correctly. (For information about the question numbering format, see "Question Numbering System" earlier in this introduction.)

The Readiness Review briefly discusses each possible answer and provides a specific reason why each answer is correct or incorrect. You should review the discussion of each possible answer to help you understand why the correct answer is the best answer among the choices given. You should understand not only the answer to the question, but the concepts on which the correct answer is based. If you feel you need more information about a topic or you do not understand the answer, use the Further Reading section in each objective to learn where you can find more information.

The answers to the questions in the Readiness Review are based on current industry specifications and standards. However, the information provided by the answers is subject to change as technology improves and changes.

Exam Objectives Summary

The Implementing and Supporting Microsoft Windows NT Server 4.0 certification exam (Exam 70-067) measures your ability to implement, administer, and trouble-shoot information systems that incorporate Windows NT Server version 4.0 in a simple computing environment. Such an environment might include one or more servers, a single domain, and a single location; and it might have file-sharing and print-sharing capabilities. Before taking the exam, you should be proficient in the job skills discussed in the following sections. These sections provide the exam ob-jectives and the corresponding objective numbers (which you can use to reference the questions in the Readiness Review electronic assessment and book) grouped by Objective Domains.

Objective Domain 1: Planning

The objectives in Objective Domain 1 are as follows:

- Objective 1.1 (70-067.01.01)—Choose a file system.

- Objective 1.2 (70-067.01.02)—Choose a fault-tolerance method.

- Objective 1.3 (70-067.01.03)—Choose a protocol for various situations.

Objective Domain 2: Installation and Configuration

The objectives in Objective Domain 2 are as follows:

- Objective 2.1 (70-067.02.01)—Install Windows NT Server on x86-based (CISC) platforms.

- Objective 2.2 (70-067.02.02)—Install Windows NT Server using various installa-tion methods and procedures.

- Objective 2.3 (70-067.02.03)—Install Windows NT Server to serve a variety of roles.

- Objective 2.4 (70-067.02.04)—Install the most common network protocols and configure protocol binding order and activity.

- Objective 2.5 (70-067.02.05)—Configure network adapters.

- Objective 2.6 (70-067.02.06)—Configure Windows NT Server core services.

- Objective 2.7 (70-067.02.07)—Configure peripherals and devices.

- Objective 2.8 (70-067.02.08)—Configure hard disks to meet various requirements.

- Objective 2.9 (70-067.02.09)—Configure printers.

- Objective 2.10 (70-067.02.10)—Configure a Windows NT Server computer for access by various types of clients.

Objective Domain 3: Managing Resources

The objectives in Objective Domain 3 are as follows:

- Objective 3.1 (70-067.03.01)—Manage user and group accounts.

- Objective 3.2 (70-067.03.02)—Create and manage policies and profiles for various situations.

- Objective 3.3 (70-067.03.03)—Administer remote servers from various types of clients.

- Objective 3.4 (70-067.03.04)—Manage disk resources.

Objective Domain 4: Connectivity

The objectives in Objective Domain 4 are as follows:

- Objective 4.1 (70-067.04.01)—Configure Windows NT Server for interoperability with NetWare servers by using various tools.

- Objective 4.2 (70-067.04.02)—Install and configure Remote Access Service (RAS).

Objective Domain 5: Monitoring and Optimization

The objectives in Objective Domain 5 are as follows:

- Objective 5.1 (70-067.05.01)—Monitor performance of various functions by using Performance Monitor.

- Objective 5.2 (70-067.05.02)—Identify performance bottlenecks.

Objective Domain 6: Troubleshooting

The objectives in Objective Domain 6 are as follows:

- Objective 6.1 (70-067.06.01)—Choose the appropriate course of action to take to resolve installation failures.

- Objective 6.2 (70-067.06.02)—Choose the appropriate course of action to take to resolve boot failures.

- Objective 6.3 (70-067.06.03)—Choose the appropriate course of action to take to resolve configuration errors.

- Objective 6.4 (70-067.06.04)—Choose the appropriate course of action to take to resolve printer problems.

- Objective 6.5 (70-067.06.05)—Choose the appropriate course of action to take to resolve RAS problems.

- Objective 6.6 (70-067.06.06)—Choose the appropriate course of action to take to resolve connectivity problems.

- Objective 6.7 (70-067.06.07)—Choose the appropriate course of action to take to resolve resource access problems and permission problems.

- Objective 6.8 (70-067.06.08)—Choose the appropriate course of action to take to resolve fault-tolerance failures.

Getting More Help

A variety of resources are available to help you study for the exam. Your options include instructor-led classes, seminars, self-paced kits, or other learning materials. The materials described here are created to prepare you for MCP exams. Each training resource fits a different type of learning style and budget.

Microsoft Official Curriculum (MOC)

Microsoft Official Curriculum (MOC) courses are technical training courses developed by Microsoft product groups to educate computer professionals who use Microsoft technology. The courses are developed with the same objectives used for Microsoft certification, and MOC courses are available to support most exams for the MCSE certification. The courses are available in instructor-led, online, or self-paced formats to fit your preferred learning style.

Self-Paced Training

Microsoft Press self-paced training kits cover a variety of Microsoft technical products. The self-paced kits, which are based on MOC courses, feature self-paced lessons, hands-on practices, multimedia presentations, practice files, and demonstration software. They can help you understand the concepts and get the experience you need to prepare for the corresponding MCP exam.To help you prepare for the Implementing and Supporting Microsoft Windows NT Server 4.0 70-067 MCP exam, Microsoft has written the *Microsoft Windows NT Technical Support Training* kit and the *Microsoft Windows NT Network Administration Training* kit. With these official self-paced training kits, you can learn the fundamentals of administrating and supporting network technology using Microsoft Windows NT 4.0. These kits give you training for the real world by offering hands-on training through CD-ROM–based network simulation exercises.

MCP Approved Study Guides

MCP Approved Study Guides, available through several organizations, are learning tools that help you prepare for MCP exams. The study guides are available in a variety of formats to match your learning style, including books, compact discs, online content, and videos. These guides come in a wide range of prices to fit your budget.

Microsoft Seminar Series

Microsoft Solution Providers and other organizations are often a source of information to help you prepare for an MCP exam. For example, many solution providers will present seminars to help industry professionals understand a particular product technology such as networking. For information on all Microsoft-sponsored events, visit http://www.microsoft.com/events.

Planning

Planning a Windows NT installation is the first domain objective for the 70-067 Microsoft Windows NT Server exam. This objective tests your ability to choose a file system (FAT or NTFS), and a fault-tolerance method based on an understanding of fault-tolerance features and the categories of Windows NT operating system fault tolerance. This objective also covers the common protocol suites and your ability to determine which are necessary to communicate with other clients and servers in the network. Good planning makes for an efficient Windows NT Server installation process and decreases the likelihood of configuration problems or system failure.

Tested Skills and Suggested Practices

The skills you need to successfully master the Planning domain objective on the exam include:

- Recommending a file system, either FAT or NTFS, based on a variety of system requirements.

  - Practice1: Read about the features and limitations of the FAT and NTFS file systems.

  - Practice 2: Evaluate scenario-based questions in which you must select the proper file system.

  - Practice 3: In the Windows NT Disk Administrator, create, delete, and format a partition.

- Determining the proper location for the system partition and boot partition.

  - Practice 1: Define the difference between a system partition and a boot partition.

  - Practice 2: Read about partition configurations as they relate to operating system functions and security.

- Identifying disk fault-tolerance options available in hardware and in the Windows NT operating system.

  - Practice 1: Study documentation on various RAID (redundant array of inexpensive disks) implementations.

  - Practice 2: Compare the levels of RAID available in Windows NT with those available in hardware-level RAID implementations.

  - Practice 3: Using Disk Administrator, view a display of disk drives to determine their configuration, and map that configuration to the ARC (Advanced RISC Computing) names found in BOOT.INI.

  - Practice 4: Create a stripe set, a mirror set, a stripe set with parity, and a volume set in the Windows NT Disk Administrator.

- Describing additional fault-tolerant features available in Windows NT.

  - Practice 1: Read about the functions and features of the Windows NT UPS (uninterruptible power supply) service and the Windows NT backup service.

  - Practice 2: Configure the UPS service to operate in Windows NT and create a power loss condition to test the automated shutdown function.

  - Practice 3: Install and test a tape drive and a controller in Windows NT.

  - Practice 4: Run NTBackup to perform a full, a differential, and an incremental backup.

- Determining the protocol or protocols that satisfy communication and application requirements in a variety of network environments.

  - Practice 1: Study the implementation details and functions provided by TCP/IP (Transmission Control Protocol/Internet Protocol), NWLink IPX/SPX (Internetwork Packet Exchange/Sequenced Packet Exchange), NetBEUI, and DLC (Data Link Control).

  - Practice 2: Install each protocol and test its primary functions. For example: install DLC and communicate with a network printer; install TCP/IP and access the Internet; install NWLink IPX/SPX and log on to a Novell NetWare file server.

  - Practice 3: Answer scenario-based questions where you choose the proper protocol or protocols to install on a network.

OBJECTIVE 1.1

Choose a file system.

Windows NT operates with three file systems: the CD File System (CDFS), the File Allocation Table (FAT), and the NT File System (NTFS). CDFS, a read-only file system used for accessing CD-ROMs, is automatically installed with Windows NT and is not part of the file system planning process.

The FAT file system and NTFS provide the operating system with a way to index, read, and write data to installed disk drives. NTFS also provides access security and auditing functions. In choosing a file system there are other considerations beyond file system features such as characteristics and compatibility. For example, although NTFS is a more secure file system, it is not compatible with other locally installed operating systems. For a comprehensive comparison of FAT and NTFS characteristics, see the titles referenced in the Further Reading section.

To successfully answer the questions for this objective, you need a firm understanding of the key terms in the following section. For definitions of these terms, refer to the Glossary in this book.

Key Terms

- 8.3 format

- Active partition

- Advanced RISC Computing (ARC) names

- Auditing

- Case preserving

- Case-sensitive file naming

- Extended partition

- File Allocation Table (FAT)

- File and object access control

- File system

- Hot fixing or sector sparing

- Local security

- Long file name (LFN)

- NT File System (NTFS)

- Partition

- Portable Operating System Interface (POSIX)

70-067.01.01.001

You are setting up a Windows NT Server 4.0 on an Intel-based computer. This server will also be employed as a test platform for testing the installation of your company's software, so you will dual-boot with Windows 95 OSR2. Which file system should you choose for the computer's 2-GB hard drive?

A. FAT

B. NTFS

C. CDFS

D. FAT32

70-067.01.01.002

You are setting up Windows NT Server 4.0 on an Intel-based computer connected to a small network. You need to configure the single 7-GB hard disk as drives C:, D:, E:, F:, and G:. How can this be done?

A. Create five primary partitions designated as drives C: through G:.

B. Create four primary partitions designated as drives C: through F:, and a single extended partition with logical drive G:.

C. Create a single primary partition designated as drive C:, and create four extended partitions with logical drives D: through G:.

D. Create a single primary partition designated as drive C:, and create a single extended partition with logical drives D: through G:.

70-067.01.01.001

You are setting up a Windows NT Server 4.0 on an Intel-based computer. This server will also be employed as a test platform for testing the installation of your company's software, so you will dual-boot with Windows 95 OSR2. Which file system should you choose for the computer's 2-GB hard drive?

▶ **Correct Answer: A**

    A. **Correct:** You are installing Windows NT Server 4.0 on an Intel-based computer which will dual-boot Windows 95 OSR2 (Operating System Release 2) and Windows NT. The only file system supported by both of these operating systems is FAT.

    B. **Incorrect:** NTFS is supported only on Windows NT Workstation or Windows NT Server. Therefore, Windows 95 OSR2 would not be accessible after the installation of Windows NT Server 4.0.

    C. **Incorrect:** CDFS is the file system used to access read-only CD-ROMs. It cannot be used to access a hard drive.

    D. **Incorrect:** FAT32 is supported on Windows 95 OSR2 and Windows 98. Windows NT does not support this file system. During the installation of Windows NT Server 4.0, this partition must be deleted and recreated if it will contain Windows NT operating system files.

70-067.01.01.002

You are setting up Windows NT Server 4.0 on an Intel-based computer connected to a small network. You need to configure the single 7-GB hard disk as drives C:, D:, E:, F:, and G:. How can this be done?

▶ **Correct Answer: D**

    A. **Incorrect:** Windows NT can support up to four primary partitions.

    B. **Incorrect:** If Windows NT is configured to support four primary partitions on a disk drive, that drive cannot support an extended partition.

    C. **Incorrect:** Windows NT can support only one extended partition per disk drive.

    D. **Correct:** You are configuring Windows NT Server 4.0 with a single 7-GB hard disk. You need to configure the hard disk with five drives (C:, D:, E:, F:, and G:). Windows NT supports up to three primary partitions and one extended partition, or four primary partitions and no extended partition per disk drive. Additionally, a primary partition must be represented by a single drive letter, while an extended partition can be subpartitioned into multiple drive letters. Therefore, creating a single primary partition as drive C: and creating a single extended partition that is subpartitioned into drives D: through G: will provide the required drive letter assignments.

Further Reading

 Microsoft Windows NT Network Administration Training kit. Review Lessons 1 and 3 in Chapter 6, "Securing Network Resources with NTFS Permissions."

 Microsoft Windows NT Server Concepts and Planning Manual. Review Chapter 7, "Protecting Data, Managing Disks, and Partitioning Disks."

 Microsoft Windows NT Server 4.0 Resource Kit. In the *Resource Guide*, review the section "Understanding ARC pathnames" in Chapter 5, "Preparing for and Performing Recovery."

 Microsoft Windows NT Technical Support Training kit. Review Lessons 1 and 2 in Chapter 5, "Managing File Systems," and Lessons 1 and 2 in Chapter 6, "Managing Partitions."

 Microsoft Windows NT Workstation Resource Kit. Review Chapter 18, "Choosing a File System."

 Networking Essentials, Second Edition training kit. Review Lesson 3 in Chapter 6, "Network Administration and Support."

 "Overview of FAT, HPFS, and NTFS File Systems." You can find this article at the Microsoft Support Online Web site (http://support.microsoft.com/support/c.asp?FR=0) by selecting "Specific article ID number" under "I want to search by," entering **Q100108** in the "My question is" field, and then clicking on the Find button.

O B J E C T I V E   1 . 2

Choose a fault-tolerance method.

Planning a Microsoft Windows NT network for data integrity and availability requires knowledge of the fault-tolerance features available through the operating system and through the server hardware. The two tested categories of Windows NT operating system fault tolerance are disk drive data redundancy (RAID 1 or 5) and power system control (UPS Service).

When planning fault tolerance, focus on the Windows NT operating system RAID implementations using the Windows NT UPS service and on implementing a backup scheme using the Windows NT Backup program. Windows NT Server supports two levels of RAID fault tolerance: RAID 1 (disk mirroring) and RAID 5 (disk striping with parity). Before implementing RAID 1 or 5 compare them, as each has different requirements and advantages. Although RAID arrays provide an important level of fault tolerance, the Windows NT operating system and the data on the drives can be compromised by an unexpected interruption in system power. Even though power failures are never planned, their effect on the Windows NT operating system can be controlled. Using the Windows NT UPS service, which works with a battery (UPS), a power failure can initiate an orderly shutdown of the system. An orderly shutdown involves writing all data stored in the operating system cache to the disk, and stopping all application services to prepare the system for a loss of power.

To successfully answer the questions for this objective, you need a firm understanding of the key terms in the following section. For definitions of these terms, refer to the Glossary in this book.

Key Terms

- Disk array

- Disk controller

- Disk duplexing

- Fault tolerance

- Redundant array of inexpensive disks (RAID)

- RAID 0 (striping)

- RAID 1 (mirror sets)

- RAID 5 (stripe sets with parity)

- RAID 10

- Uninterruptible power supply (UPS)

- Uninterruptible power supply (UPS) Service

70-067.01.02.001

You are setting up a Windows NT Server 4.0 and need to implement fault tolerance through the Windows NT Operating System. The Intel-based server has four 2-GB hard drives. The server performs a full tape backup every morning at 2:00 A.M.. Which RAID method should you implement to maximize disk space and provide fault tolerance?

A. RAID 0

B. RAID 1

C. RAID 2

D. RAID 3

E. RAID 4

F. RAID 5

70-067.01.02.001

You are setting up a Windows NT Server 4.0 and need to implement fault tolerance through the Windows NT Operating System. The Intel-based server has four 2-GB hard drives. The server performs a full tape backup every morning at 2:00 A.M.. Which RAID method should you implement to maximize disk space and provide fault tolerance?

▶ **Correct Answer: F**

A. **Incorrect:** RAID 0 (disk striping) is not a fault-tolerant solution.

B. **Incorrect:** While RAID 1 (disk mirroring) is a fault-tolerant solution which can be implemented through Disk Administrator, it reduces logical storage capacity by 50 percent.

C. **Incorrect:** RAID 2 cannot be implemented using the Windows NT operating system.

D. **Incorrect:** RAID 3 cannot be implemented using the Windows NT operating system.

E. **Incorrect:** RAID 4 cannot be implemented using the Windows NT operating system.

F. **Correct:** You are configuring a software level fault-tolerant configuration for Windows NT Server 4.0. The server contains four 2-GB hard drives, and you want to maximize disk storage capacity while implementing a fault-tolerant solution. The only two fault-tolerant solutions available in Windows NT Server are RAID1 and RAID 5. Using four disk drives, a RAID 1 solution would decrease logical disk capacity by 50 percent. A RAID 5 implementation would reduce logical disk capacity by 25 percent or one-quarter of the total physical disk capacity. In this case RAID 5 is the best solution.

70-067.01.02.002

You have assembled an Intel, Pentium-based computer with two 4.3-GB hard disks. All hardware components are listed on the Windows NT hardware compatibility list. You are installing Windows NT Server on the computer.

The required result is to provide fault tolerance for programs and data.

The first optional result is to provide fault tolerance for the boot partition.

The second optional result is to minimize the use of system memory required to support fault tolerance.

The proposed solution is to implement a mirror set.

What does the proposed solution provide?

A. The required result and all optional results.

B. The required result and one optional result.

C. The required result but none of the optional results.

D. The proposed solution does not provide the required result.

70-067.01.02.002

You have assembled an Intel, Pentium-based computer with two 4.3-GB hard disks. All hardware components are listed on the Windows NT hardware compatibility list. You are installing Windows NT Server on the computer.

The required result is to provide fault tolerance for programs and data.

The first optional result is to provide fault tolerance for the boot partition.

The second optional result is to minimize the use of system memory required to support fault tolerance.

The proposed solution is to implement a mirror set.

What does the proposed solution provide?

▶ **Correct Answer: A**

A. **Correct:** You are installing an HCL-approved Windows NT Server on an Intel, Pentium-based computer with two identically sized hard disks. The required result, to provide fault tolerance to programs and data, is achieved through the implementation of a RAID 1 (mirror set) disk configuration. The first optional result, to provide fault tolerance for the boot partition, is achieved since a mirror set can be implemented for both the boot and system partition. The second optional result, to minimize the use of system memory required to support fault tolerance, is achieved because a mirror set requires less memory to support fault tolerance than the alternative, a RAID 5 fault-tolerant solution.

B. **Incorrect:** The required result and both optional results are achieved.

C. **Incorrect:** The required result and both optional results are achieved.

D. **Incorrect:** The required result is achieved.

70-067.01.02.003

You have assembled a Pentium-based computer with two 4.3-GB hard disks. All hardware components are listed on the Windows NT hardware compatibility list. You are planning to install Windows NT Server on the computer.

The required result is to provide fault tolerance for programs and data.

The first optional result is to provide fault tolerance for the system and boot partitions.

The second optional result is to minimize the use of system memory required to support fault tolerance.

The proposed solution is to implement a stripe set with parity.

What does the proposed solution provide?

A. The required result and all optional results.

B. The required result and one optional result.

C. The required result but none of the optional results.

D. The proposed solution does not provide the required result.

70-067.01.02.003

You have assembled a Pentium-based computer with two 4.3-GB hard disks. All hardware components are listed on the Windows NT hardware compatibility list. You are planning to install Windows NT Server on the computer.

The required result is to provide fault tolerance for programs and data.

The first optional result is to provide fault tolerance for the system and boot partitions.

The second optional result is to minimize the use of system memory required to support fault tolerance.

The proposed solution is to implement a stripe set with parity.

What does the proposed solution provide?

▶ **Correct Answer: C**

A. **Incorrect:** Only the required result is achieved. The first optional result, to provide fault tolerance for the system and boot partitions, and the second optional result, to minimize the use of system memory required to support fault tolerance, is not achieved.

B. **Incorrect:** The required result is achieved, but none of the optional results are achieved.

C. **Correct:** You are installing an HCL-approved Windows NT Server on an Intel, Pentium-based computer with two identically sized hard disks. The required result, to provide fault tolerance to programs and data, is achieved through the implementation of a RAID 5 (disk striping with parity) disk configuration. The first optional result, to provide fault tolerance for the boot partition, is not achieved since a stripe set with parity cannot be implemented on the boot or the system partition. The second optional result, to minimize the use of system memory required to support fault tolerance, is not achieved because a RAID 5 requires more memory to support fault tolerance than the alternative, a RAID 1 fault-tolerant solution.

D. **Incorrect:** The required result is achieved.

70-067.01.02.004

You have assembled a Pentium-based computer with one 4.3-GB hard disk. All hardware components are listed on the Windows NT hardware compatibility list. You will install Windows NT Server on the computer.

The required result is to select a file system for use on the computer to support Windows NT Server.

The first optional result is to prepare the computer for dual booting with MS-DOS.

The second optional result is to prepare the computer for supporting file-level security.

The proposed solution is to format the hard disk as a single FAT32 (large disk support) partition.

What does the proposed solution provide?

A. The required result and all optional results.

B. The required result and one optional result.

C. The required result but none of the optional results.

D. The proposed solution does not provide the required result.

70-067.01.02.004

You have assembled a Pentium-based computer with one 4.3-GB hard disk. All hardware components are listed on the Windows NT hardware compatibility list. You will install Windows NT Server on the computer.

The required result is to select a file system for use on the computer to support Windows NT Server.

The first optional result is to prepare the computer for dual booting with MS-DOS.

The second optional result is to prepare the computer for supporting file-level security.

The proposed solution is to format the hard disk as a single FAT32 (large disk support) partition.

What does the proposed solution provide?

▶ **Correct Answer: D**

A. **Incorrect:** The required result is not achieved.

B. **Incorrect:** The required result is not achieved.

C. **Incorrect:** The required result is not achieved.

D. **Correct:** The proposed solution does not provide the required result. You are installing an HCL-approved Windows NT Server on an Intel, Pentium-based computer with one hard disk. The required result, to select a file system for use on the computer to support Windows NT Server, is not achieved by formatting the disk drive with FAT32. Windows NT does not support the FAT32 file system. The first two optional results are not considered since the required result is not achieved.

70-067.01.02.005

You have assembled a Pentium-based computer with one 4.3-GB hard disk. All hardware components are listed on the Windows NT hardware compatibility list. You will install Windows NT Server on the computer.

The required result is to select a file system for use on the computer to support Windows NT Server.

The first optional result is to prepare the computer for dual booting with MS-DOS.

The second optional result is to prepare the computer for supporting file-level security.

The proposed solution is to format the hard disk as a single NTFS partition.

What does the proposed solution provide?

A. The required result and all optional results.

B. The required result and one optional result.

C. The required result but none of the optional results.

D. The proposed solution does not provide the required result.

70-067.01.02.005

You have assembled a Pentium-based computer with one 4.3-GB hard disk. All hardware components are listed on the Windows NT hardware compatibility list. You will install Windows NT Server on the computer.

The required result is to select a file system for use on the computer to support Windows NT Server.

The first optional result is to prepare the computer for dual booting with MS-DOS.

The second optional result is to prepare the computer for supporting file-level security.

The proposed solution is to format the hard disk as a single NTFS partition.

What does the proposed solution provide?

▶ **Correct Answer: B**

A. **Incorrect:** The required result and the second optional result are achieved. However, the first optional result, to prepare the computer for dual booting with MS-DOS, is not achieved.

B. **Correct:** You are installing an HCL-approved Windows NT Server on an Intel, Pentium-based computer with one hard disk. The required result, to select a file system for use on the computer to support Windows NT Server, is achieved by formatting the disk drive with NTFS. Windows NT supports NTFS. The first optional result, to prepare the computer for dual booting with MS-DOS, is not achieved because DOS cannot access an NTFS formatted drive. The second optional result, to prepare the computer to support file-level security, is achieved since NTFS supports directory-level and file-level security (also called local permissions).

C. **Incorrect:** The required result and one optional result are achieved.

D. **Incorrect:** The required result is achieved.

70-067.01.02.006

You have assembled a Pentium-based computer with one 4.3-GB hard disk. All hardware components are listed on the Windows NT hardware compatibility list. You will install Windows NT Server on the computer.

The required result is to select a file system for use on the computer to support Windows NT Server.

The first optional result is to prepare the computer for dual booting with MS-DOS.

The second optional result is to prepare the computer for supporting file-level security.

The proposed solution is to format the hard disk as a single FAT partition.

What does the proposed solution provide?

A. The required result and all optional results.

B. The required result and one optional result.

C. The required result but none of the optional results.

D. The proposed solution does not provide the required result.

70-067.01.02.006

You have assembled a Pentium-based computer with one 4.3-GB hard disk. All hardware components are listed on the Windows NT hardware compatibility list. You will install Windows NT Server on the computer.

The required result is to select a file system for use on the computer to support Windows NT Server.

The first optional result is to prepare the computer for dual booting with MS-DOS.

The second optional result is to prepare the computer for supporting file-level security.

The proposed solution is to format the hard disk as a single FAT partition.

What does the proposed solution provide?

▶ **Correct Answer: B**

A. **Incorrect:** The required result and the first optional result are achieved. However, the second optional result, to prepare the computer for supporting file-level security, is not achieved.

B. **Correct:** You are installing an HCL-approved Windows NT Server on an Intel, Pentium-based computer with one hard disk. The required result, to select a file system for use on the computer to support Windows NT Server, is achieved by formatting the disk drive with the FAT file system. Windows NT supports FAT. The first optional result, to prepare the computer for dual booting with MS-DOS, is achieved since DOS's native drive format is FAT. The second optional result, to prepare the computer for supporting file-level security, is not achieved since FAT does not support directory-level and file-level security.

C. **Incorrect:** The required result and one optional result are achieved

D. **Incorrect:** The required result is achieved.

Further Reading

 Microsoft Windows NT Server 4.0 Resource Kit. In the *Resource Guide*, review Chapter 4, "Planning a Reliable Configuration," on planning a reliable and fault-tolerant disk configuration and configuring your mass storage.

 Networking Essentials, Second Edition training kit. Review Chapter 6, "Network Administration and Support."

 Microsoft Windows NT Network Administration Training kit. Review Lesson 2 in Chapter 11, "Backing Up and Restoring Files."

 Microsoft Windows NT Network Administration Training kit. Review the "NTFS Permissions Planning" and "Backup Planning" worksheets in Appendix A for the exam. If you are working through this kit, and plan to implement Windows NT Server, all of the planning worksheets should be completed.

 Microsoft Windows NT Technical Support Training kit. Review Chapter 7, "Managing Fault Tolerance."

 Microsoft Windows NT Server 4.0 Enterprise Technologies Training Kit: Supporting Windows NT Server in the Enterprise. Review Lesson 2 in Chapter 1, "Planning the Enterprise with Microsoft Windows NT Server 4.0." This chapter covers objectives 1.1 and 1.2.

OBJECTIVE 1.3

Choose a protocol for various situations.

When planning to integrate Windows NT into a network environment, you must first determine what protocol or protocols are necessary to communicate with other computers (clients or servers) in the network. Protocol requirements vary by network and application support. Although many protocols are used for communications on a network, NetBEUI, NWLink IPX/SPX, TCP/IP, and DLC contain the most common communication components to consider during the planning phase. If you do not provide support for the proper protocols, computers cannot communicate with each other. Resources such as printers, servers, and other shared devices will not be accessible. To avoid access problems in a network and create an efficiently utilized network, it is ideal to standardize on a single protocol.

NetBEUI is a common protocol for small, single-segment networks where routing is not necessary. Because of its small size and efficiency, NetBEUI is also an ideal protocol for low bandwidth, remote access communications. NWLink IPX/SPX is Microsoft's implementation of Novell's IPX/SPX protocol suite. Using NWLink IPX/SPX, Windows NT computers can communicate with and provide access to Novell NetWare servers locally or across routed networks. TCP/IP is ideal for Internet, intranet, and other routed networks. It is particularly effective for large to very large multi-segmented networks that are linked to remote sites by way of dedicated WAN connections. The three protocols just described support a wide variety of applications. DLC, on the other hand, is designed to support network-connected printers and SNA networks typically used for host access to IBM mainframes and mini-computers.

The key to planning protocol support for a network is to first assess the current environment and then select a protocol that can serve that environment. For example, if Windows NT computers interoperate in a network composed of Novell NetWare servers, you need to use the NWLink IPX/SPX protocol. If your network contains only Windows NT servers, you can use NetBEUI, NWLink IPX/SPX, or TCP/IP, depending on application support requirements and the network configuration (single segment or routed). However, if you must support a private wide area network (WAN) and Internet access, TCP/IP will provide access to both.

To successfully answer the questions for this objective, you need a firm understanding of the key terms in the following section. For definitions of these terms, refer to the Glossary in this book.

Key Terms

- Data Link Control (DLC)

- Internet

- Intranet

- NetBEUI

- Novell NetWare

- NWLink Internet Protocol Exchange/Sequenced Packet Exchange (NWLink IPX/SPX)

- Protocol suite

- Router

- Routing

- System Network Architecture (SNA)

- Transmission Control Protocol/Internet Protocol (TCP/IP)

- Wide area network (WAN)

70-067.01.03.001

You are setting up a Windows NT 4.0 network. There are three Windows NT 4.0 Servers, 250 Windows NT 4.0 Workstations, and two routers dividing the network into three segments. The research and development department of your company has indicated that Internet access is critical to their research effort. Which protocol should you choose?

A. DLC

B. TCP/IP

C. NetBEUI

D. NWLink IPX/SPX

70-067.01.03.002

You are setting up a small Windows NT 4.0 network and need a fast and efficient protocol. There is one Windows NT 4.0 Server and 15 Windows NT 4.0 Workstations. Your company does not expect to expand this network, and Internet connectivity is not required. Which protocol should you choose?

A. DLC

B. TCP/IP

C. NetBEUI

D. NWLink IPX/SPX

70-067.01.03.001

You are setting up a Windows NT 4.0 network. There are three Windows NT 4.0 Servers, 250 Windows NT 4.0 Workstations, and two routers dividing the network into three segments. The research and development department of your company has indicated that Internet access is critical to their research effort. Which protocol should you choose?

▶ **Correct Answer: B**

A. **Incorrect:** The DLC protocol is used to support SNA networks and network connected printers. This protocol does not provide Internet access.

B. **Correct:** Your company has indicated that Internet access is critical to their research effort. Since Windows NT will be used for both the clients and the servers, TCP/IP can be installed on the computers and support Internet access. Additionally, TCP/IP is a routable protocol, which means that it can travel through the routers that divide the network.

C. **Incorrect:** The NetBEUI protocol is not routable and cannot provide Internet access.

D. **Incorrect:** While IPX/SPX is routable, it cannot directly provide Internet access. Third-party software can be used to provide gateway services to the Internet but this is not the best solution.

70-067.01.03.002

You are setting up a small Windows NT 4.0 network and need a fast and efficient protocol. There is one Windows NT 4.0 Server and 15 Windows NT 4.0 Workstations. Your company does not expect to expand this network, and Internet connectivity is not required. Which protocol should you choose?

▶ **Correct Answer: C**

A. **Incorrect:** The DLC protocol is used to support SNA networks and network connected printers. This protocol is fast and efficient but it does not provide file and print services, which is a common function in most networks.

B. **Incorrect:** TCP/IP is a robust and configurable protocol; however, it is not considered efficient. This is not the best choice for a small, static network that does not require Internet access.

C. **Correct:** NetBEUI is a fast and efficient protocol and is ideal for small networks.

D. **Incorrect:** NWLink IPX/SPX is a routable and robust protocol. While IPX/SPX is easier to configure than TCP/IP, NetBEUI is a simpler protocol, and therefore, a better choice for this small network.

70-067.01.03.003

You are planning to upgrade a client's NetWare 3.12 network with a new Windows NT Server 4.0 computer.

The required result is to select a communications protocol for the Windows NT Server 4.0 computer.

The first optional result is to support connectivity to the Internet.

The second optional result is to support connectivity between Microsoft clients and NetWare 3.12 servers.

The proposed solution is to install TCP/IP and NWLink IPX/SPX Compatible Transport.

What does the proposed solution provide?

A. The required result and all optional results.

B. The required result and one optional result.

C. The required result but none of the optional results.

D. The proposed solution does not provide the required result.

70-067.01.03.003

You are planning to upgrade a client's NetWare 3.12 network with a new Windows NT Server 4.0 computer.

The required result is to select a communications protocol for the Windows NT Server 4.0 computer.

The first optional result is to support connectivity to the Internet.

The second optional result is to support connectivity between Microsoft clients and NetWare 3.12 servers.

The proposed solution is to install TCP/IP and NWLink IPX/SPX Compatible Transport.

What does the proposed solution provide?

▶ **Correct Answer: A**

A. **Correct:** You are upgrading a NetWare 3.12 network with a Windows NT Server 4.0 computer. The required result, to select a communications protocol for the Windows NT Server 4.0 computer, is achieved through the proposed solution, installing TCP/IP and NWLink IPX/SPX on the Windows NT Server. The first optional result, to support connectivity to the Internet, is achieved by installing TCP/IP on the Windows NT Server and any clients that require this support. Note that the optional solution does not state that Internet access is required, just that the protocol supports this type of connectivity. The second optional result, to support connectivity between Microsoft clients and NetWare 3.12 servers, is achieved by installing the NWLink IPX/SPX protocol. This alone will not provide access; however, it does support connectivity as the optional result suggests.

B. **Incorrect:** The required result is achieved, but none of the optional results are achieved.

C. **Incorrect:** The required result and both optional results are achieved.

D. **Incorrect:** The required result is achieved.

70-067.01.03.004

Your network environment includes computers running Windows NT Server and UNIX. You need to print from your UNIX-based computer to a network printer attached to a Windows NT Server machine.

Which protocol is required to support the LPD service?

A. DLC

B. FPNW

C. TCP/IP

D. NetBEUI

70-067.01.03.005

You are planning to upgrade a client's NetWare 3.12 network with a new Windows NT Server 4.0 computer.

The required result is to select a communications protocol for the Windows NT Server 4.0 computer.

The first optional result is to support connectivity to the Internet.

The second optional result is to support connectivity between Microsoft clients and NetWare 3.12 servers.

The proposed solution is to install TCP/IP.

What does the proposed solution provide?

A. The required result and all optional results.

B. The required result and one optional result.

C. The required result but none of the optional results.

D. The proposed solution does not provide the required result.

70-067.01.03.004

Your network environment includes computers running Windows NT Server and UNIX. You need to print from your UNIX-based computer to a network printer attached to a Windows NT Server machine.

Which protocol is required to support the LPD service?

► **Correct Answer: C**

A. **Incorrect:** The DLC protocol can be used for network connected printers. However, the DLC protocol does not support the Line Printer Daemon service.

B. **Incorrect:** File and Print Services for NetWare allows a Windows NT Server to emulate the functions of a Novell NetWare 3.x server. This is a service, not a protocol.

C. **Correct:** TCP/IP is the only protocol that supports the LPD service. Both clients running Windows NT or UNIX and the TCP/IP protocol can print through the LPD service.

D. **Incorrect:** The NetBEUI protocol does not support the LPD service.

70-067.01.03.005

You are planning to upgrade a client's NetWare 3.12 network with a new Windows NT Server 4.0 computer.

The required result is to select a communications protocol for the Windows NT Server 4.0 computer.

The first optional result is to support connectivity to the Internet.

The second optional result is to support connectivity between Microsoft clients and NetWare 3.12 servers.

The proposed solution is to install TCP/IP.

What does the proposed solution provide?

► **Correct Answer: B**

A. **Incorrect:** The required result and the first optional result are achieved. However, the second optional result, to support connectivity between Microsoft clients and the NetWare 3.12 servers, is not achieved.

B. **Correct:** You are upgrading a client's NetWare 3.12 network with a Windows NT Server. The required result, to select a communications protocol for the Windows NT Server 4.0 computer, is achieved by installing TCP/IP. The first optional result, to support connectivity to the Internet, is also achieved by installing the TCP/IP protocol. The second optional result, to support connectivity between Microsoft clients and NetWare 3.12 server, is not achieved since the IPX/SPX protocol is not installed.

C. **Incorrect:** The required result and one of the optional results are achieved.

D. **Incorrect:** The required result is achieved.

Further Reading

 Microsoft Windows NT Server Network Supplement Manual. Review Chapters 1–4 on TCP/IP, and Chapters 12 and 13 on IPX/SPX.

 Microsoft Windows NT Server Resource Kit: Networking Guide. Review Chapter 5, "Network Services: Enterprise Level—Preparations for Configuring Services."

 Networking Essentials, Second Edition. Review Lesson 4 in Chapter 3, "How a Network Functions," Lessons 1 and 2 in Chapter 5, "Network Operations," and Lessons 2 and 3 in Chapter 7, "Larger Networks."

 Microsoft Windows NT Technical Support Training kit. Review Lessons 2–4 in Chapter 10, "Configuring Windows NT Protocols," Lesson 1 in Chapter 13, "Internetworking and Intranetworking," and Lesson 1 in Chapter 14, "Interoperating with Novell NetWare."

 Microsoft Windows NT Server 4.0 Enterprise Technologies Training Kit. In *Supporting Microsoft Windows NT Server in the Enterprise*, review Lessons 4 and 6 in Chapter 4, "Connectivity."

Installation and Configuration

The installation and configuration of Windows NT Server is the second domain objective for the 70-067 exam. Because Windows NT is a sophisticated network operating system loaded with options, the installation process is complex and requires the installer to make many choices. This objective tests your understanding of the available installation and configuration options and processes that enable you to install operating systems correctly, avoid the configuration problems that result from a bad installation, and troubleshoot failed installations.

Tested Skills and Suggested Practices

The skills you need to successfully master the Installation and Configuration Objective Domain on the exam include:

- Installing a Windows NT Server.

    - Practice 1: Run several Windows NT installations and watch the installation screens carefully so that you can visualize and explain the stages of the installation process.

    - Practice 2: Review the Windows NT installation process so that you are clear on what you are seeing during Practice 1.

    - Practice 3: Run both an Express and Custom setup to determine what basic options are available during an Express setup and what additional setup options are provided by a Custom setup.

    - Practice 4: Configure and run an Over the Network Installation of Windows NT Server.

    - Practice 5: Create a primary domain controller during installation. If a second computer is available, create a backup domain controller to join the domain created by the primary domain controller.

    - Practice 6: Install Windows NT Server as a member server and note the differences in the installation process from a domain controller installation.

- Running Network Client Administrator.

  - Practice 1: Create a Network Installation Startup Disk. Run the startup disk to install Windows 95 on a client.

  - Practice 2: Make an installation disk set and configure a network adapter driver using the NDIS 3 driver for MS-DOS.

  - Practice 3: Copy the Client Based Network Administration tools and install the Windows NT Server tools to a Windows 95 client.

- Installing the protocol or protocols that will satisfy communication and application requirements in a variety of network environments.

  - Practice 1: Install each protocol and test its primary functions. Install TCP/IP and ping a host on the network. Install NWLink IPX/SPX and Gateway Services for NetWare to provide access to a Novell NetWare file server through a Windows NT server.

  - Practice 2: Explore the Bindings tab located in the Network dialog box, which can be accessed through Control Panel or the Network Neighborhood Properties sheet. Modify the NetBIOS Interface binding order after installing multiple protocols.

- Configuring an ISA, EISA and PCI network adapter for operations on a Windows NT Server.

  - Practice 1: Using an ISA NIC, change the IRQ on the adapter via either a hardware jumper, a DIP switch, or through software. Then configure the installed adapter driver through Windows NT Server to see if the adapter will function. If it doesn't function, use the Resources tab in Windows NT Diagnostics to determine an available interrupt.

  - Practice 2: Using an EISA NIC, change the IRQ on the adapter through the EISA configuration routine. Then follow the configuration procedure shown in Practice 1.

  - Practice 3: Using a PCI NIC, determine the IRQ used by the adapter through the Resources tab in Windows NT Diagnostics. Windows NT Diagnostics is contained in the Administrative Tools (Common) group. Then view the properties of the PCI NIC through the Adapters tab in the Network dialog box. Note the memory address and I/O port in use and return to the Resources tab in Windows NT Diagnostics to find these settings.

- Understanding the core services, their role in a Windows NT network, and how the services are configured.

  - Practice 1: Run the Services program in Control Panel to view the core Windows NT Server services. Next, stop a service, and then attempt to complete a procedure that this service provides. For example, stop the Workstation service and then try to connect to a network resource from the Windows NT Server. Also, stop the Server service and try to log on to the Windows NT Server from a workstation on the network.

- Practice 2: Configure a service like the License Manager to manual startup using the Services program in Control Panel. Next, restart the server to verify that the License Manger service is not running. Then, from a Windows NT CMD prompt, start the License Manager service using the NET START service name command.

- Installing and configuring peripheral devices for operation in Windows NT Server.

  - Practice 1: Install and configure a modem or ISDN dial-up adapter as a dial-out (dial-up networking) device or dial-in (RAS Server) device.

  - Practice 2: Install and configure a SCSI adapter during Windows NT Setup. If available, install a tape device and configure a tape device driver for backup operation.

  - Practice 3: Connect UPS to a Windows NT Server and configure the Windows NT UPS Service to interact with the UPS. Simulate a power failure to verify that the UPS Service is communicating with the UPS.

Caution Complete this procedure on a non-production system.

  - Practice 4: From Control Panel, run the Mouse program and view the device driver installed under the General tab. Repeat this procedure using the Keyboard program. Next, run the Display program and under the Settings tab/Display Type button, view the display driver information. Next, run the Devices program and find each of the devices and their startup settings. Finally, run Windows NT Diagnostics and locate the mouse, keyboard, and such display device driver resource settings as IRQ, I/O, DMA, and Memory.

- Configuring hard disks during the Windows NT installation process, both in the Windows NT Disk Administrator contained in the Administrative Tools (Common) group and from the Windows NT CMD prompt.

Caution The following practice skills should only be completed on a test system.

  - Practice 1: Maintain the existing partitions on disks in the system and install Windows NT Server on a FAT or NTFS partition.

  - Practice 2: Install Windows NT Server again, this time deleting all partitions on a disk drive in the system. Then, recreate a 1-GB partition and install

Windows NT Server on this partition. During setup, choose to format the partition as NTFS.

- Practice 3: After installation is completed, enter Disk Administrator and create a mirror set from the 1-GB partition created in the previous step.

- Practice 4: If enough disks are available in the server, create a stripe set, a volume set, and a stripe set with parity.

Note If the number of disks and available capacity are minimal, you can delete the stripe set, and recreate a stripe set with parity with a minimum of three hard drives. If necessary a volume set can be created with two separate partitions on a single drive.

- Practice 5: Convert a FAT partition to NTFS using the Convert command.

- Installing and configuring printers to interact with print devices on the network.

  - Practice 1: Install a printer for a print device on the network. Then, send a print job to the printer. Next, create a second printer to the same print device and set the priority for the second printer lower than the first printer. Send two print jobs, one to each printer, to verify that the printer with the higher priority prints to the print device first.

  - Practice 2: Install a second print device that accepts print jobs from the same printer configured in Practice 1. Once this is configured, send multiple print jobs to the printer to verify that the printer pool is properly configured.

  - Practice 3: Explore all of the properties of an installed printer. Also, from the Printers window, access the File menu Server Properties option. Whenever you encounter an option that is not familiar, select it and press the F1 key for pop-up menu hints.

- Creating a Windows NT Server domain controller that will support a variety of clients.

  - Practice: Log on to the domain controller while running a Windows NT Workstation client, a Windows 95 client, and an MS-DOS client. Note the steps that must be taken to configure each of these client operating systems for logon to the server.

OBJECTIVE 2.1

Install Windows NT Server on *x86*-based (CISC) platforms.

The first step in any installation routine should be to test the existing system to verify that it meets minimum requirements and can be upgraded. It is also important to know beforehand how the Windows NT Server installation program interacts with previously installed operating systems and applications.

The following table shows the minimum system requirements for installing Windows NT Server 4.0 on a computer containing an *x86* based processor (*x86* is synonymous with Intel-based or CISC-based processors).

Resource	Requirement
CPU	Either a 32-bit CISC processor 80486/33 or higher, or a supported RISC processor, MIPS R4400 or R5000, DEC/Compaq Alpha AXP and a PReP-compliant Motorola/IBM PowerPC chip.
Disk space requirements	124 MB on CISC, or158 MB on RISC
Display	Standard VGA
Memory (RAM)	16 MB on CISC, 16 MB on RISC

Note Support has ended for the MIPS and PPC processors after Windows NT 4. In addition, some CISC-based non-Intel processors cannot run in 80486-emulation mode for applications that require it. For the purpose of test preparation, focus on the CISC-based installation routine.

The ideal installation environment for Windows NT Server is a computer on the Microsoft hardware compatibility list (HCL) that does not contain any previously installed operating systems. Microsoft does not support hardware absent from the HCL since it has not been certified to run Windows NT. To check the HCL, go to http://www.microsoft.com/hwtest/hcl. If this URL is not accessible, go to http://www.microsoft.com and search using "HCL" (without quotes) as your search text.

To successfully answer the questions for this objective, you need a firm understanding of the key terms in the following section. For definitions of these terms, refer to the Glossary in this book.

Key Terms

- Case preserving

- Case sensitive

- Complex Instructions Set Computing (CISC) processor

- Computer name

- Convert.exe

- Emergency Repair Disk (ERD)

- Hardware Compatibility List (HCL)

- Member server

- Reduced Instruction Set Computing (RISC) processor

- Roaming profile

- User profile

- Windows NT domain

- Windows NT domain controller

- Windows or Windows NT workgroup

- Winnt.exe

- Winnt32.exe

70-067.02.01.001

You are installing Windows NT Server 4.0 on an Intel-based computer running MS-DOS 6.2. Which command should you use to install Windows NT Server?

A. WINNT

B. WINNT32

C. SETUPLDR

D. WINNT32 /b

70-067.02.01.002

Using the United States version of Windows NT Server, which media can be used to complete an installation on an Intel-based computer? (Choose all that apply.)

A. Floppy disk

B. Local CD-ROM

C. Shared folder on a server

D. Shared CD-ROM on a server

70-067.02.01.001

You are installing Windows NT Server 4.0 on an Intel-based computer running MS-DOS 6.2. Which command should you use to install Windows NT Server?

▶ **Correct Answer: A**

A. **Correct:** When you install Windows NT Server 4.0 on an Intel-based computer running MS-DOS 6.2, you must use the 16-bit Windows NT installation routine, winnt.exe.

B. **Incorrect:** WINNT32 is the 32-bit version of the Windows NT installation routine. This version of the installation routine is only used when upgrading or installing Windows NT on a computer that is running Windows NT.

C. **Incorrect:** SETUPLDR is the Windows NT installation program used on RISC-based platforms such as the Alpha.

D. **Incorrect:** WINNT32 /b is the 32-bit version of the Windows NT installation routine running as a "floppyless" installation. The /b switch tells the installation routine to copy the Windows NT installation boot files to the computer's system partition rather than to floppy disks. Therefore, floppy disks do not need to be loaded or removed by the user during the installation process.

70-067.02.01.002

Using the United States version of Windows NT Server, which media can be used to complete an installation on an Intel-based computer? (Choose all that apply.)

▶ **Correct Answers: B, C, and D**

A. **Incorrect:** Floppy disk installation of Windows NT Server is not permitted in the United States, but is permitted outside of the United States. Windows NT 3.5x supports this method of installation regardless of geographical region.

B. **Correct:** In the United States, a local CD-ROM installation is permitted, and is the most common installation method.

C. **Correct:** Using a shared folder on a server is also called an "Over the Network" installation and is permitted. This method of installation provides the ability to fully automate and customize the installation routine.

D. **Correct:** Sharing a Windows NT Server CD-ROM over the network is similar to performing a local CD-ROM installation of Windows NT Server.

70-067.02.01.003

You are installing Windows NT Server 4.0 on a new Intel-based computer. The computer came pre-loaded with Windows 95 Revision B.

Which command should you use to install Windows NT Server 4.0 without creating setup floppy disks during installation?

A. WINNT /b

B. WINNT /n

C. WINNT32 /b

D. WINNT32 /n

70-067.02.01.003

You are installing Windows NT Server 4.0 on a new Intel-based computer. The computer came pre-loaded with Windows 95 Revision B.

Which command should you use to install Windows NT Server 4.0 without creating setup floppy disks during installation?

▶   **Correct Answer: A**

  A. **Correct:** To install Windows NT Server 4.0 without creating floppy disks on a Windows 95 computer, the 16-bit version of the Windows NT installer, WINNT, is run with the floppyless installation switch, /b.

  B. **Incorrect:** WINNT /n is an invalid command.

  C. **Incorrect:** WINNT32 /b is the 32-bit version of the Windows NT installation routine running as a "floppyless" installation. The /b switch tells the installation routine to copy the Windows NT installation boot files to the computer's system partition rather than to floppy disks. Therefore, floppy disks do not need to be loaded or removed by the user during the installation process.

  D. **Incorrect:** WINNT32 /n is an invalid command.

70-067.02.01.004

You need to install Windows NT Server 4.0 on a Pentium-based computer currently running Windows NT Server 3.51. The required result is to install Windows NT Server 4.0.

The first optional result is to avoid reloading software currently running on the computer.

The second optional result is to avoid having to create and use setup boot disks during the installation.

The proposed solution is to use the WINNT32 /b command to install Windows NT Server 4.0 to the same directory as Windows NT Server 3.51.

What does the proposed solution provide?

A. The required result and both optional results.

B. The required result and one optional result.

C. The required result but none of the optional results.

D. The proposed solution does not provide the required result.

70-067.02.01.004

You need to install Windows NT Server 4.0 on a Pentium-based computer currently running Windows NT Server 3.51. The required result is to install Windows NT Server 4.0.

The first optional result is to avoid reloading software currently running on the computer.

The second optional result is to avoid having to create and use setup boot disks during the installation.

The proposed solution is to use the WINNT32 /b command to install Windows NT Server 4.0 to the same directory as Windows NT Server 3.51.

What does the proposed solution provide?

▶ **Correct Answer: A**

A. **Correct:** The required result and both the optional results are achieved. The WINNT32 command is the 32-bit version of the installation routine. This command is used to install or, in this case, upgrade the currently running version of Windows NT Server. During the upgrade process, all currently installed applications will be preserved after the installation. Therefore, the first optional result, to avoid reloading software currently running on the computer, is achieved. And because the /b command line switch was included, the installation was run without floppy disks. Therefore, the second optional result, to avoid having to create and use setup boot disks during installation, is achieved.

B. **Incorrect:** Both optional results are achieved.

C. **Incorrect:** Again, both optional results are achieved.

D. **Incorrect:** The required result is achieved.

70-067.02.01.005

You need to install Windows NT Server 4.0 on a Pentium-based computer currently running Windows NT Server 3.51. You do not have the setup boot disks.

The required result is to install Windows NT Server 4.0.

The first optional result is to avoid reloading software currently running on the computer.

The second optional result is to avoid having to create and use setup boot disks during the installation.

The proposed solution is to use the WINNT32 /x command to install Windows NT Server 4.0 to the same directory as Windows NT Server 3.51.

What does the proposed solution provide?

A. The required result and both optional results.

B. The required result and one optional result.

C. The required result but none of the optional results.

D. The proposed solution does not provide the required result.

70-067.02.01.005

You need to install Windows NT Server 4.0 on a Pentium-based computer currently running Windows NT Server 3.51. You do not have the setup boot disks.

The required result is to install Windows NT Server 4.0.

The first optional result is to avoid reloading software currently running on the computer.

The second optional result is to avoid having to create and use setup boot disks during the installation.

The proposed solution is to use the WINNT32 /x command to install Windows NT Server 4.0 to the same directory as Windows NT Server 3.51.

What does the proposed solution provide?

▶ **Correct Answer: D**

A. **Incorrect:** The required result is not achieved.

B. **Incorrect:** The required result is not achieved.

C. **Incorrect:** The required result is not achieved.

D. **Correct:** The proposed solution does not provide the required result. Although the WINN32 installation routine is the correct program for upgrading Windows NT 3.51 Server to Windows NT 4.0 Server, the /x switch assumes that you are using setup floppy diskettes. The /x switch prevents the installation routine from creating setup boot floppies. Therefore, when WINNT32 /x is used the installation routine immediately requests the setup boot floppies. However, the question claims that you do not have the setup boot floppies and therefore the installation will fail.

70-067.02.01.006

You need to install Windows NT Server 4.0 on a Pentium-based computer currently running Windows NT Server 3.51. You do not have the setup boot disks.

The required result is to install Windows NT Server 4.0.

The first optional result is to avoid reloading software currently running on the computer.

The second optional result is to avoid having to create and use setup boot disks during the installation.

The proposed solution is to use the WINNT32 /b command to install Windows NT Server 4.0 to a different directory than the Windows 3.51 installation.

What does the proposed solution provide?

A. The required result and both optional results.

B. The required result and one optional result.

C. The required result but none of the optional results.

D. The proposed solution does not provide the required result.

70-067.02.01.006

You need to install Windows NT Server 4.0 on a Pentium-based computer currently running Windows NT Server 3.51. You do not have the setup boot disks.

The required result is to install Windows NT Server 4.0.

The first optional result is to avoid reloading software currently running on the computer.

The second optional result is to avoid having to create and use setup boot disks during the installation.

The proposed solution is to use the WINNT32 /b command to install Windows NT Server 4.0 to a different directory than the Windows 3.51 installation.

What does the proposed solution provide?

► **Correct Answer: B**

A. **Incorrect:** While the required result is achieved, only the second optional result is achieved.

B. **Correct:** The required result, to install Windows NT Server 4.0 is achieved; however, the first optional result, to avoid reloading software that was installed into Windows NT 3.51, is not achieved. The proposed solution specifies that Windows NT Server 4.0 is installed to a different directory than the Windows NT 3.51 installation. When Windows NT Server 4.0 is installed in this way, the current version of Windows NT is not upgraded. Therefore, any applications installed in the original environment are not included in the new installation. The second optional result, to avoid having to create and use setup boot disks during the installation is achieved since the proposed solution specifies that the WINNT32 /b command should be used for this installation.

C. **Incorrect:** The required result and one of the optional results are achieved.

D. **Incorrect:** The required result is achieved.

70-067.02.01.007

You need to install Windows NT Server 4.0 on a Pentium-based computer currently running Windows NT Server 3.51. You do not have the setup boot disks.

The required result is to install Windows NT Server 4.0.

The first optional result is to avoid reloading software currently running on the computer.

The second optional result is to avoid having to create and use setup boot disks during the installation.

The proposed solution is to use the WINNT32 command to install Windows NT Server 4.0 to the same directory as the Windows NT 3.51 installation.

What does the proposed solution provide?

A. The required result and all optional results.

B. The required result and one optional result.

C. The required result but none of the optional results.

D. The proposed solution does not provide the required result.

70-067.02.01.007

You need to install Windows NT Server 4.0 on a Pentium-based computer currently running Windows NT Server 3.51. You do not have the setup boot disks.

The required result is to install Windows NT Server 4.0.

The first optional result is to avoid reloading software currently running on the computer.

The second optional result is to avoid having to create and use setup boot disks during the installation.

The proposed solution is to use the WINNT32 command to install Windows NT Server 4.0 to the same directory as the Windows NT 3.51 installation.

What does the proposed solution provide?

▶ **Correct Answer: B**

A. **Incorrect:** While the required result is achieved, only the second optional result is achieved.

B. **Correct:** The required result is achieved, to install Windows NT Server 4.0. The proposed solution states that you will run the WINNT32 command, which begins the installation of Windows NT Server 4.0 on a computer already running Windows NT. The first optional result, to avoid reloading software currently running on the computer, is achieved since the proposed solution states that Windows NT Server 4.0 will be installed in the same directory currently running Windows NT 3.51. However, the second proposed solution is not achieved since the proposed solution uses the WINNT32 command without switches. When this command is launched, the installation routine will ask that you insert setup boot floppies to complete the installation.

C. **Incorrect:** The required result and one of the optional results are achieved.

D. **Incorrect:** The required result is achieved.

Further Reading

 "Computing, Networking, Printing, and Scanning Acronyms." You can find this article at the Microsoft Support Online Web site (http://support.microsoft.com/support/c.asp?FR=0) by selecting "Specific article ID number" under "I want to search by," entering **Q86179** in the "My question is" field, and then clicking on the Find button.

 "How to Create Windows NT Boot Floppy Disks." You can find this article at the Microsoft Support Online Web site (http://support.microsoft.com/support/c.asp?FR=0) by selecting "Specific article ID number" under "I want to search by," entering **Q131735** in the "My question is" field, and then clicking on the Find button.

 Microsoft Windows NT Technical Support Training kit. Review Chapter 1 "Overview of Windows NT" and Lessons 1 and 2 in Chapter 2, "Installing Windows NT."

 Microsoft Windows NT Server Start Here Manual. Chapters 5–8 provide a step-by-step look at the installation process for review.

 "Windows NT Partitioning Rules During Setup." You can find this article at the Microsoft Support Online Web site (http://support.microsoft.com/support/c.asp?FR=0) by selecting "Specific article ID number" under "I want to search by," entering **Q138364** in the "My question is" field, and then clicking on the Find button.

OBJECTIVE   2.2

Install Windows NT Server using various installation methods and procedures.

Although Windows NT Server can be installed a number of ways, the most common methods are via CD-ROM or with the Windows NT setup diskettes. A CD-ROM installation is manual and requires that you answer all of the questions presented during the installation process. Using the appropriate switches with the winnt.exe or winnt32.exe utilities, you can complete installation even if you have misplaced the three setup diskettes. For CD-ROM installation you can also use the /ox switch to generate the necessary diskettes during installation. For server-based installation, the diskettes may be avoided altogether by using the /b switch.

For network environments, where customization and automation are required, the Windows NT Server distribution files can be copied to a network share. Then, the setup files can be customized and automated to rapidly deploy Windows NT across the network. Any file server can be used as the distribution point for the Windows NT Server "Over the Network" installation. For example, using a NetWare server, a Windows NT Server automated installation routine can be designed that installs Windows NT Server, a specific network adapter, and TCP/IP configured to use DHCP. This process can occur without user intervention. Automation is achieved using setup switches, /w, /u, and /s to augment the WINNT or WINNT32 installation command.

After Windows NT Server is installed, it can be used to assist in the installation of client network drivers and Windows 95, thereby enabling computers on the network to use the services provided by Windows NT Server. The utility available for this purpose is called the Network Client Administrator, which can be found in the Start menu under Administrative Tools on Windows NT Server.

To successfully answer the questions for this objective, you need a firm understanding of the key terms in the following section. For definitions of these terms, refer to the Glossary in this book.

Key Terms

- Answer file

- Client network drivers

- Floppyless installation

- Network Client Administrator

- Network share

- Redirector

- Setup switches

- Source directory

- Uniqueness Database File (UDF)

70-067.02.02.001

How must a server be configured to create a Windows NT 4.0 Server domain?

A. Member server

B. Backup domain controller

C. Primary domain controller

70-067.02.02.002

How many primary domain controllers are required to serve a Windows NT 4.0 single domain network with 1,000 clients?

A. 1

B. 2

C. 3

D. 5

70-067.02.02.001

How must a server be configured to create a Windows NT 4.0 Server domain?

▶ **Correct Answer: C**

  A. **Incorrect:** Installing a Windows NT Server as a member server does not allow for the creation of a domain, because the server cannot act as a domain controller. Installing a Windows NT Server as a member server allows the server to join a domain or a workgroup and to create a workgroup.

  B. **Incorrect:** Installing a Windows NT Server as a backup domain controller (BDC) does not allow for the creation of a domain. Although a BDC is a domain controller, it can only join an existing domain.

  C. **Correct:** Since, during the installation of a primary domain controller (PDC), the setup routine requests a unique name for the domain, a PDC is used to create a domain. BDCs, member servers, and clients can join the domain after the installation of the PDC.

70-067.02.02.002

How many primary domain controllers are required to serve a Windows NT 4.0 single domain network with 1,000 clients?

▶ **Correct Answer: A**

  A. **Correct:** Regardless of the size of the network, only one primary domain controller (PDC) can be created for a single domain network. Each domain can contain only one PDC and as many BDCs as are required to support the domain users.

  B. **Incorrect:** No more than one PDC can exist in a domain.

  C. **Incorrect:** No more than one PDC can exist in a domain.

  D. **Incorrect:** No more than one PDC can exist in a domain.

70-067.02.02.003

What is created by Windows NT Server Setup to uniquely identify every domain created, regardless of the names provided during the setup routine?

A. Domain name

B. NetBIOS name

C. Server identifier

D. Security identifier

70-067.02.02.004

The ACCT domain needs to be divided into the AP and AR domains. The ACCT domain is composed of a primary domain controller, two backup domain controllers, and eight member servers. One of the backup domain controllers from the ACCT domain needs to be reconfigured as a backup domain controller in the AP domain.

How can the existing backup domain controller on the ACCT domain be reconfigured to function as the backup domain controller in the AP domain?

A. Reinstall Windows NT Server 4.0.

B. Change the domain name from ACCT to AP.

C. Change the security identifier using the User Manager for Domains Properties tab.

D. Promote the ACCT backup domain controller to a primary domain controller on the AP domain, and demote the primary domain controller to a backup domain controller.

70-067.02.02.003

What is created by Windows NT Server Setup to uniquely identify every domain created, regardless of the names provided during the setup routine?

▶ **Correct Answer: D**

A. **Incorrect:** During the setup routine, one of the names provided by the person performing the installation routine is the domain name.

B. **Incorrect:** During the setup routine, one of the names provided by the person performing the installation routine is the NetBIOS name, also called a computer name.

C. **Incorrect:** There is no server identifier in Windows NT.

D. **Correct:** The security identifier or SID is a unique number that underlies many system services. For example, each user, computer name, and domain name object is given a unique SID, which is then used by network services to identify these objects. During the installation of a Windows NT Server PDC, the installation routine creates a unique SID for the domain.

70-067.02.02.004

The ACCT domain needs to be divided into the AP and AR domains. The ACCT domain is composed of a primary domain controller, two backup domain controllers, and eight member servers. One of the backup domain controllers from the ACCT domain needs to be reconfigured as a backup domain controller in the AP domain.

How can the existing backup domain controller on the ACCT domain be reconfigured to function as the backup domain controller in the AP domain?

▶ **Correct Answer: A**

A. **Correct:** The question states that the ACCT domain must be divided into two domains, AP and AR. The ACCT domain contains a PDC, two BDCs, and eight member servers. One BDC will be removed and reconfigured as a BDC in the AP domain. Since it is not possible to move a BDC to another domain, the only option is to reinstall, not upgrade, Windows NT Server as a BDC in the new domain.

B. **Incorrect:** Simply changing the domain name from ACCT to AP will not work since a BDC built for one domain cannot be moved to another domain. Only a Windows NT Server member server can join another domain.

C. **Incorrect:** User Manager for Domains does not include an option to change the SID of one domain to the SID of another.

D. **Incorrect:** While it is possible to promote a BDC to a PDC within a domain, this procedure cannot be used to move a BDC from one domain to another.

70-067.02.02.005

Which servers can authenticate users in a Windows NT 4.0 domain? (Choose two.)

A. Member servers

B. Backup domain controllers

C. Primary domain controllers

D. Any Windows NT Workstation computer

70-067.02.02.006

The ACCT domain on a network needs to be divided into the AP and AR domains. Three member servers from the ACCT domain will serve as member servers in the AP domain.

What should you do to reconfigure the member servers on the ACCT domain so they can function as member servers in the AP domain?

A. Reinstall Windows NT Server 4.0.

B. Have the servers join the AP domain.

C. Change the security identifier using the User Manager for Domain's properties.

D. Promote the ACCT member server to a primary domain controller on the AP domain, and demote the primary domain controller to a member server.

70-067.02.02.005

Which servers can authenticate users in a Windows NT 4.0 domain? (Choose two.)

▶ **Correct Answers: B and C**

    A. **Incorrect:** Member servers can join a domain, but they are not able to authenticate users into a Windows NT 4.0 domain. Member servers do not maintain a copy of the domain security accounts manager (SAM) database used to authenticate users. Additionally, a member server does not run the NetLogon service which is used to authenticate users to the domain.

    B. **Correct:** A BDC contains a copy of the domain SAM database and runs the NetLogon service. Therefore, a BDC can authenticate users to the domain.

    C. **Correct:** A PDC contains the master SAM database for the domain. Additionally, the PDC runs the NetLogon service. Therefore, a PDC can authenticate users to the domain.

    D. **Incorrect:** Like a member server, a Windows NT Workstation does not maintain the domain SAM database and does not run the NetLogon service. Therefore, a Windows NT Workstation is unable to authenticate users to the domain.

70-067.02.02.006

The ACCT domain on a network needs to be divided into the AP and AR domains. Three member servers from the ACCT domain will serve as member servers in the AP domain.

What should you do to reconfigure the member servers on the ACCT domain so they can function as member servers in the AP domain?

▶ **Correct Answer: B**

    A. **Incorrect:** It is not necessary to reinstall Windows NT Server 4.0 on a member server to move from the ACCT domain to the AP domain. Unlike a PDC or BDC, a member server is not bound to a single domain.

    B. **Correct:** From the Change Domain button in the Control Panel–Network program, a member server can join a domain. In addition, all versions of Windows NT must register their computer account in the new domain. This can be accomplished from the same Change Domain button or through Server Manager. In either case, administrator equivalent access to the PDC is necessary to initiate a computer account in the domain.

    C. **Incorrect:** User Manager for Domains does not include an option to change the SID of one domain to the SID of another.

    D. **Incorrect:** A member server can not change its role to domain controller. A server must be installed as a BDC to be promoted to a PDC. Through the process of promotion, the PDC in the domain is automatically demoted to a BDC, if it is online. A PDC cannot be directly demoted to BDC. Additionally, BDC to PDC promotion can only be accomplished within the domain controller's current domain.

70-067.02.02.007

The ACCT domain has a PDC, two BDCs, and eight member servers. The ACCT domain needs to be divided into the AP and AR domains, each with a PDC, two BDCs, and four member servers. Three new servers have been purchased.

The required result is to create the AP and AR domains.

The first optional result is to configure two BDCs for each domain and split the member servers between the two domains.

The second optional result is to make the conversion as efficient as possible.

The proposed solution is to reinstall Windows NT Server on the existing PDC and both BDCs for the AP domain, install Windows NT Server on the three new computers as the PDC and BDCs of the AR domain, and reinstall Windows NT Server on all eight member servers for the AP and AR domains.

What does the proposed solution provide?

A. The required result and both optional results.

B. The required result and one optional result.

C. The required result but none of the optional results.

D. The proposed solution does not provide the required result.

70-067.02.02.007

The ACCT domain has a PDC, two BDCs, and eight member servers. The ACCT domain needs to be divided into the AP and AR domains, each with a PDC, two BDCs, and four member servers. Three new servers have been purchased.

The required result is to create the AP and AR domains.

The first optional result is to configure two BDCs for each domain and split the member servers between the two domains.

The second optional result is to make the conversion as efficient as possible.

The proposed solution is to reinstall Windows NT Server on the existing PDC and both BDCs for the AP domain, install Windows NT Server on the three new computers as the PDC and BDCs of the AR domain, and reinstall Windows NT Server on all eight member servers for the AP and AR domains.

What does the proposed solution provide?

▶ **Correct Answer: B**

A. **Incorrect:** The required result and the first optional result are achieved. However, the second optional result, to make the conversion process as efficient as possible, is not achieved.

B. **Correct:** The required result, to create the AP and AR domains, is achieved. The proposed solution directs you to reinstall Windows NT Server on the exiting PDC for the ACCT domain. During the reinstallation of the PDC, the AP domain can be created. The AR domain is created by installing Windows NT Server as a PDC on one of the three new computers.

The first optional result is to configure two BDCs for each domain and split the member servers between the two domains. During the reinstallation of the BDCs from the ACCT domain, these computers can be directed to join the AP domain. Next, the three new computers are installed and configured as the PDC and two BDCs that join the AR domain. To complete the requirements for the first optional result, Windows NT Server is reinstalled on four of the member servers and, during this process, directed to join the AP domain. Windows NT Server is then reinstalled on the other four member servers and directed to join the AR domain. Therefore, the first optional result is fulfilled.

As you may have guessed from this lengthy explanation, the second optional result, to make the conversion as efficient as possible, is not achieved. It is not efficient to reinstall Windows NT Server in order to replace the ACCT domain with a new domain name. It is more efficient to rename the ACCT domain on the original PDC to AP and then direct the BDCs to join this renamed domain. Therefore, only the required result and the first optional result are achieved.

C. **Incorrect:** The required result and one of the optional results are achieved.

D. **Incorrect:** The required result is achieved.

70-067.02.02.008

The ACCT domain has a PDC, two BDCs, and eight member servers. The ACCT domain needs to be divided into the AP and AR domains, each with a PDC, two BDCs, and four member servers. Three new servers have been purchased.

The required result is to create the AP and AR domains.

The first optional result is to configure two BDCs for each domain and split the member servers between the two domains.

The second optional result is to make the conversion as efficient as possible.

The proposed solution is to reinstall Windows NT Server on the existing PDC and both BDCs for the AP domain, install Windows NT Server on the three new computers as the PDC and BDCs of the AR domain, and reinstall Windows NT Server on four of the eight member servers to become part of the AR domain.

What does the proposed solution provide?

A. The required result and both optional results.

B. The required result and one optional result.

C. The required result but none of the optional results.

D. The proposed solution does not provide the required result.

70-067.02.02.008

The ACCT domain has a PDC, two BDCs, and eight member servers. The ACCT domain needs to be divided into the AP and AR domains, each with a PDC, two BDCs, and four member servers. Three new servers have been purchased.

The required result is to create the AP and AR domains.

The first optional result is to configure two BDCs for each domain and split the member servers between the two domains.

The second optional result is to make the conversion as efficient as possible.

The proposed solution is to reinstall Windows NT Server on the existing PDC and both BDCs for the AP domain, install Windows NT Server on the three new computers as the PDC and BDCs of the AR domain, and reinstall Windows NT Server on four of the eight member servers to become part of the AR domain.

What does the proposed solution provide?

▶ **Correct Answer: C**

A. **Incorrect:** Only the required result is achieved. The first optional result, to configure two BDCs for each domain and split the member servers between the two domains and the second optional result, to make the conversion process as efficient as possible, is not achieved.

B. **Incorrect:** The required result is achieved, but none of the optional results are achieved

C. **Correct:** The required result, to create the AP and AR domains, is achieved. The proposed solution directs you to reinstall Windows NT Server on the exiting PDC for the ACCT domain. During the reinstallation of the PDC, the AP domain can be created. The AR domain is created by installing Windows NT Server as a PDC on one of the three new computers.

The first optional result, to configure two BDCs in each domain and split the member servers between the two domains, is only partially achieved. During the reinstallation of the BDCs from the ACCT domain, these computers can be directed to join the AP domain. Next, the two remaining new computers are installed and configured as BDCs that join the AR domain. Windows NT Server is then reinstalled on four of the member servers and, during this process, directed to join the AR domain. However, no procedure is provided for reconfiguring the other four member servers to become part of the AP domain. Therefore, the first optional result is not fulfilled.

As with the previous question, the second optional result, to make the conversion as efficient as possible, is not achieved. It is not efficient to reinstall Windows NT Server in order to create a new domain name. Instead, it is more efficient to rename the ACCT domain on the original PDC to AP and then direct the BDCs to join this renamed domain. Therefore, only the required result and the first optional result are achieved.

D. **Incorrect:** The required result is achieved.

70-067.02.02.009

The ACCT domain has a PDC, two BDCs, and eight member servers. The ACCT domain needs to be divided into the AP and AR domains, each with a PDC, two BDCs, and four member servers. Three new servers have been purchased.

The required result is to create the AP and AR domains.

The first optional result is to configure two BDCs for each domain and split the member servers between the two domains.

The second optional result is to make the conversion as efficient as possible.

The proposed solution is to reinstall Windows NT Server on the existing PDC and both BDCs for the AP domain, install Windows NT Server on the three new computers as the PDC and BDCs of the AR domain, and have member servers join the appropriate domain.

What does the proposed solution provide?

A. The required result and both optional results.

B. The required result and one optional result.

C. The required result but none of the optional results.

D. The proposed solution does not provide the required result.

70-067.02.02.009

The ACCT domain has a PDC, two BDCs, and eight member servers. The ACCT domain needs to be divided into the AP and AR domains, each with a PDC, two BDCs, and four member servers. Three new servers have been purchased.

The required result is to create the AP and AR domains.

The first optional result is to configure two BDCs for each domain and split the member servers between the two domains.

The second optional result is to make the conversion as efficient as possible.

The proposed solution is to reinstall Windows NT Server on the existing PDC and both BDCs for the AP domain, install Windows NT Server on the three new computers as the PDC and BDCs of the AR domain, and have member servers join the appropriate domain.

What does the proposed solution provide?

▶   **Correct Answer: B**

A. **Incorrect:** The required result and the first optional result are achieved. However, the second optional result, to make the conversion process as efficient as possible, is not achieved.

B. **Correct:** The required result, to create the AP and AR domains, is achieved. The proposed solution directs you to reinstall Windows NT Server on the existing PDC for the ACCT domain. During the reinstallation of the PDC, the AP domain can be created. The AR domain is created by installing Windows NT Server as a PDC on one of the three new computers.

   The first optional result is to configure two BDCs for each domain and split the member servers between the two domains. During the reinstallation of the BDCs from the ACCT domain, these computers can be directed to join the AP domain. Next, the three new computers are installed and configured as the PDC and two BDCs that join the AR domain. To complete the requirements for the first optional result, four member servers are reconfigured to join the AP domain and the other four member servers are reconfigured to join the AR domain. Therefore, the first optional result is fulfilled.

   While reconfiguring the member servers to the new domains is efficient, the second optional result, to make the entire conversion as efficient as possible, is not achieved. It is not efficient to reinstall Windows NT Server in order to replace the ACCT domain with a new domain name. Instead, it is more efficient to rename the ACCT domain on the original PDC to AP and then direct the BDCs to join this renamed domain. Therefore, only the required result and the first optional result are achieved.

C. **Incorrect:** The required result and one optional result are achieved.

D. **Incorrect:** The required result is achieved.

70-067.02.02.010

The ACCT domain has a PDC, two BDCs, and eight member servers. The ACCT domain needs to be divided into the AP and AR domains, each with a PDC, two BDCs, and four member servers. Three new servers have been purchased.

The required result is to create the AP and AR domains.

The first optional result is to configure two BDCs for each domain and split the member servers between the two domains.

The second optional result is to make the conversion as efficient as possible.

The proposed solution is to rename the ACCT domain to the AP domain, install Windows NT Server on the three new computers as the PDC and BDCs of the AR domain, and have member servers join the appropriate domain.

What does the proposed solution provide?

A. The required result and both optional results.

B. The required result and one optional result.

C. The required result but none of the optional results.

D. The proposed solution does not provide the required result.

70-067.02.02.010

The ACCT domain has a PDC, two BDCs, and eight member servers. The ACCT domain needs to be divided into the AP and AR domains, each with a PDC, two BDCs, and four member servers. Three new servers have been purchased.

The required result is to create the AP and AR domains.

The first optional result is to configure two BDCs for each domain and split the member servers between the two domains.

The second optional result is to make the conversion as efficient as possible.

The proposed solution is to rename the ACCT domain to the AP domain, install Windows NT Server on the three new computers as the PDC and BDCs of the AR domain, and have member servers join the appropriate domain.

What does the proposed solution provide?

▶ **Correct Answer: A**

A. **Correct:** The required result, to create the AP and AR domains, is achieved. The proposed solution directs you to rename the ACCT domain to the AP domain. Note that for the domain renaming to be complete this procedure should be started at the ACCT PDC, and then completed on both ACCT BDCs. The AR domain is created by installing Windows NT Server as a PDC on one of the three new computers.

The first optional result is to configure two BDCs for each domain and split the member servers between the two domains. Since the ACCT domain is renamed as the AP domain, the two BDCs of the ACCT domain become the BDCs of the new AP domain. Since the AP domain contains the same domain SID used for the ACCT domain, the reconfiguration will be successful. Next, the two remaining new computers are installed and configured as BDCs that join the AR domain. To complete the requirements for the first optional result, the member servers are reconfigured to join the appropriate domain. Therefore, the first optional result is fulfilled.

Renaming the current PDC and BDCs from ACCT to AP, installing three Windows NT Servers, one PDC and two BDCs, and reconfiguring the member servers to join appropriate domain names is the most efficient way to complete the network reconfiguration. Thus, the second optional result, to make the conversion as efficient as possible, is achieved.

B. **Incorrect:** The required result and both optional results are achieved.

C. **Incorrect:** The required result and both optional results are achieved.

D. **Incorrect:** The required result is achieved.

Further Reading

 "Description of OS/2 LAN Manager Device Drivers and NDIS." You can find this article at the Microsoft Support Online Web site (http://support.microsoft.com/support/c.asp?FR=0) by selecting "Specific article ID number" under "I want to search by," entering **Q51088** in the "My question is" field, and then clicking on the Find button.

 "Microsoft Network Client and LAN Manager 2.2c Comparison." You can find this article at the Microsoft Support Online Web site (http://support.microsoft.com/support/c.asp?FR=0) by selecting "Specific article ID number" under "I want to search by," entering **Q124175** in the "My question is" field, and then clicking on the Find button.

 Microsoft Windows NT Technical Support Training kit. Review Lesson 5 in Chapter 2, "Installing Windows NT." Lesson 5 provides you with practice on customizing and installing Windows NT using the "Over the Network" installation method, and explains how to remove Windows NT.

 Microsoft Windows NT Server Concepts and Planning Manual. Chapter 11, "Managing Client Administration," provides you with a comprehensive review of the Network Client Administrator program.

OBJECTIVE 2.3

Install Windows NT Server to serve a variety of roles.

Windows NT Server can be installed to act as either a file and print server or as an application server. Under certain circumstances it is appropriate to configure a computer to act as both. For example, in small networks it would be practical to install a Windows NT Server to act as both an Exchange e-mail (application) server and as a file and print server.

A Windows NT Server file and print server not only provides shared disk and printer devices for users to store files and print documents on, it is also a domain controller. As such, it maintains a central repository of user names and groups that can be referenced and authenticated throughout the network. Using this server, an administrative user in the domain can manage all clients that are part of their domain, or a trusted domain.

There are two types of domain controllers: a Primary Domain Controller (PDC), and a Backup Domain Controller (BDC). The PDC stores the only modifiable database of user accounts and groups in the domain. This database is called the Security Accounts Manager (SAM). A BDC provides a real-time, read-only, backup of the SAM database.

Besides playing the role of two domain controllers, a Windows NT Server can also play the role of member server. A member server is not involved in domain-based user and group account management. Instead, a member server either joins an existing domain or joins a workgroup on the network. Removing the domain management requirement from the server frees up the server for other tasks. It is common for a member server to act as an application server and run resource intensive services, such as SQL Server or Exchange Server.

During the installation of Windows NT Server, you must decide whether the computer will act as a PDC, BDC, or member server. If you choose to configure your server as a PDC, you must define a unique domain name. If you choose to configure it as a BDC, you must join a domain. However, if you configure a computer as a member server, you can join a domain, create a workgroup, or join a workgroup. The computer name, domain, or workgroup name information must be configured during the installation process.

To successfully answer the questions for this objective, you need a firm understanding of the key terms in the following section. For definitions of these terms, refer to the Glossary in this book.

Key Terms

- Application server

- File and print server

- Security identifier (SID)

- Trusted domain

- Windows NT Server BDC

- Windows NT Server member server

- Windows NT Server PDC

70-067.02.03.001

You need to upgrade a Windows NT Server 3.51 machine on your network to Windows NT Server 4.0. You have copied the \I386 directory from the Windows NT Server 4.0 CD-ROM to a server and created an answer file named UNATTEND.TXT to automate the installation.

After mapping a network drive to the \I386 directory on the network server, which command should you issue to install Windows NT Server 4.0?

A. WINNT /U

B. WINNT /N:UNATTEND.TXT

C. WINNT32 /U:UNATTEND.TXT

D. WINNT32 /A:UNATTEND.TXT

E. WINNT32 /UDF:UNATTEND.TXT

70-067.02.03.001

You need to upgrade a Windows NT Server 3.51 machine on your network to Windows NT Server 4.0. You have copied the \I386 directory from the Windows NT Server 4.0 CD-ROM to a server and created an answer file named UNATTEND.TXT to automate the installation.

After mapping a network drive to the \I386 directory on the network server, which command should you issue to install Windows NT Server 4.0?

▶ **Correct Answer: C**

A. **Incorrect:** This question states that you need to upgrade a networked computer from Windows NT Server 3.51 to Windows NT Server 4.0. It also states that you have taken all necessary steps to perform an "Over the Network" installation. The answer suggests that you use the 16-bit WINNT installation routine, which will not work on a Windows NT Server 3.51 installation. Additionally, the /U switch must be followed by the name of a file used for an unattended installation of Windows NT.

B. **Incorrect:** The /N switch is not a legal Windows NT installation switch. Additionally, the WINNT 16-bit installation routine will not work on a Windows NT 3.51 installation.

C. **Correct:** To upgrade Windows NT 3.51, the correct command is WINNT32. The /u:answer_file switch following the command allows you to automate the installation of Windows NT Server 4.0, over the network. This command specifies the location of an answer file that provides answers the user would otherwise be prompted for during Setup. In this example, the default automated installation file, UNATTEND.TXT, is being used for the installation.

D. **Incorrect:** While the WINNT32 command is the correct command to upgrade Windows NT 3.51 to Windows NT 4, the switch following WINNT32 is incorrect.

E. **Incorrect:** The /UDF switch is used in conjunction with the /U switch to customize the installation of Windows NT further.

70-067.02.03.002

You need to install Windows NT Server 4.0 on a number of computers using an unattended installation. You are using an answer file named UNATTEND.TXT and a Uniqueness Database File named MYSERVERS.TXT, both placed in the \I386 directory on the C: drive of a network server. All computers connect to the C:\I386 directory share using the logical M: drive.

What is the correct command syntax to install Windows NT Server on the computer identified as server1 currently running MS-DOS?

A. WINNT /U:server1 /UDF:server1

B. WINNT32 /UDF:server1 /UDF MYSERVERS.TXT

C. WINNT /U:UNATTEND.TXT /UDF:server1 /MYSERVERS.TXT

D. WINNT /S:M:\ /U:UNATTEND.TXT /UDF:server1, M:\MYSERVERS.TXT

70-067.02.03.002

You need to install Windows NT Server 4.0 on a number of computers using an unattended installation. You are using an answer file named UNATTEND.TXT and a Uniqueness Database File named MYSERVERS.TXT, both placed in the \I386 directory on the C: drive of a network server. All computers connect to the C:\I386 directory share using the logical M: drive.

What is the correct command syntax to install Windows NT Server on the computer identified as server1 currently running MS-DOS?

▶ **Correct Answer: D**

A. **Incorrect:** While WINNT is the correct 16-bit installation routine for a computer running MS-DOS, the syntax specified for the /U and /UDF command is incorrect.

B. **Incorrect:** WINNT32 is not the correct routine for installing Windows NT on an MS-DOS computer. Additionally, /U is not specified in this unattended installation while the uniqueness database file switch is specified twice.

C. **Incorrect:** WINNT is the correct 16-bit installation routine for an MS-DOS computer. However, no source directory is specified for the unattended installation, there is no comma between the uniqueness ID and the name of the uniqueness database file, MYSERVERS.TXT. Additionally, there is a forward slash preceding the name of the uniqueness database file.

D. **Correct:** The WINNT command is the correct installation routine for a computer running MS-DOS. The /S switch specifies the source directory of the installation files, M:. The UNATTEND.TXT file is stored in the source directory, M: and the /UDF syntax tells the WINNT command to merge any sections of MYSERVERS.TXT containing the server1 identifier into the setup routine.

70-067.02.03.003

You are planning to install Windows NT Server 4.0 on a Pentium-based computer running Windows NT 3.51 which has a CD-ROM drive installed as drive E:. While you have the Windows NT Server 4.0 compact disc, you have lost the NT Server setup floppy disks. All hardware devices are listed on the HCL.

The required result is to install Windows NT Server 4.0.

The first optional result is to replace the Windows NT Server setup floppy disks that are needed to complete an installation of Windows NT Server from a compact disc.

The second optional result is to provide the capability to use the Windows NT Server Emergency Repair Disk in case of a boot failure.

The proposed solution is to mount the Windows NT Server 4.0 compact disc and run E:\I386\ WINNT32 /OX.

What does the proposed solution provide?

A. The required result and all optional results.

B. The required result and one optional result.

C. The required result but none of the optional results.

D. The proposed solution does not provide the required result.

70-067.02.03.003

You are planning to install Windows NT Server 4.0 on a Pentium-based computer running Windows NT 3.51 which has a CD-ROM drive installed as drive E:. While you have the Windows NT Server 4.0 compact disc, you have lost the NT Server setup floppy disks. All hardware devices are listed on the HCL.

The required result is to install Windows NT Server 4.0.

The first optional result is to replace the Windows NT Server setup floppy disks that are needed to complete an installation of Windows NT Server from a compact disc.

The second optional result is to provide the capability to use the Windows NT Server Emergency Repair Disk in case of a boot failure.

The proposed solution is to mount the Windows NT Server 4.0 compact disc and run E:\I386\ WINNT32 /OX.

What does the proposed solution provide?

▶   **Correct Answer: D**

A. **Incorrect:** The required result is not achieved and only one optional result, to replace the Windows NT Server setup floppy disks, is achieved.

B. **Incorrect:** Since the required result is not achieved, you can immediately conclude that the only correct answer is D

C. **Incorrect:** Since the required result is not achieved, you can immediately conclude that the only correct answer is D.

D. **Correct:** The proposed solution suggests that you run the WINNT32 /ox command. This command will create the lost setup boot floppies; however, it will not run the installation of Windows NT. Therefore, the required result, to install Windows NT Server 4.0, is not achieved.

Further Reading

 Microsoft Windows NT Technical Support Training kit. Review Lessons 2 and 3 in Chapter 2, "Installing Windows NT." These lessons list the important preparation steps for an installation of Windows NT, and procedures for adding a Windows NT computer account to a domain.

 Microsoft Windows NT Resource Kit. Chapter 2, "Microsoft Corporation Worldwide Network Background" is an examination of how Microsoft Corporation configured their Worldwide Network which will give you insight on how to configure domains in a large network.

OBJECTIVE 2.4

Install the most common network protocols and configure protocol binding order and activity.

The three most common protocols used for networking Windows NT Server are NetBEUI, NWLink IPX/SPX, and TCP/IP. This objective explores how these protocols are configured to operate in a Windows NT network. Enhanced Windows NT protocol services such as WINS are also included in this objective. Before testing your knowledge of protocol configuration, review Objective 1.3 on protocol features and characteristics.

To successfully answer the questions for this objective, you need a firm understanding of the key terms in the following section. For definitions of these terms, refer to the Glossary in this book.

Key Terms

- Bindings

- Domain Name System (DNS)

- Dynamic Host Configuration Protocol (DHCP)

- File and Print Services for NetWare (FPNW)

- Frame

- Gateway

- Internal network number

- LMHOSTS

- Multi-homed computer

- Network Basic Input/Output System (NetBIOS)

- Routing

- Routing Information Protocol (RIP)

- Service Advertising Protocol (SAP)

- Windows Internet Naming Server (WINS)

70-067.02.04.001

You are setting up a network that has four Windows NT Server 4.0 computers and 70 workstations that use either Windows 95 or Windows NT Workstation 4.0. Two routers will be used to control the flow of network traffic. There are plans to connect the network to the Internet.

Which protocol should you use to network these computers?

A. DHCP

B. TCP/IP

C. IPX/SPX

D. NetBEUI

70-067.02.04.001

You are setting up a network that has four Windows NT Server 4.0 computers and 70 workstations that use either Windows 95 or Windows NT Workstation 4.0. Two routers will be used to control the flow of network traffic. There are plans to connect the network to the Internet.

Which protocol should you use to network these computers?

▶ **Correct Answer: B**

A. **Incorrect:** The Dynamic Host Configuration Protocol (DHCP) is a service designed to dynamically assign TCP/IP configuration information to DCHP enabled clients. While it could be considered part of the TCP/IP protocol suite, it, in itself, does not provide basic protocol connection services.

B. **Correct:** The question states that you will be configuring a network of four Windows NT Server 4.0 computers, and 70 workstations that use either Windows 95 or Windows NT Workstation 4.0. Any of the common protocols, NetBEUI, IPX/SPX, or TCP/IP, can service a network with this number of servers and clients. Then the question specifies that routers will be used to control the flow of network traffic. In this case, NetBEUI cannot be used since it is not a routable protocol. Finally, the question explains that there are plans to connect the network to the Internet. Since TCP/IP is the protocol used for Internet communications, IPX/SPX is eliminated and the correct answer is B, TCP/IP.

C. **Incorrect:** IPX/SPX is not used for Internet communications.

D. **Incorrect:** NetBEUI is not a routable protocol.

70-067.02.04.002

You are adding five Windows NT 4.0 Servers to an existing network that contains a single UNIX server and three NetWare 3.12 servers. Which protocols should you configure on the Windows NT Servers so they can communicate with the other servers? (Choose two.)

A. DHCP

B. TCP/IP

C. NetBEUI

D. UNIX Transport

E. NWLink IPX/SPX

70-067.02.04.002

You are adding five Windows NT 4.0 Servers to an existing network that contains a single UNIX server and three NetWare 3.12 servers. Which protocols should you configure on the Windows NT Servers so they can communicate with the other servers? (Choose two.)

▶ **Correct Answers: B and E**

A. **Incorrect:** The Dynamic Host Configuration Protocol (DHCP) is a service designed to dynamically assign TCP/IP configuration information to DCHP enabled clients. While it could be considered part of the TCP/IP protocol suite, it, in itself, does not provide basic protocol connection services.

B. **Correct:** Since you are adding five Windows NT 4.0 Servers to an existing network that contains a single UNIX server, you should configure TCP/IP on the Windows NT Servers so that they can communicate with the UNIX host. UNIX native protocol is TCP/IP.

C. **Incorrect:** The NetBEUI protocol cannot be used to communicate with a UNIX host or a NetWare server.

D. **Incorrect:** UNIX Transport is not a protocol.

E. **Correct:** Since you are adding five Windows NT 4.0 Servers to an existing network that contains three NetWare 3.12 servers, you should configure IPX/SPX on the Windows NT Servers so that they can communicate with the NetWare servers.

Note IPX/SPX alone will not provide client or gateway services to the NetWare server. See the Connectivity domain objective for details on configuring Windows NT Server for interoperability with NetWare.

70-067.02.04.003

You are setting up a backup domain controller and need to see the primary domain controller's IP configuration. Which command can you use on the PDC to view its TCP/IP configuration?

A. ping

B. ping /all

C. ipconfig /all

D. ipconfig /host

E. winipcfg

70-067.02.04.003

You are setting up a backup domain controller and need to see the primary domain controller's IP configuration. Which command can you use on the PDC to view its TCP/IP configuration?

▶ **Correct Answer: C**

A. **Incorrect:** Packet Internet Groper (ping) is a TCP/IP command used to verify connections to one or more remote hosts. The ping utility uses the ICMP echo request and echo reply packets to determine whether a particular IP system on a network is functional. The ping utility is useful for diagnosing IP network or router failures but is used mainly for determining the IP configuration of the PDC.

B. **Incorrect:** The ping utility does not function with switches. Therefore the /all switch is invalid.

C. **Correct:** The command to use on a computer running Windows NT to view its TCP/IP configuration information is ipconfig /all. This utility displays all current TCP/IP network configuration values. If ipconfig is entered without switches, the response is a display of basic TCP/IP configuration values, including IP address, subnet mask, and default gateway. Using the /all switch displays additional details like primary and secondary WINS server addresses, NetBIOS broadcast type and DNS address information.

D. **Incorrect:** While the ipconfig utility does support switches, the /host switch is invalid. The command syntax for the ipconfig utility is: ipconfig [/all | /renew [adapter] | /release [adapter]]. For more information on these switches, see Appendix A, "TCP/IP Utilities Reference," in *Internetworking with Microsoft TCP/IP on Microsoft Windows NT.4.0.*

E. **Incorrect:** The winipcfg utility is used on a Windows 95 or Windows 98 computer to view TCP/IP configuration information. Notice that the ipconfig command functions on a Windows 98 computer.

70-067.02.04.004

You are setting up TCP/IP on a Windows NT Server 4.0 Intel-based computer that has an IP address of 200.200.200.8. What is the command used to test the network connectivity from the server to the primary domain controller whose IP address is 200.200.200.5?

A. ping 200.200.200.5

B. ping 200.200.200.8

C. ipconfig 200.200.200.5

D. ipconfig 200.200.200.8

70-067.02.04.004

You are setting up TCP/IP on a Windows NT Server 4.0 Intel-based computer that has an IP address of 200.200.200.8. What is the command used to test the network connectivity from the server to the primary domain controller whose IP address is 200.200.200.5?

▶ **Correct Answer: A**

A. **Correct:** You are asked what command is used to test network connectivity from a computer with an IP address of 200.200.200.8 to a PDC with an IP address of 200.200.200.5. The ping utility is used to test the connection. Review the answer to the previous question for details on the ping utility. Using ping, you request a reply from 200.200.200.5 by specifying this IP address after the ping command or ping 200.200.200.5.

B. **Incorrect:** After TCP/IP is configured on a computer, it is common to ping the address of the local computer. However, this is not the best answer since your goal is to test connectivity from the server to the PDC.

C. **Incorrect:** The ipconfig utility is not used to test connectivity between two TCP/ip hosts. Additionally, it is not valid to specify an IP address following the ipconfig command. This utility can only be used for local IP address information.

D. **Incorrect:** The ipconfig utility is not used to test connectivity between two TCP/ip hosts. Additionally, it is not valid to specify an IP address following the ipconfig command. This utility can only be used for local IP address information.

70-067.02.04.005

You are the administrator of a NetWare 3.12 LAN using the 802.2 frame type over 10BaseT.

The required result is to connect a Windows NT Server–based computer named NTS4MIS1 to the LAN.

The first optional result is to configure NTS4MIS1 to act as an IPX router.

The second optional result is to allow NTS4MIS1 to communicate with NetWare servers.

The proposed solution is to install a compatible network adapter card on NTS4MIS1, connect the adapter to the network hub, install NWLink, and enable RIP routing over IPX.

What does the proposed solution provide?

A. The required result and all optional results.

B. The required result and one optional results.

C. The required result but none of the optional results.

D. The proposed solution does not provide the required result.

70-067.02.04.005

You are the administrator of a NetWare 3.12 LAN using the 802.2 frame type over 10BaseT.

The required result is to connect a Windows NT Server–based computer named NTS4MIS1 to the LAN.

The first optional result is to configure NTS4MIS1 to act as an IPX router.

The second optional result is to allow NTS4MIS1 to communicate with NetWare servers.

The proposed solution is to install a compatible network adapter card on NTS4MIS1, connect the adapter to the network hub, install NWLink, and enable RIP routing over IPX.

What does the proposed solution provide?

▶ **Correct Answer: C**

A. **Incorrect:** Only the required result, to connect a Windows NT Server–based computer named NTS4MIS1 to the LAN, is achieved. The first optional result, to configure NTS4MIS1 to act as an IPX router and the second optional result, to allow NTS4MIS1 to communicate with NetWare servers, is not achieved.

B. **Incorrect:** The required result is achieved, but none of the optional results are achieved

C. **Correct:** Only the required result, to connect a Windows NT Server–based computer named NTS4MIS1 to the LAN, is achieved. The first optional result, to configure NTS4MIS1 to act as an IPX router is not achieved, because there is only one network adapter in the server. For a Windows NT Server to act as a router, two network adapters must be installed. The second optional result, to allow NTS4MIS1 to communicate with NetWare servers, is not achieved. While the IPX/SPX protocol allows the Windows NT Server to use the same protocol as the NetWare servers on the LAN, this protocol alone does not enable communication between these two server types. To access NetBIOS applications running on the NetWare server, the Windows NT Server requires the NWLink NetBIOS protocol layer. To provide logon capability from the Windows NT Server to the NetWare server, Gateway Services for NetWare must be installed on the Windows NT Server. This technology will be discussed in the Connectivity domain objective.

D. **Incorrect.** The required result is achieved.

Further Reading

 Microsoft Windows NT Server Networking Supplement Manual. Chapters 1–4 provide specific reference material on implementing TCP/IP in Windows NT.

 Microsoft Windows NT Server Resource Kit: Microsoft Windows NT Networking Guide. The Introduction, Chapters 1, 5–10, and 13, and Appendix F provide an architectural overview of how transport protocols and networking services fit into the structure of the Windows NT operating system.

 Microsoft Windows NT Technical Support Training kit. Chapter 10, "Configuring Windows NT Protocols," provides you with a comprehensive discussion of the transport protocols supported in Windows NT and how to configure them for proper operation.

OBJECTIVE 2.5

Configure network adapters.

Just like protocols, network adapters are installed and configured through the Network program in Control Panel. Before network adapter drivers can be installed, the network adapter(s) must be installed and configured. Installing a single network adapter is a relatively straightforward procedure. The installation of multiple network adapters in a computer requires attention to hardware configuration. Pay attention to the following rules to ensure proper operation:

- Both adapters must be configured to use their network adapter drivers as specified under the Adapters tab in the Network dialog box.

- Unless you are using third-party load-balancing or network fault-tolerance hardware or software, each network adapter must be connected to distinct network segments.

- Each protocol that will be supported must be installed and configured for use on each network adapter. For example, the TCP/IP protocol must be configured to use a valid IP address and subnet mask for each segment of the network.

- If the multi-homed computer will be used for routing, either a static route or routes must be configured or the RIP Service must be installed. Additionally, only one gateway address should be configured for a single network adapter in the computer.

To successfully answer the questions for this objective, you need a firm understanding of the key terms in the following section. For definitions of these terms, refer to the Glossary in this book.

Key Terms

- Base memory address

- Interrupts

- I/O addresses

- Network adapter

- Network adapter driver

70-067.02.05.001

A Windows NT Server 4.0 using 10BaseT Ethernet with the 802.3 frame type needs to communicate with a NetWare 4.11 server using 10BaseT Ethernet with the 802.2 frame type. Both servers are connected to the same IPX network. What is the fastest way to accomplish this?

A. Add a network interface card to the NetWare 4.11 computer.

B. Reconfigure the NetWare 4.11 computer to use the 802.2 frame type and reconfigure all clients using 802.3 to use 802.2.

C. Configure the Windows NT 4.0 computer to use multiple frame types.

D. Add a network interface card to the Windows NT Server 4.0 computer.

70-067.02.05.001

A Windows NT Server 4.0 using 10BaseT Ethernet with the 802.3 frame type needs to communicate with a NetWare 4.11 server using 10BaseT Ethernet with the 802.2 frame type. Both servers are connected to the same IPX network. What is the fastest way to accomplish this?

▶ **Correct Answer: C**

    A. **Incorrect:** A Windows NT Server 4.0 using 10BaseT Ethernet and running the 802.3 frame type needs to communicate with a NetWare 4.11 server also using 10BaseT Ethernet but running the 802.2 frame type. Both servers are connected through their respective network adapters to the same IPX network. While a network adapter could be added to the NetWare 4.11 server, it cannot be attached to the same network.

    B. **Incorrect:** Although a NetWare server can be reconfigured to run the 802.2 frame type, depending on the size of the network, reconfiguring all clients to use 802.2 could be a lengthy process. While running a single frame type is the best solution to use the network efficiently, it is not, as the question asks, the fastest way to accomplish this task.

    C. **Correct:** Configuring the Windows NT Server to use multiple frame types, 802.2 and 802.3, is the fastest way to accomplish connectivity between the NetWare server and the Windows NT Server. Notice that the NetWare server can also be configured for multiple frame types, but this is not necessary to accomplish this task.

    D. **Incorrect:** Adding a network adapter to the Windows NT Server will not work for the same reason that adding a network card to the NetWare server will not work to accomplish this task.

70-067.02.05.002

There are two NetWare 3.12 servers on your LAN, and you want to install a Windows NT Server 4.0 computer named NTSRV4LA. You install a compatible network adapter card in NTSRV4LA, set the binding for NWLink, and connect NTSRV4LA to the LAN.

The required result is to provide connectivity between the Internet and NTSRV4LA.

The first optional result is to configure NTSRV4LA to act as an IPX router.

The second optional result is to prevent Internet users from accessing your LAN without permission.

The proposed solution is to install an additional network adapter, configure it with only TCP/IP, and connect it to the Internet. Use the Routing tab in the NWLink IPX/SPX Properties box to enable Routing Information Protocol (RIP).

What does the proposed solution provide?

A. The required result and all optional results.

B. The required result and one optional result.

C. The required result but none of the optional results.

D. The proposed solution does not provide the required result.

70-067.02.05.002

There are two NetWare 3.12 servers on your LAN, and you want to install a Windows NT Server 4.0 computer named NTSRV4LA. You install a compatible network adapter card in NTSRV4LA, set the binding for NWLink, and connect NTSRV4LA to the LAN.

The required result is to provide connectivity between the Internet and NTSRV4LA.

The first optional result is to configure NTSRV4LA to act as an IPX router.

The second optional result is to prevent Internet users from accessing your LAN without permission.

The proposed solution is to install an additional network adapter, configure it with only TCP/IP, and connect it to the Internet. Use the Routing tab in the NWLink IPX/SPX Properties box to enable Routing Information Protocol (RIP).

What does the proposed solution provide?

▶ **Correct Answer: B**

A. **Incorrect:** The required result and the second optional result are achieved. However, the first optional result is not achieved.

B. **Correct:** The required result, to provide connectivity between the Internet and the Windows NT Server, NTSRV4LA, is achieved. The proposed solution, to install a network adapter, configure it with only TCP/IP, and connect it to the Internet, allows this server to access the Internet. The first optional result, to configure NTSRV4LA to act as an IPX router, is not achieved since only one network adapter is bound to the IPX/SPX protocol. To achieve routing over IPX/SPX, both network adapters must be bound to IPX/SPX and the RIP for NWLink IPX/SPX Compatible Transport must be installed. The second optional result, to prevent Internet users from accessing your LAN without permission, is achieved through protocol isolation. On NTSRV4LA, IPX/SPX is bound to the network adapter connected to the internal network while the other network adapter is bound to only TCP/IP. The Routing tab in the IPX/SPX Properties box is not available since IPX/SPX is only bound to one network adapter.

C. **Incorrect:** The required result and one of the optional results are achieved.

D. **Incorrect:** The required result is achieved.

70-067.02.05.003

You are adding a sound card to your Windows NT Server 4.0 computer. The sound card must use IRQ 10. IRQ10 is the IRQ your network adapter is currently using. How can you change the network adapter's IRQ to IRQ 6?

A. In the Control Panel, click on the Network icon, click on the Services tab, select the appropriate adapter, click on Properties, and change the IRQ to 6.

B. In the Control Panel, click on the Network icon, click on the Adapters tab, select the appropriate adapter, click on Properties, and change the IRQ to 6.

C. In the Control Panel, click on the Network icon, click on the Adapters tab, select the appropriate adapter, click on Properties, click on Setup, and change the IRQ to 6.

D. In the Control Panel, click on the Network icon, click on the Services tab, select the appropriate adapter, click on Properties, click on Setup, and change the IRQ to 6.

70-067.02.05.003

You are adding a sound card to your Windows NT Server 4.0 computer. The sound card must use IRQ 10. IRQ10 is the IRQ your network adapter is currently using. How can you change the network adapter's IRQ to IRQ 6?

▶ **Correct Answer: B**

A. **Incorrect:** The Services tab in the Control Panel–Network program is used to configure and view installed network services. It is not used to adjust the driver configuration of a network adapter.

B. **Correct:** To change the IRQ settings for a network adapter, you must select the Adapters tab in the Control Panel–Network program and then select the Properties button.

C. **Incorrect:** This is a fictitious navigation procedure. It is important that you can visualize navigation procedures to efficiently administer a system running Windows NT.

D. **Incorrect:** As explained in option A, network adapters are not configured from the Services tab.

70-067.02.05.004

There are two NetWare 3.12 servers on your LAN, and you want to install a Windows NT Server 4.0 computer named NTSRV4LA.

You install a compatible network adapter card in NTSRV4LA, set the binding for NWLink, and connect it to the LAN.

The required result is to provide connectivity between the Internet and NTSRV4LA.

The first optional result is to configure NTSRV4LA to act as an IPX router.

The second optional result is to prevent Internet users from accessing your LAN without permission.

The proposed solution is to install an additional network adapter card, configure it with only TCP/IP, and connect it to the Internet. Install RIP for IP.

What does the proposed solution provide?

A. The required result and all optional results.

B. The required result and one optional result.

C. The required result but none of the optional results.

D. The proposed solution does not provide the required result.

70-067.02.05.004

There are two NetWare 3.12 servers on your LAN, and you want to install a Windows NT Server 4.0 computer named NTSRV4LA.

You install a compatible network adapter card in NTSRV4LA, set the binding for NWLink, and connect it to the LAN.

The required result is to provide connectivity between the Internet and NTSRV4LA.

The first optional result is to configure NTSRV4LA to act as an IPX router.

The second optional result is to prevent Internet users from accessing your LAN without permission.

The proposed solution is to install an additional network adapter card, configure it with only TCP/IP, and connect it to the Internet. Install RIP for IP.

What does the proposed solution provide?

▶ **Correct Answer: B**

A. **Incorrect:** The required result, to provide connectivity between the Internet and NTSRV4LA, and the second optional result, to prevent Internet users from accessing your LAN without permission, are achieved. However, the first optional result, to configure NTSRV4LA to act as an IPX router, is not achieved.

B. **Correct:** The question explains that a network adapter bound to NWLink IPX/SPX has been installed on the Windows NT Server, NTSRV4LA.

   The proposed solution states that an additional network adapter is installed into NTSRV4LA, bound to TCP/IP, and connected to the Internet. RIP for IP is also installed on this card. RIP for IP can be configured for a single network adapter to provide dynamic routing information to other computers connected to the same network. However, NTSRV4LA is connected to the internal LAN using only NWLink IPX/SPX. Therefore, the dynamic routing information collected on NTSRV4LA is only accessible by NTSRV4LA.

   This does satisfy the required result, to provide connectivity between the Internet and NTSRV4LA.

   This protocol isolation also satisfies the second optional result, to prevent Internet users from accessing your LAN without permission. The first optional result, to configure NTSRV4LA to act as an IPX router, is not achieved because both adapters are not running IPX/SPX and the RIP for NWLink IPX/SPX Compatible Transport service is not installed.

C. **Incorrect:** The required result and one of the optional results are achieved.

D. **Incorrect:** The required result is achieved.

70-067.02.05.005

Your Windows NT Server domain environment includes five domain controllers and 31 other servers supporting 10,000 users. All computers are running TCP/IP. When members of the TECHPUB group copy a large volume of data to a server named ALNTS40TP1, network performance suffers.

The required result is to improve the performance of the network while continuing to support all users' needs.

The first optional result is to reduce administrative overhead.

The second optional result is to provide dynamic IP routing.

The proposed solution is to install a new network adapter card on ALNTS40TP1, and install RIP for IP. Create a subnet for members of the TECHPUB group, and connect it to the new adapter card.

What does the proposed solution provide?

A. The required result and all optional results.

B. The required result and one optional result.

C. The required result but none of the optional results.

D. The proposed solution does not provide the required result.

70-067.02.05.005

Your Windows NT Server domain environment includes five domain controllers and 31 other servers supporting 10,000 users. All computers are running TCP/IP. When members of the TECHPUB group copy a large volume of data to a server named ALNTS40TP1, network performance suffers.

The required result is to improve the performance of the network while continuing to support all users' needs.

The first optional result is to reduce administrative overhead.

The second optional result is to provide dynamic IP routing.

The proposed solution is to install a new network adapter card on ALNTS40TP1, and install RIP for IP. Create a subnet for members of the TECHPUB group, and connect it to the new adapter card.

What does the proposed solution provide?

▶ **Correct Answer: A**

A. **Correct:** The required result, to improve the performance of the network while continuing to support all users' needs, is achieved by installing a network adapter on ALNTS40TP1, and creating a subnet for this adapter that connects all members of the TECHPUB group directly to the server. This isolates TECHPUB network traffic to an exclusive subnetwork. The first optional result, to reduce administrative overhead, is achieved by installing the RIP for IP service. This service provides a dynamically updated routing table. Therefore, it is unnecessary to create static routes to remote IP networks. The second optional result, to provide dynamic IP routing, is also achieved through the RIP for IP service installation.

B. **Incorrect:** The required result and both optional results are achieved.

C. **Incorrect:** The required result and both optional results are achieved.

D. **Incorrect:** The required result is achieved.

Further Reading

 Modern Operating Systems by Andrew S. Tanenbaum (1992). Chapter 5 on Input/Output is an excellent operating system fundamentals reference.

 Networking Essentials, Second Edition. Lesson 3 in Chapter 2, "Connecting Network Components," provides you with information on configuring network adapters for proper operation in a network.

 On the web, search for Network Technical Discussion and Microsoft Systems Journal (http://channels.microsoft.com/msj). This site provides a detailed discussion of the Windows NT network architecture.

OBJECTIVE 2.6

Configure Windows NT Server core services.

A critical feature of Windows NT is its ability to run services as background processes. A service is simply an application that runs behind the scenes to provide a wide range of capabilities to both local and network users. For example, the server service allows network users to connect and use files and printers located on the computer running the Server service. If the same computer running the Server service is running the Workstation service, then the local user can also connect to remote network resources.

For some services to operate optimally, they must be configured. Service configuration is accomplished through Control Panel programs or separate applications. The Server service is modified from the Control Panel–Network program–Services tab. The Services program in Control Panel can also be used to start, stop, pause, and configure the startup and logon behavior of installed services.

To successfully answer the questions for this objective, you need a firm understanding of the key terms in the following section. For definitions of these terms, refer to the Glossary in this book.

Key Terms

- Directory Replicator service

- Domain synchronization

- Export directory

- Import directory

- License logging service

- License Manager

- Logon validation or authentication

- NetLogon service

- Pass-through authentication

- Per-seat licensing

- Per-server licensing

- REPL$

- Workstation service or redirector

70-067.02.06.001

You are setting up directory replication on a network with 2 Windows NT Server 4.0 computers, 15 Windows NT Workstation 4.0 computers, 10 Windows NT Workstation 3.51, and 15 Windows 95 computers. Which operating system on the network can serve as an export server?

A. Windows 95

B. Windows NT Server 4.0

C. Windows NT 4.0 Workstation

D. Windows NT Workstation 3.51

70-067.02.06.002

What is the default path shared as REPL$ when starting the Directory Replicator service?

A. Systemroot\Repl\Export

B. Systemroot\Repl\Import

C. Systemroot\System32\Repl\Export

D. Systemroot\System32\Repl\Import

70-067.02.06.001

You are setting up directory replication on a network with 2 Windows NT Server 4.0 computers, 15 Windows NT Workstation 4.0 computers, 10 Windows NT Workstation 3.51, and 15 Windows 95 computers. Which operating system on the network can serve as an export server?

▶ **Correct Answer: B**

A. **Incorrect:** Windows 95 computers cannot run the Directory Replicator service; therefore, they cannot be used as import or export servers for a network configured for directory replication.

B. **Correct:** Windows NT Server 4.0, running the Directory Replicator service, is the only operating system that can serve as an export server. If necessary, this operating system can also serve as an import server.

C. **Incorrect:** While Windows NT 4.0 Workstation can run the Directory Replicator service, it can only act as an import server.

D. **Incorrect:** While Windows NT 3.51 Workstation can run the Directory Replicator service, it can only act as an import server.

70-067.02.06.002

What is the default path shared as REPL$ when starting the Directory Replicator service?

▶ **Correct Answer: C**

A. **Incorrect:** By default, this is not a valid path on a Windows NT computer.

B. **Incorrect:** By default, this is not a valid path on a Windows NT computer.

C. **Correct:** When the Directory Replicator service is started, it automatically creates the REPL$ share to the \systemroot\System32\Repl\Export directory. Starting from this share, files and subdirectories can be copied to import servers on the network. Through Server Manager, the default export path can be changed.

D. **Incorrect:** The import directory \systemroot\System32\Repl\Import is the location where files exported by the Directory Replicator service are copied.

70-067.02.06.003

Where are the settings that control directory replication stored in the Windows NT Server 4.0 Registry?

A. HKEY_CLASSES_ROOT

B. HKEY_CURRENT_USER

C. HKEY_LOCAL_MACHINE

D. HKEY_CURRENT_CONFIG

70-067.02.06.003

Where are the settings that control directory replication stored in the Windows NT Server 4.0 Registry?

▶ **Correct Answer: C**

A. **Incorrect:** The HKEY_CLASSES_ROOT Registry subkey stores configuration information, OLE, and file class association data. Therefore, the Directory Replicator service information is not stored in this subkey.

B. **Incorrect:** The HKEY_CURRENT_USER Registry subkey stores user-specific data for the currently logged on user. Note that this information is also a subtree of HKEY_USERS, the security identifier tree.

C. **Correct:** The HKEY_LOCAL_MACHINE Registry subkey contains configuration information about the local computer. The keys under HKEY_LOCAL_MACHINE are grouped into five subkeys. They are ...\HARDWARE, ...\SAM, ...\SECURITY, ...\SOFTWARE, and ...\SYSTEM. The Directory Replicator service settings are stored in HKEY_LOCAL_MACHINE\system\ CurrentControlSet\Services\Replicator.

D. **Incorrect:** The HKEY_CURRENT_CONFIG subtree contains configuration data for the hardware profile currently in use on the computer. This subtree is actually an alias pointing to HKEY_LOCAL_MACHINE\System\CurrentControlSet\HardwareProfiles\Current. The contents of the Hardware Profiles\Current subkey appear in this subtree.

70-067.02.06.004

Your company is installing a Windows NT 4.0 network. The license you purchased with Windows NT Server 4.0 is a 15-client license. The company has 25 employees, each of whom have their own workstation and require network access.

The company operates on two shifts. During the first shift, there are never more than 13 employees at work, and during the second shift, there are never more than 14 employees at work.

Which Windows NT Server 4.0 licensing mode must be selected to enable everyone to access the network?

A. Per Seat

B. Per Server

C. Per Network

D. Per Computer

E. Per Workstation

70-067.02.06.004

Your company is installing a Windows NT 4.0 network. The license you purchased with Windows NT Server 4.0 is a 15-client license. The company has 25 employees, each of whom have their own workstation and require network access.

The company operates on two shifts. During the first shift, there are never more than 13 employees at work, and during the second shift, there are never more than 14 employees at work.

Which Windows NT Server 4.0 licensing mode must be selected to enable everyone to access the network?

▶ **Correct Answer: B**

A. **Incorrect:** Fifteen client licenses were purchased, but the network contains a total of 25 employees, each of whom have their own workstations. The only way to legally configure this network for all workstations using per-seat licensing is by purchasing 25 client licenses.

B. **Correct:** Per-server licensing is the proper selection for this network. Since 15 licenses were purchased, and no more than 14 users access the server simultaneously, per-server, or concurrent-server licensing, is the correct choice.

C. **Incorrect:** Microsoft does not use a licensing mode called "Per Network."

D. **Incorrect:** Microsoft does not use a licensing mode called, "Per Computer."

E. **Incorrect:** Microsoft does not use a licensing mode called, "Per Workstation."

70-067.02.06.005

Your company is reconfiguring its Windows NT 4.0 network. The license you purchased with Windows NT Server 4.0 is a 15-client license. The company has 25 employees, each of whom have their own workstation and require network access.

In the past, the company has operated on two shifts where there were no more than 14 employees working at any given time. The company is migrating to a single shift with 25 simultaneous users. You are going to add a server when the migration occurs. The addition of the server makes it necessary to change the current server's licensing mode from per-server to per-seat licensing.

What should you do to change the server licensing mode?

A. Purchase a 10-client license and do nothing further.

B. Purchase a 10-client license and reinstall Windows NT Server 4.0 so the per-seat option can be selected during setup.

C. Purchase a 10-client license, go to the licensing icon in the control panel, and change the licensing mode from per-server to per-seat.

D. Purchase a 10-client license, go to the licensing icon in the administrative tools, and change the licensing mode from per-server to per-seat.

70-067.02.06.005

Your company is reconfiguring its Windows NT 4.0 network. The license you purchased with Windows NT Server 4.0 is a 15-client license. The company has 25 employees, each of whom have their own workstation and require network access.

In the past, the company has operated on two shifts where there were no more than 14 employees working at any given time. The company is migrating to a single shift with 25 simultaneous users. You are going to add a server when the migration occurs. The addition of the server makes it necessary to change the current server's licensing mode from per-server to per-seat licensing.

What should you do to change the server licensing mode?

▶ **Correct Answer: C**

A. **Incorrect:** While this is the first step in meeting the new licensing requirements, supporting 25 users on two Windows NT Servers, the server must be configured for this new licensing mode.

B. **Incorrect:** While it is possible to reinstall Windows NT Server, and change the licensing mode during reinstallation, this is an inefficient method for configuring the server for per-seat licensing.

C. **Correct:** To reconfigure the Windows NT Server for per-seat licensing, it is necessary to launch Control Panel, open the Licensing program and change the licensing mode from per-server to per-seat. This procedure can be completed on both Windows NT Servers.

D. **Incorrect:** The License Manager under the Windows NT Administrative Tools menu allows you to manage the licensing mode you have configured for the network. However, the Licensing program in Control Panel must be used first to configure the licensing mode.

Further Reading

 Microsoft Windows NT Server Resource Kit. In the *Networking Guide*, see Chapter 2 for a detailed explanation of the NetLogon Service function.

 Microsoft Windows NT Technical Support Training kit. Lessons 1 and 2 in Chapter 9, "The Windows NT Networking Environment," reinforce your understanding of how the Windows NT components fit together to provide networking services to clients in the network. Lessons 2–4 in Chapter 16, "Implementing File Synchronization and Directory Replication," provide you with practice labs for the Directory Replicator service.

 Microsoft Windows NT Server Concepts and Planning Manual. Review Chapter 12, "Licensing and License Manager" for a description of Windows NT licensing, and procedures for implementing the License Manager in Windows NT.

OBJECTIVE 2.7

Configure peripherals and devices.

After devices have been installed into a Windows NT Server, device drivers must be configured to allow the operating system to work with the new hardware. Device drivers can be installed and configured during or after the installation process. All installed device drivers appear in the Control Panel–Devices program. Through the Devices program, device drivers are stopped and started, and their startup behavior is changed. Hardware profiles, configured through the System program–Hardware Profiles tab, are also enabled and disabled from the Devices program. The devices commonly installed into a Windows NT Server include: communication and SCSI devices, tape devices, UPS devices, and the UPS Service, mouse, display, and keyboard drivers.

To successfully answer the questions for this objective, you need a firm understanding of the key terms in the following section. For definitions of these terms, refer to the Glossary in this book.

Key Terms

- Devices applet
- Integrated Service Digital Network (ISDN) adapter
- Modem
- Ports applet
- Remote UPS shutdown
- Small Computer System Interface (SCSI)
- Tape Devices applet
- Uninterruptible power supply (UPS) applet
- UPS low battery signal at least two minutes before shutdown
- UPS power failure signal
- UPS Service
- X.25 PAD

70-067.02.07.001

Which type of connection does Windows NT Server 4.0 use to communicate with an uninterruptible power supply (UPS)?

A. Serial

B. Parallel

70-067.02.07.002

How many serial ports can be configured on a Windows NT Server 4.0 computer?

A. 63

B. 64

C. 255

D. 256

70-067.02.07.003

What is the correct ARC path syntax to indicate a SCSI drive with the SCSI controller BIOS disabled?

A. scsi(w)disk(x)partition(y)rdisk(z)

B. scsi(w)disk(x)rdisk(y)partition(z)

C. multi(w)rdisk(x)disk(y)partition(z)

D. multi(w)disk(x)rdisk(y)partition(z)

70-067.02.07.001

Which type of connection does Windows NT Server 4.0 use to communicate with an uninterruptible power supply (UPS)?

▶ **Correct Answer: A**

A. **Correct:** The Windows NT UPS Service uses a serial connection to communicate with a UPS. Three voltage signals can be sent from the UPS to the UPS Service. The three signals tell the UPS Service when a power failure occurs, when the UPS is running low on battery power, and when the UPS triggers the UPS Service to shut down the server.

B. **Incorrect:** The parallel port is not used by the UPS to communicate with the UPS Service.

70-067.02.07.002

How many serial ports can be configured on a Windows NT Server 4.0 computer?

▶ **Correct Answer: D**

A. **Incorrect:** See the explanation for answer D.

B. **Incorrect:** See the explanation for answer D.

C. **Incorrect:** See the explanation for answer D.

D. **Correct:** Using a multi-port serial card, a Windows NT Server can support 256 asynchronous connections. A multi-port serial card is typically used to provide this number of RS232 connections.

70-067.02.07.003

What is the correct ARC path syntax to indicate a SCSI drive with the SCSI controller BIOS disabled?

▶ **Correct Answer: B**

A. **Incorrect:** The disk value is always followed by the rdisk value. Therefore, the syntax used in option A is not the correct ARC path syntax to indicate any Windows NT boot partition.

B. **Correct:** The syntax for an ARC path always starts with a controller designation, either multi or scsi. For a scsi controller with a disabled BIOS, the ARC path always begins with scsi. Next, the disk value designates scsi disk technology, while rdisk designates ide or esdi disk technology. Both of these value names are present in this order, even though only one of them is in use. Finally, the Partition value designates the volume on the disk where Windows NT is installed (also called the boot partition). Therefore, this is the correct ARC path syntax.

C. **Incorrect:** The multi ARC path designation is used for a scsi controller with its BIOS enabled, or any other controller technology (ide or esdi). Remember also that the disk value always precedes the rdisk value.

D. **Incorrect:** The multi ARC path designation is used for a scsi controller with its BIOS enabled, or any other controller technology (ide or esdi).

70-067.02.07.004

Which Control Panel icon is used to install a tape device driver on a Windows NT Server 4.0 computer?

A. System

B. Server

C. Devices

D. Services

E. Tape Devices

F. SCSI Adapters

70-067.02.07.004

Which Control Panel icon is used to install a tape device driver on a Windows NT Server 4.0 computer?

▶ **Correct Answer: E**

A. **Incorrect:** The System program in Control Panel is used to view general information, such as the version and build of Windows NT. It is also used to configure application performance for foreground applications, configure virtual memory, adjust and add environment variables, modify startup and shutdown settings, and configure hardware and user profiles.

B. **Incorrect:** The Server program in Control Panel is an application for viewing and managing user connections, shares, alerts, and replication settings. This application allows you to configure the same information as does the Properties sheet of a computer displayed through Server Manager. The difference is that Server Manager allows you to view the properties of any registered computer running Windows NT in the domain, while the Server program only allows you to view the properties of the local computer.

C. **Incorrect:** The Devices program in Control Panel is used to stop, start, and modify the startup behavior of device drivers. It can also be used to enable and disable hardware profiles configured through the System program–Hardware Profiles tab.

D. **Incorrect:** The Services program in Control Panel can be used to start, stop, pause, and configure the startup and logon behavior of installed services.

E. **Correct:** The Tape Device program is used to install a tape device driver on a Windows NT Server 4.0 computer.

F. **Incorrect:** The SCSI Adapters program in Control Panel is used to load and configure SCSI adapter device drivers, and IDE CD-ROM device drivers into Windows NT. Before a SCSI tape device driver can be loaded, its corresponding SCSI device driver must be loaded through this program.

70-067.02.07.005

If your internal modem is not supported by RAS, how can you configure Windows NT Server to establish RAS connections?

A. Add modem commands to Modem.inf.

B. Configure the modem to use software compression.

C. Modify the Registry settings for the modem to include modem commands.

D. Create a script file containing modem commands that will run each time the modem is activated.

70-067.02.07.005

If your internal modem is not supported by RAS, how can you configure Windows NT Server to establish RAS connections?

▶ **Correct Answer: A**

A. **Correct:** If an internal modem is not supported by RAS, the Modem.inf file can be modified to include modem commands specific to the installed modem. The Modem.inf file lists all modems supported by Remote Access, along with the command and response strings each modem needs for correct operation. When you select a modem during Remote Access installation, the Setup program associates the selected modem with the specified communication port. Remote Access connection utilities read Modem.inf to obtain the command strings for the modem associated with each communication port. You can find Modem.inf in the \systemroot\system32\ras directory. Updated Modem.inf files are available from modem manufacturers or on the Microsoft Web site. For more information, *see* Appendix C, "Understanding Modem.inf," of the *Microsoft Windows NT Server Networking Supplement Manual*.

B. **Incorrect:** Configuring a modem to use software compression does not provide modem command support to a modem not listed in Modem.inf.

C. **Incorrect:** The Registry does not contain modem command sequences. To read about the Registry settings for RAS, see Appendix A of the *Microsoft Windows NT Server Networking Supplement Manual*.

D. **Incorrect:** Script files can be used to automate common connection tasks for RAS. There is a new, well-documented script language in Script.doc titled: "Dial-Up Scripting Command Language For Dial-Up Networking Scripting Support." Three example script files are included with Windows NT 4.0: Pppmenu.scp, Slip.scp, and Slipmenu.scp. These three files and Script.doc are in the Windows NT 4.0 %SystemRoot%\System32\RAS directory.

70-067.02.07.006

Which file is required only on Intel-based systems that boot from a SCSI hard disk with the SCSI adapter BIOS disabled?

A. *.pal

B. Osloader.exe

C. Bootsect.dos

D. Ntbootdd.sys

E. Ntdetect.com

70-067.02.07.006

Which file is required only on Intel-based systems that boot from a SCSI hard disk with the SCSI adapter BIOS disabled?

▶ **Correct Answer: D**

A. **Incorrect:** The *.pal files are stored on the system partition in the \Os\Winnt40 directory of Alpha-based computers and are involved in Windows NT startup.

B. **Incorrect:** The Boot Loader menu and functionality that is implemented by NTLDR on *x*86-based systems is not needed on Advanced RISC Computing (ARC)–based systems. This is because ARC-based systems have the NTLDR functionality built into the system firmware. The initial stages of the Windows NT load sequence is handled by osloader.exe. Notice that osloader.exe reads hardware information from the hardware POST routine so ntdetect.com is not used.

C. **Incorrect:** The boot record on the system is saved as bootsect.dos, regardless of what operating system was installed on the system prior to the installation of Windows NT. Bootsect.dos is loaded if the previous operating system on the boot loader menu is selected.

D. **Correct:** This file is required only on Intel-based systems that boot from a SCSI hard disk with the SCSI adapter BIOS disabled. Ntbootdd.sys is the Windows NT SCSI device driver for the boot device. It loads the "SCSI miniport" low-level hardware device drivers. On SCSI adapters, where the BIOS is enabled, these drivers are loaded using BIOS Int13 calls in real mode. When the BIOS is disabled, this same function is handled by ntbootdd.sys.

E. **Incorrect:** This is the Windows NT *x*86 hardware detection program. This program runs during the boot process on *x*86 based systems, and populates the Registry with hardware information.

70-067.02.07.007

What is the correct ARC path syntax to indicate a SCSI drive with the SCSI controller BIOS enabled?

A. scsi(w)disk(x)partition(y)rdisk(z)

B. scsi(w)disk(x)rdisk(y)partition(z)

C. multi(w)rdisk(x)disk(y)partition(z)

D. multi(w)disk(x)rdisk(y)partition(z)

70-067.02.07.007

What is the correct ARC path syntax to indicate a SCSI drive with the SCSI controller BIOS enabled?

▶ **Correct Answer: D**

A. **Incorrect:** The question asks for the ARC path for a SCSI drive with the SCSI controller BIOS enabled. For a SCSI controller with the BIOS disabled, the ARC path always begins with scsi. For a SCSI controller with the BIOS enabled, or any other driver controller technology, the ARC path always begins with multi.

B. **Incorrect:** Like option A, this ARC path begins with scsi rather than multi.

C. **Incorrect:** The disk value always precedes the rdisk value. This option lists rdisk first.

D. **Correct:** The syntax for an ARC path always starts with either a multi or scsi controller designation. Since this ARC path is for a SCSI controller with the BIOS enabled, multi is correct. Next, the disk value designates SCSI disk technology while rdisk designates ide or esdi disk technology. Both of these value names are present in this order, although only one of them is in use. Finally, the Partition value designates the volume on the disk where Windows NT is installed (the boot partition). Therefore, this is the correct ARC path syntax.

Further Reading

 Microsoft Windows NT Resource Kit: Microsoft Windows NT Resource Guide. Chapter 3 provides a single source for understanding how disk resources are managed in Windows NT.

 Microsoft Windows NT Resource Kit: Microsoft Windows NT Resource Guide. Chapter 5, "Preparing for and Performing Recovery Using UPS," explains how to install a UPS, and configure the UPS service to interact with the UPS.

 Microsoft Windows NT Server 4.0 Resource Kit: Supplement 1. Chapter 4, "Using ISDN, Windows NT Architecture Supporting ISDN, Configuring Windows NT Server for ISDN and Alternatives to ISDN," explains how to configure ISDN, and how to use high-speed dial-up methods in RAS.

 Microsoft Windows NT Server 4.0 Resource Kit: Supplement 2. "Nt40card.hlp" offers assistance with network adapters and SCSI card configuration.

 Microsoft Windows NT Technical Support Training kit. Lesson 2 in Chapter 3, "Configuring the Windows NT Environment," provides an additional review on how the Control Panel programs can be used to modify the configuration of Windows NT.

O B J E C T I V E 2 . 8

Configure hard disks to meet various requirements.

You can configure disk drives in Windows NT in many different ways. This objective tests your ability to allocate disk capacity, format disk drives, build disk redundancy, implement disk security, and achieve optimum performance from your disk drives.

To successfully answer the questions for this objective, you need a firm understanding of the key terms in the following section. For definitions of these terms, refer to the Glossary in this book.

Key Terms

- Advanced RISC Computing (ARC)

- Boot.ini

- Disk Administrator Orphan

- Disk Administrator Regenerate

- Mirror set

- Share level permissions

- Stripe set

- Volume set

70-067.02.08.001

Your company has a small network consisting of a single Windows NT 4.0 Server and seven Windows 95 clients. The server has two identical 4-GB SCSI hard drives. Windows NT fault tolerance needs to be implemented on the server. If there is a problem with the server's hard disk, you want to be able to remove it and use the other hard drive. Which Windows NT fault-tolerance method can you implement without adding any new hardware?

A. RAID 0

B. RAID 1

C. RAID 2

D. RAID 3

E. RAID 4

F. RAID 5

70-067.02.08.001

Your company has a small network consisting of a single Windows NT 4.0 Server and seven Windows 95 clients. The server has two identical 4-GB SCSI hard drives. Windows NT fault tolerance needs to be implemented on the server. If there is a problem with the server's hard disk, you want to be able to remove it and use the other hard drive. Which Windows NT fault-tolerance method can you implement without adding any new hardware?

▶   **Correct Answer: B**

   A. **Incorrect:** The question states that Windows NT fault tolerance needs to be implemented on the server. RAID 0 is not a fault-tolerant feature.

   B. **Correct:** The question states that the server has two identical 4-GB SCSI hard drives. Windows NT fault tolerance needs to be implemented on the server. RAID 1 allows for data to be duplicated across the two drives. Additionally, if there is a problem with the server's hard disk, you can re-move a hard drive and continue to use the operational drive. To maintain fault tolerance, the missing drive should be replaced and remirrored to the existing drive.

   C. **Incorrect:** RAID 2 uses extra check disks which have data bits striped across the data and check disks. The data includes an interleaved Hamming code, which can be used to detect and correct single bit errors as well as to detect double bit errors. This RAID implementation is not available in Windows NT Server software level RAID.

   D. **Incorrect:** RAID 3 uses a single redundant check disk (sometimes referred to as a parity disk) for each group of drives. Data written to the RAID 3 disk array is bit-striped across the data disks. This RAID implementation is not available in Windows NT Server software level RAID.

   E. **Incorrect:** RAID 4 dedicates one entire disk for storing check data, allowing data from a failed drive to be easily recovered. This RAID implementation is not available in Windows NT Server software level RAID.

   F. **Incorrect:** RAID 5 dedicates the equivalent of one entire disk for storing check data but distributes the check data over all the drives in the group. While Windows NT Server supports RAID 5, the minimum number of disks required to implement this fault-tolerant solution is 3 disks.

70-067.02.08.002

Your company needs to implement Windows NT fault tolerance on their network server. Their main server has nine 4-GB hard drives. If one disk fails, you want to be able to reconstruct the data that was on the hard disk. What Windows NT fault-tolerance method should you use?

A. RAID 0

B. RAID 1

C. RAID 2

D. RAID 3

E. RAID 4

F. RAID 5

70-067.02.08.002

Your company needs to implement Windows NT fault tolerance on their network server. Their main server has nine 4-GB hard drives. If one disk fails, you want to be able to reconstruct the data that was on the hard disk. What Windows NT fault-tolerance method should you use?

▶ **Correct Answer: F**

A. **Incorrect:** The question states that Windows NT fault tolerance needs to be implemented on the server. RAID 0 is not a fault-tolerant feature.

B. **Incorrect:** RAID 1 is a fault-tolerant option available in Windows NT Server, and requires an even number of drives. The question states that the server has nine 4-GB hard drives.

C. **Incorrect:** RAID 2 uses extra check disks which have data bits striped across the data and the check disks. The data includes an interleaved Hamming code, which can be used to detect and correct single bit errors, as well as to detect double bit errors. This RAID implementation is not available in Windows NT Server software level RAID.

D. **Incorrect:** RAID 3 uses a single redundant check disk (sometimes referred to as a parity disk) for each group of drives. Data written to the RAID 3 disk array is bit-striped across the data disks. This RAID implementation is not available in Windows NT Server software level RAID.

E. **Incorrect:** RAID 4 dedicates one entire disk for storing check data in order to allow data from a failed drive to be easily recovered. This RAID implementation is not available in Windows NT Server software level RAID.

F. **Correct:** RAID 5 dedicates the equivalent of one entire disk to storing check data, but distributes the check data over all the drives in the group. Windows NT Server supports RAID 5 and can use anywhere from 3 to 32 disks to implement this fault-tolerant solution. Therefore, nine drives can be used. In this configuration, one-ninth of the total space stores parity data. Using this parity information, data on a failed disk can be reconstructed in memory. The failed drive should be replaced as soon as possible because read and write performance suffers when a RAID 5 must calculate disk data from parity information.

70-067.02.08.003

Your company needs to implement fault tolerance on a network server. The server has ten 4-GB hard drives. How much usable disk space will they have if they choose to use a stripe set with parity on this server?

A. 20 GB

B. 28 GB

C. 30 GB

D. 36 GB

E. 38 GB

70-067.02.08.004

You need to implement fault tolerance on a network server. The server has two 8-GB hard drives. How much usable disk space will result if you choose to mirror the disks on this server?

A. 5 GB

B. 6 GB

C. 8 GB

D. 10 GB

E. 12 GB

F. 16 GB

70-067.02.08.003

Your company needs to implement fault tolerance on a network server. The server has ten 4-GB hard drives. How much usable disk space will they have if they choose to use a stripe set with parity on this server?

▶ **Correct Answer: D**

A. **Incorrect:** See the explanation for answer D.

B. **Incorrect:** See the explanation for answer D.

C. **Incorrect:** See the explanation for answer D.

D. **Correct:** Striping with parity or RAID 5 dedicates a portion of the array to storing parity information. The overhead storage required for RAID 5 is calculated this way:

Number of drives in RAID 5 array = n, Parity overhead = 1/n

In this question, if you have a RAID 5 array consisting of ten 4-GB drives, the parity overhead is one-tenth, or 4-GB.

Total storage is total drive size minus overhead. In this example, that would be 40 GB minus 4 GB, or 36 GB total user storage.

E. **Incorrect:** See the explanation for answer D.

70-067.02.08.004

You need to implement fault tolerance on a network server. The server has two 8-GB hard drives. How much usable disk space will result if you choose to mirror the disks on this server?

▶ **Correct Answer: C**

A. **Incorrect:** See the explanation for answer C.

B. **Incorrect:** See the explanation for answer C.

C. **Correct:** RAID 1, mirroring and duplexing, storage overhead is always fifty percent. Therefore, two 8-GB drives in a mirrored configuration yield 8 GB of total useable storage.

D. **Incorrect:** See the explanation for answer C.

E. **Incorrect:** See the explanation for answer C.

F. **Incorrect:** See the explanation for answer C.

70-067.02.08.005

A Windows NT Server 4.0 computer is using a stripe set. Each of the ten 4-GB hard drives has a single partition. How large are the units of data that are written to the stripe set formatted to NTFS?

A. 16 KB

B. 32 KB

C. 64 KB

D. 128 KB

E. 256 KB

F. 512 KB

70-067.02.08.006

A Windows NT Server contains four identical 8-GB SCSI hard disks. You need to provide a Windows NT fault-tolerance solution for the server while maximizing storage space. Which Windows NT fault-tolerance solution should you implement?

A. Disk mirroring

B. Disk duplexing

C. Disk striping with ECC

D. Disk striping with parity

70-067.02.08.005

A Windows NT Server 4.0 computer is using a stripe set. Each of the ten 4-GB hard drives has a single partition. How large are the units of data that are written to the stripe set formatted to NTFS?

▶ **Correct Answer: C**

A. **Incorrect:** See the explanation for answer C.

B. **Incorrect:** See the explanation for answer C.

C. **Correct:** All file systems used by Windows NT organize the hard disk based upon cluster (or allocation unit) size, which represents the smallest amount of disk space which can be allocated to hold a file. If no cluster size is specified during format, NTFS picks defaults, which are based on the size of the partition. These defaults have been selected to reduce the amount of space lost and to reduce the amount of fragmentation on the partition. For any partition size greater than 32 GB, the cluster size is 64 KB. A stripe set of ten 4-GB hard drives has a single partition of 40 GB, so the cluster size is 64 KB.

D. **Incorrect:** See the explanation for answer C.

E. **Incorrect:** See the explanation for answer C.

F. **Incorrect:** See the explanation for answer C.

70-067.02.08.006

A Windows NT Server contains four identical 8-GB SCSI hard disks. You need to provide a Windows NT fault-tolerance solution for the server while maximizing storage space. Which Windows NT fault-tolerance solution should you implement?

▶ **Correct Answer: D**

A. **Incorrect:** RAID 1, mirroring and duplexing, storage overhead is always fifty percent. Therefore, four 8-GB drives in a mirrored configuration yields only 16 GB of total useable storage.

B. **Incorrect:** Disk duplexing is a RAID 1 implementation using two disk I/O channels on a single disk controller, or two disk controllers each connected to a drive in the mirror set. Since this is a RAID 1 implementation, fifty percent of disk capacity is lost to the mirror.

C. **Incorrect:** This is not a supported Windows NT RAID implementation.

D. **Correct:** Striping with parity or RAID 5 provides the most storage capacity of any Windows NT fault tolerant solution. The storage overhead required for this RAID 5 implementation is:

For four 8-GB drives, parity overhead is one-quarter, or 8 GB.

Total storage is total drive size minus overhead. In this example, this amounts to 32 GB minus 8 GB, or 24 GB of total user storage.

70-067.02.08.007

Your company is implementing a Windows NT 4.0 network. You want to be able to restrict access to some files on a server's hard drive. Which file system is required?

A. HPFS

B. NTFS

C. FAT16

D. FAT32

70-067.02.08.007

Your company is implementing a Windows NT 4.0 network. You want to be able to restrict access to some files on a server's hard drive. Which file system is required?

▶ **Correct Answer: B**

A. **Incorrect:** HPFS is not supported in Windows NT Server 4.0. Since you want to be able to restrict access to some files on a server's hard drive in a Windows NT 4.0 network, HPFS cannot be used. HPFS is supported in Windows NT 3.51 and OS/2.

B. **Correct:** NTFS provides local security. Therefore, this is the file system you should choose to restrict access to some files on a server's hard drive. NTFS permissions can be applied to directories, files, or both.

C. **Incorrect:** FAT16 is the FAT file system supported in Windows NT. This file system does not provide local security. As with NTFS, network-based share level security can be applied but FAT restricts access at the directory level, not at the file level. Additionally, FAT only functions over the network. Therefore, a user that logs on locally to the Windows NT server can access files protected through share-level security.

D. **Incorrect:** The FAT32 file system is supported in Windows 95 and Windows 98. Windows NT 3.51 and 4.0 do not support this file system.

Further Reading

 Microsoft Windows NT Network Administration Training kit. Chapter 6, "Securing Network Resources with NTFS Permissions," provides a comprehensive discussion of NTFS local permissions, and exercises to practice the application of local security to an NTFS partition.

 Microsoft Windows NT Technical Support Training kit. Lessons 1 and 2 in Chapter 6, "Managing Partitions," provide practice with disk management through Disk Administrator, and a simulated exercise to create a volume set.

 Microsoft Windows NT Workstation: Resource Kit Version 4.0. Chapter 17, "Disk and File System Basics," describes the organization, contents, and purpose of the information on hard disks.

OBJECTIVE 2.9

Configure printers.

This objective reviews printer configuration procedures and options, and printer security available in Windows NT Server. One printer can be installed during the Windows NT Server installation process and more printers can be installed after the installation process. A *printer* in Windows NT is a software device driver, whereas a *print device* is the hardware to which print jobs are sent. Printers can be configured to service multiple print devices, or multiple printers can direct print jobs to a single print device.

Printers are added to Windows NT Server by a user with Full Control print permission. The Add Printer option found in the Start–Settings–Printer window allows for the installation of a printer. A printer is configured through the properties of an installed printer. The most common of these configuration procedures include:

- Specifying the proper driver for the printer under the General tab.

- Selecting a port or ports where print devices are connected.

- Configuring printer pooling through the Ports tab.

- Scheduling print jobs and setting print priorities to each printer.

- Sharing a printer on the network through the Sharing tab.

- Controlling access and auditing printer use.

To successfully answer the questions for this objective, you need a firm understanding of the key terms in the following section. For definitions of these terms, refer to the Glossary in this book.

Key Terms

- Local printing devices

- Logical port

- Network interface printing device

- Physical port

- Printer

- Print device

- Print monitors

- Printer pool

- Printer router (WINSPOOL.DRV)

- Print spooler

- Remote printing device

70-067.02.09.001

Your network has a single Windows NT Server 4.0 system, three Windows 95 client computers, and three Windows NT Workstation 4.0 client computers. All computers print to a Hewlett-Packard 4Si printer connected to the server. You need to install an updated driver for the 4Si printer. Which computers need to have the updated driver installed on their hard drive?

A. Only Windows NT Server

B. Only Windows 95 and Windows NT Server

C. Only Windows NT Server and Windows NT Workstation computers

D. Windows 95, Windows NT Server, and Windows NT Workstation computers

70-067.02.09.002

Which Windows NT 4.0 Server default local groups are allowed full control print permissions and print administration capabilities? (Choose three.)

A. Users

B. Server Operators

C. Administrators

D. Print Operators

E. Backup Operators

70-067.02.09.001

Your network has a single Windows NT Server 4.0 system, three Windows 95 client computers, and three Windows NT Workstation 4.0 client computers. All computers print to a Hewlett-Packard 4Si printer connected to the server. You need to install an updated driver for the 4Si printer. Which computers need to have the updated driver installed on their hard drive?

▶ **Correct Answer: B**

A. **Incorrect:** Both the Windows NT Server and the Windows 95 computers require the updated driver installation on their hard drive.

B. **Correct:** Windows 95 clients do not automatically obtain printer drivers from Windows NT version 4.0 print servers in the same way that Windows NT clients do. Windows NT clients automatically download the printer driver from the server when a newer version of the driver is installed on the Windows NT Server print server.

The Windows 95 clients use a technology called "Point and Print" to download the printer driver and some printer settings to the client only when the client runs the Windows 95, Add Printer Wizard application. This procedure is only run the first time that the printer is installed. Therefore, an updated printer driver must be installed on the Windows 95 client. Additionally, the updated driver must be installed on the Windows NT Server print server so Windows NT Workstation clients will receive the updated driver when they print.

C. **Incorrect:** Only the Windows NT Server and the Windows 95 computers require the updated driver. Windows NT Workstation clients automatically download the updated driver from the Windows NT Server.

D. **Incorrect:** Only the Windows NT Server and the Windows 95 computers require the updated driver. Windows NT Workstation clients automatically download the updated driver from the Windows NT Server.

70-067.02.09.002

Which Windows NT 4.0 Server default local groups are allowed full control print permissions and print administration capabilities? (Choose three.)

▶ **Correct Answers: B, C, and D**

A. **Incorrect:** By default, the Users local group is given only print permission to printers attached to the print server. Users can print, pause, or delete their own jobs.

B. **Correct:** By default, Server Operators are granted Full Control rights to the print server.

C. **Correct:** By default, Administrators are granted Full Control rights to the print server.

D. **Correct:** By default, Print Operators are granted Full Control rights to the print server.

E. **Incorrect:** Backup Operators are not granted rights to printers attached to the print server.

70-067.02.09.003

How can you distribute print jobs to the next available print device on a heavily used printer connected to a Windows NT Server–based computer?

A. Print Queue

B. Printing Pool

C. Printer Spool

D. Network Queue

E. Network Printer

70-067.02.09.004

You have a network printer connected directly to a Windows NT Server–based computer that supports print jobs from three Windows for Workgroups 3.11 computers and itself. You need to upgrade to a new driver for the printer. On which computers should you install the new print driver?

A. Only the server

B. Only one Windows 3.11 computer

C. Only the three Windows 3.11 computers

D. All Windows 3.11 computers and the server

70-067.02.09.003

How can you distribute print jobs to the next available print device on a heavily used printer connected to a Windows NT Server–based computer?

▶ **Correct Answer: B**

A. **Incorrect:** In Windows NT terminology, a queue refers to a group of documents waiting to be printed.

B. **Correct:** A printing pool consists of two or more identical print devices associated with one printer. This allows for the distribution of print jobs to multiple printing devices, thus providing an effective method of distributing print jobs.

C. **Incorrect:** A printer spool is another name for a print queue.

D. **Incorrect:** This is not Windows NT printing terminology.

E. **Incorrect:** While connecting a printer to the network can improve the speed at which jobs are sent to the printer, this does not assist in distributing print jobs to the next available print device.

70-067.02.09.004

You have a network printer connected directly to a Windows NT Server–based computer that supports print jobs from three Windows for Workgroups 3.11 computers and itself. You need to upgrade to a new driver for the printer. On which computers should you install the new print driver?

▶ **Correct Answer: D**

A. **Incorrect:** Updating only the server's printer driver does not provide a driver update to the Windows for Workgroups 3.11 clients. Each operating system platform, Windows 95, Windows NT, WFW, or Windows 3.x, uses a driver specifically designed for their environment. Note that a Windows NT 4.0 Workstation and Windows NT 4.0 Server use the same printer drivers while a Windows NT 3.5x computer uses different printer drivers.

B. **Incorrect:** All clients require driver updates.

C. **Incorrect:** If print jobs will be sent from the Windows NT Server, this driver must be updated as well.

D. **Correct:** All clients and the server should receive print driver updates. This way, printing occurs from all platforms to all print devices using updated print drivers.

70-067.02.09.005

A single network printing device handles all of the print jobs from both the Data Processing group and the Executives group. Company executives belong to the Executives group, and they all print time-sensitive data. You need to set up printer priorities so print jobs sent by members of the Executives group print before print jobs sent to the printer by the Data Processing group. You configure two printers, the Executive printer and the Data Processing printer, as pointing to the same print device.

Which priority should be assigned to the Executive printer so the executives will have the highest possible print priority to this printing device?

A. 9

B. 10

C. 49

D. 99

E. 149

F. 199

70-067.02.09.005

A single network printing device handles all of the print jobs from both the Data Processing group and the Executives group. Company executives belong to the Executives group, and they all print time-sensitive data. You need to set up printer priorities so print jobs sent by members of the Executives group print before print jobs sent to the printer by the Data Processing group. You configure two printers, the Executive printer and the Data Processing printer, as pointing to the same print device.

Which priority should be assigned to the Executive printer so the executives will have the highest possible print priority to this printing device?

▶ **Correct Answer: D**

A. **Incorrect:** This is not the highest possible printing priority.

B. **Incorrect:** This is not the highest possible printing priority.

C. **Incorrect:** This is not the highest possible printing priority.

D. **Correct:** The highest printer priority setting is 99. By default, all printers are set to the lowest priority, 1. Therefore, the Data Processing printer priority to the printing device is 1, while the Executive printing priority to the printing device is set to 99. When a member of the Executive group prints to the Executive printer, their jobs will be printed before print jobs from members of the Data Processing group.

E. **Incorrect:** This is higher than the highest possible printing priority.

F. **Incorrect:** This is higher than the highest possible printing priority.

Further Reading

 Microsoft Windows NT Network Administration Training kit. Review Chapter 7, "Setting Up a Network Print Server," and Chapter 8, "Administering a Network Print Server." These chapters provide a comprehensive discussion of the creation and management of printers in Windows NT, and include practice exercises for hands-on training.

 Microsoft Windows NT Server Manual. For more details on print server setup and configuration in Windows NT, review Chapter 5, "Setting Up Print Servers," in the *Concepts and Planning Manual.*

 Microsoft Windows NT Server Resource Kit: Microsoft Windows NT Networking Guide. Chapter 14, "Using DLC with Windows NT," provides details on the DLC protocol and how it is used to provide print services and SNA network services.

 Microsoft Windows NT Server Resource Kit. In the *Microsoft Windows NT Resource Guide,* review all the documentation in Chapter 2 except "Troubleshooting Printing Problems." This is one of the most comprehensive references for printing in Windows NT networks.

OBJECTIVE   2.10

Configure a Windows NT Server computer for access by various types of clients.

This objective tests your ability to determine configuration of a Windows NT Server for client access. Configuring an NT Server for various types of clients depends on protocol support requirements, resources, client needs, server licensing issues, and UNIX hosts, which must be made accessible through Windows NT Server services. As described in Objective 2.4, NetBEUI, NWLink IPX/SPX, and TCP/IP are the protocols most commonly used for client connectivity. MS-DOS, Windows 95, and Windows NT Workstation can use any of these protocols to establish a connection with a Windows NT Server. While NetBEUI requires little to no configuration, IPX/SPX and TCP/IP require careful server configuration for access by these clients.

To successfully answer the questions for this objective, you need a firm understanding of the key terms in the following section. For definitions of these terms, refer to the Glossary in this book.

Key Terms

- BOOTP relay agent

- HOSTS file

- LMHOSTS file

- Logon Script

- Microsoft Networking

- Multi-Protocol Router (MPR)

- Policy file

- Profiles

- RFC1542

- User Manager for Domains

70-067.02.10.001

Which protocols are supported with the Microsoft Network Client Version 3.0 for MS-DOS? (Choose four.)

A. IPX

B. DLC

C. TCP/IP

D. NetBEUI

E. DNS resolution using WINS

F. SPX

70-067.02.10.001

Which protocols are supported with the Microsoft Network Client Version 3.0 for MS-DOS? (Choose four.)

▶ **Correct Answers: A, B, C, and D**

A. **Correct:** The IPX protocol is supported by the Microsoft Network Client Version 3.0.

B. **Correct:** The Data Link Control (DLC) protocol, used in SNA networks, and for sending print jobs to a network-connected printer running the DLC protocol, is supported by the Microsoft Network Client Version 3.0. A client running the Microsoft Network Client Version 3.0 and DLS can send print jobs directly to a network-connected printer supporting DLC.

C. **Correct:** The TCP/IP protocol suite is supported by the Microsoft Network Client Version 3.0.

D. **Correct:** The NetBEUI protocol is supported by the Microsoft Network Client Version 3.0.

E. **Incorrect:** This is not a protocol.

F. **Incorrect:** The NWLink protocol shipped with Microsoft Network Client supports only IPX. SPX is not supported.

70-067.02.10.002

Your company has some legacy computers running MS-DOS, and you need to integrate them into your TCP/IP network environment.

The required result is to provide automatic configuration of TCP/IP for MS-DOS–based computers with Microsoft Network Client 3.0 installed.

The first optional result is to configure DNS name resolution using WINS for the MS-DOS client computers.

The second optional result is to configure WINS name resolution for the MS-DOS client computers.

The proposed solution is to configure a DHCP server for use with the MS-DOS client computers.

What does the proposed solution provide?

A. The required result and all optional results.

B. The required result and one optional result.

C. The required result but none of the optional results.

D. The proposed solution does not provide the required result.

70-067.02.10.002

Your company has some legacy computers running MS-DOS, and you need to integrate them into your TCP/IP network environment.

The required result is to provide automatic configuration of TCP/IP for MS-DOS–based computers with Microsoft Network Client 3.0 installed.

The first optional result is to configure DNS name resolution using WINS for the MS-DOS client computers.

The second optional result is to configure WINS name resolution for the MS-DOS client computers.

The proposed solution is to configure a DHCP server for use with the MS-DOS client computers.

What does the proposed solution provide?

▶ **Correct Answer: B**

A. **Incorrect:** The required result and the second optional result are achieved. However, the first optional result, to configure DNS name resolution using WINS for the MS-DOS client computers, is not achieved.

B. **Correct:** The required result, to provide automatic configuration of TCP/IP for MS-DOS–based computers running the Microsoft Network Client 3.0, is achieved. The default configuration for this client using TCP/IP is DHCP enabled. Therefore, since the proposed solution is to configure a DHCP server for use with the MS-DOS client, the MS-DOS client will receive a dynamically assigned IP address, subnet mask, and as an option, a default gateway. The first optional result, to configure DNS name resolution using WINS is not supported by the MS-DOS client. Therefore, this optional result is not achieved. The second optional result, to configure WINS name resolution for the MS-DOS clients, is achieved. An MS-DOS client that uses DHCP will automatically receive the address for a WINS server on the network.

C. **Incorrect:** The required result and one optional result are achieved.

D. **Incorrect:** The required result is achieved.

70-067.02.10.003

Which command can you use to connect to a shared directory using Microsoft Network Client Version 3.0 for MS-DOS?

A. Net use

B. Net view

C. Net start

D. Net connect

70-067.02.10.003

Which command can you use to connect to a shared directory using Microsoft Network Client Version 3.0 for MS-DOS?

▶ **Correct Answer: A**

A. **Correct:** The net use command is used to connect to both drive and printer shares on the network.

B. **Incorrect:** The net view command is used to view available resources on computers that broadcast available share on the network.

C. **Incorrect:** The net start command is used to stop and start services on a Windows NT computer.

D. **Incorrect:** Net connect is not a valid net command.

70-067.02.10.004

Your TCP/IP network environment includes some legacy computers running Windows for Workgroups 3.11, and you need to configure your Windows NT Server–based computer to support them.

The required result is to provide logon validation for three users who will connect to the network using Windows for Workgroup computers.

The first optional result is to configure the Windows for Workgroup computers to use DHCP.

The second optional result is to configure the Windows for Workgroup computers to use WINS.

The proposed solution is to configure the necessary user accounts, passwords, and permissions for the three users. Set up the Microsoft TCP/IP-32 3.11 driver, configure the computers running Windows for Workgroups to join the Windows NT domain, and configure the Windows NT Server to run the DHCP Server service.

What does the proposed solution provide?

A. The required result and all optional results.

B. The required result and one optional result.

C. The required result but none of the optional results.

D. The proposed solution does not provide the required result.

70-067.02.10.004

Your TCP/IP network environment includes some legacy computers running Windows for Workgroups 3.11, and you need to configure your Windows NT Server–based computer to support them.

The required result is to provide logon validation for three users who will connect to the network using Windows for Workgroup computers.

The first optional result is to configure the Windows for Workgroup computers to use DHCP.

The second optional result is to configure the Windows for Workgroup computers to use WINS.

The proposed solution is to configure the necessary user accounts, passwords, and permissions for the three users. Set up the Microsoft TCP/IP-32 3.11 driver, configure the computers running Windows for Workgroups to join the Windows NT domain, and configure the Windows NT Server to run the DHCP Server service.

What does the proposed solution provide?

▶ **Correct Answer: A**

A. **Correct:** The required result is to provide logon validation for three users who will connect to the network using Windows for Workgroups computers. This is achieved on the server by configuring the necessary user accounts, password, and permissions. On the client, this is achieved by setting up the Microsoft TCP/IP-32 3.11 driver on the computers running Windows for Workgroups, and configuring them to join the Windows NT domain.

   The first optional result, to configure the Windows for Workgroup computers to use DHCP, is achieved through the setup of the TCP/IP-32 driver and the support of DHCP by configuring the DHCP Server service on a Windows NT Server. The second optional result, to configure the Windows for Workgroup computers to use WINS, is achieved by the setup of the Microsoft TCP/IP-32 3.11 driver on the clients. Note that the DHCP server can also be configured to deliver WINS server information to the Windows for Workgroup clients.

B. **Incorrect:** The required result and both optional results are achieved.

C. **Incorrect:** The required result and both optional results are achieved.

D. **Incorrect:** The required result is achieved.

70-067.02.10.005

Your TCP/IP network environment includes some legacy computers running Windows for Workgroups 3.11, and you need to configure your Windows NT Server–based computer to support them.

The required result is to provide logon validation for three users who will connect to the network using Windows for Workgroup computers.

The first optional result is to configure the Windows for Workgroup computers to use DHCP.

The second optional result is to configure the Windows for Workgroup computers to use WINS.

The proposed solution is to configure the necessary user accounts, passwords, and permissions for the three users. Set up the Microsoft TCP/IP for Windows for Workgroups 3.11 driver, configure the computers running Windows for Workgroups to join the Windows NT domain, and configure the Windows NT Server to run the DHCP Server service.

What does the proposed solution provide?

A. The required result and all optional results.

B. The required result and one optional result.

C. The required result but none of the optional results.

D. The proposed solution does not provide the required result.

70-067.02.10.005

Your TCP/IP network environment includes some legacy computers running Windows for Workgroups 3.11, and you need to configure your Windows NT Server–based computer to support them.

The required result is to provide logon validation for three users who will connect to the network using Windows for Workgroup computers.

The first optional result is to configure the Windows for Workgroup computers to use DHCP.

The second optional result is to configure the Windows for Workgroup computers to use WINS.

The proposed solution is to configure the necessary user accounts, passwords, and permissions for the three users. Setup the Microsoft TCP/IP for Windows for Workgroups 3.11 driver, configure the computers running Windows for Workgroups to join the Windows NT domain, and configure the Windows NT Server to run the DHCP Server service.

What does the proposed solution provide?

▶   **Correct Answer: C**

  A. **Incorrect:** Only the required result is achieved. The first optional result, to configure the Windows for Workgroup computers to use DHCP, and the second optional result, to configure the Windows for Workgroup computers to use WINS, is not achieved.

  B. **Incorrect:** The required result is achieved, but none of the optional results are achieved.

  C. **Correct:** The required result, to provide logon validation for three users who will connect to the network using Windows for Workgroup computers, is achieved. In the proposed solution, the necessary user account, password, and permissions are configured on the server. Additionally, the Microsoft TCP/IP for Windows for Workgroups 3.11 driver is installed on the clients, and the clients are configured to join the domain. The first optional result, to configure the Windows for Workgroup computers to use DHCP, and the second optional result, to configure the Windows for Workgroup computers to use WINS, are not achieved. This is because the Microsoft TCP/IP for Windows for Workgroups 3.11 driver does not support DHCP or WINS.

  Microsoft TCP/IP for Windows for Workgroups includes the NDIS 2 protocol to support connecting computers running Windows for Workgroups or computers running Windows for Workgroups to Windows NT and Windows NT Advanced Server. It does not include any TCP/IP utilities or support for DHCP or WINS. However, support for Windows Sockets is provided

  D. **Incorrect:** The required result is achieved.

Further Reading

 Microsoft Windows NT Technical Support Training kit. Chapter 11, "Windows NT Networking Services" focuses on implementing TCP/IP in a Microsoft network, and includes practice exercises.

 Microsoft Windows NT Server 4.0 Enterprise Technologies Training Kit. In *Supporting Windows NT Server in the Enterprise*, Lessons 1–4 in Chapter 4 provide details on managing DCHP, WINS, and DNS. The text also discusses the configuration of routable protocols in a Windows NT network.

 Microsoft Windows NT Server Manual. In Chapter 1 of the *Concepts and Planning Manual,* review the following sections: "Managing Windows NT Server Domains," "Network Building Blocks–An Overview," "Computers that Can Participate in a Domain," "Windows NT Computer Accounts," "Computers that Can Interact with Domain Computers," and "How User Logons Work." These sections explain how to configure computers to function in a Microsoft network.

Managing Resources

Managing resources in a Windows NT network is the third domain objective tested by the 70-067 Windows NT Server 4.0 exam. This objective covers how to maintain a secure operating system and how to ease network administration with User Manager and User Manager for Domains. With User Manager tools you can manage the SAM database and Windows NT groups. You also can configure user rights, user account policies, and enable auditing with these tools. Understanding how to use tools that perform all these functions is paramount to your success on the Windows NT Server exam. Beyond these two tools, Objective Domain 3 also covers how user account management supports profile policies, system policies, and remote administration.

Tested Skills and Suggested Practices

The skills you need to successfully master the Managing Resources Objective Domain on the exam include:

- Configuring user accounts, groups, profiles and policies for a variety of network environments.

    - Practice 1: Create and adjust user account configurations in Windows NT Workstation using User Manager, and in Windows NT Server using User Manager for Domains.

    - Practice 2: Create a template user account from which to create user accounts. Rename the template account. Attempt to delete a built-in group through User Manager for Domains. Rename the built-in guest user account.

    - Practice 3: Study the function of each built-in user and group. You should be able to discern which users and groups are automatically created on a Windows NT Workstation and which groups are automatically created on a Windows NT Server member server and domain controller.

- Practice 4: Using User Manager for Domains, create both local and global groups. Add global groups to local groups and add users to global groups. Grant local groups or users various rights through the User Rights Policy dialog box. Then, log on as a user with the granted right and test the user's ability to perform the assigned task.

- Practice 5: Configure account restrictions and enable auditing through User Manager for Domains.

- Practice 6: Create a Windows NT profile and assign it to a user account. Copy the profile to a network share, and configure the user-profile setting inside User Manager for Domains so that it functions as a roaming profile.

- Practice 7: Create a global system policy using the System Policy Editor. After the ntconfig.pol file is saved in the net-logon directory, log on the network from a Windows NT computer to observe the effects of using the System Policy Editor on the system policy.

- Providing Windows NT administration remotely.

  - Practice 1: Install server tools on a Windows 9x client and a Windows NT Workstation client.

  - Practice 2: Run the server tools on Windows 9x and Windows NT Workstation in order to understand the differences between the functions available on each platform.

- Creating secure and functional access to disk resources.

  - Practice 1: Create and share a directory (directory1) on a Windows NT Server using the Windows NT Explorer. Call the share: "share1." Using Server Manager installed on a Windows 9x computer, create another share for directory1 located on the Windows NT Server, and call this share: "share2." Remove the Everyone group from share1, and specify a local user that should be given access. Adjust rights on the share so that Read-Only access is granted to this user. Remove the Everyone group, and assign a different user to share2. Give this user Full Control rights. Create a third share, and call it "share3," assign it to the same location, and assign both users No Access to the share. Log on from the Windows 9x computer under each user configuration to test their access rights to the various share names.

- Practice 2: Use the Convert utility if the partition you used for Practice 1 is not already formatted as NTFS. Next, assign local permissions to the directory used for sharing in Practice 1. Assign both user accounts from Practice 1 with read permission. Log on each user account to see the effect of setting read permission on the directory.

- Practice 3: Log on as administrator to the Windows NT Server and copy files into the directory created in Practice 1. View the file-level permissions of a file you copied into this directory. Set the local permissions on a file to No Access for one of the users from Practices 1 and 2. Move this file to another directory on the same partition. View the local permissions to the file. Now, copy the file to a different NTFS partition and view the local permissions of the file. Next, copy the file to a FAT partition and notice that no local permissions can be set on the file.

OBJECTIVE 3.1

Manage user and group accounts.

The exam questions related to Objective 3.1 test your knowledge of the basic characteristics of user accounts in Windows NT Server 4.0, and the role of user rights and how to configure them in User Manager for Domains.

Depending on decisions you make during the installation of Windows NT, either two or three user accounts are created. If a Windows NT Server is configured as a PDC, only two built-in accounts are created: the Administrator and the Guest. The Administrator account has full control over the server and the Guest account has limited rights to the system. If a Windows NT Server is configured as a member server, an additional user, to which you attach a name during installation, is created. On a member server this account is the Administrator equivalent.

In Windows NT Server–User Manager for Domains, User Rights are configured from the Policies–User Rights menu option. User Rights can be assigned to users and groups. With the exception of a domain environment, these rights apply only to the computer where the rights are configured. In a domain environment, user rights extend to all domain controllers within the domain. You will find it more efficient to grant user rights to groups and add users to these groups than to add individual users in the User Rights Policy dialog box. To streamline the process even further, many built-in groups are created when Windows NT is installed.

To successfully answer the questions for this objective, you need a firm understanding of several key terms, and of the most common built-in local and global groups and the types of Windows NT installations that contain them. For definitions of the key terms, refer to the Glossary in this book.

Key Terms

- Access control entry (ACE)

- Access control list (ACL)

- Access token

- Account policy

- Auditing

- Built-in group

- Built-in users

- Global group

- Local group

- Lockout After

- Lockout Duration

- Maximum password age

- Minimum password age

- Minimum password length

- Password uniqueness

- Reset Count After

- Security Accounts Manager (SAM) database

- Security Identifier (SID)

- Share rights

- Shares

- Trust relationship

- User Manager

- User Manager for Domains

- User rights

70-067.03.01.001

Your network has two domains, ACCT and MNGR. The Executive group is a global group of the MNGR domain and needs to access a color laser printer on the ACCT domain's PDC. The appropriate trust relationships have been established.

What should you do to allow the Executive global group to access the color laser printer?

A. The Executive group must be added to the local group in the ACCT domain.

B. The Executive group must be added to the local group in the MNGR domain.

C. The Executive group must be added to the global group in the ACCT domain.

D. The Executive group must be added to the local group in the MNGR domain, and the local group then must be added to the global group in the ACCT domain.

70-067.03.01.001

Your network has two domains, ACCT and MNGR. The Executive group is a global group of the MNGR domain and needs to access a color laser printer on the ACCT domain's PDC. The appropriate trust relationships have been established.

What should you do to allow the Executive global group to access the color laser printer?

▶ **Correct Answer: A**

A. **Correct:** Your network contains two domains, ACCT and MNGR. The Executive global group is defined in the MNGR domain. Members of this group require access to a resource, namely a color printer in the ACCT domain. The most efficient way to provide access is by adding the Executive global group in the MNGR domain to a local group in the ACCT domain. The assumption is that the local group in the ACCT domain has rights to the color laser printer. Keep in mind that a local group can contain both users and global groups.

B. **Incorrect:** Adding the Executive global group to a local group in the MNGR domain does not provide users in the Executive global group with rights to resources in the ACCT domain.

C. **Incorrect:** A global group cannot be added to another global group. Global groups can only contain user accounts within the domain in which they are defined.

D. **Incorrect:** The second part of this answer suggests that a global group be added to another global group. This is not the case; global groups can only contain user accounts within the domain in which they are defined.

70-067.03.01.002

Sally is the network administrator of a large Windows NT 4.0 network. She accepted a position at another company, and her assistant, Jane, is going to replace her as the network administrator. Sally has permissions, group memberships, and rights that Jane does not have.

What is the best way to ensure that Jane has exactly the same rights, group memberships, and permissions as Sally does when Sally leaves the company?

A. Make Jane the Administrator, and delete Sally's account.

B. Rename Sally's user account for Jane and change the password.

C. Delete Sally's account, and add the appropriate rights and permissions for Jane.

D. Look in the HKEY_CURRENT_USER Registry key while Sally is logged on and copy the security identifier. Log on as Jane, and paste the security identifier in the appropriate Registry key.

70-067.03.01.002

Sally is the network administrator of a large Windows NT 4.0 network. She accepted a position at another company, and her assistant, Jane, is going to replace her as the network administrator. Sally has permissions, group memberships, and rights that Jane does not have.

What is the best way to ensure that Jane has exactly the same rights, group memberships, and permissions as Sally does when Sally leaves the company?

▶ **Correct Answer: B**

A. **Incorrect:** This option may give Jane the same rights as Sally; however, it does not automatically admit Jane to the same groups, or allow her the same user rights.

B. **Correct:** Renaming a user account is the most efficient way to ensure that all permissions, group memberships, and rights are maintained when one user replaces another. When Sally is renamed to Jane, she will use the same SID used previously by Sally.

C. **Incorrect:** Deleting Sally's account and then creating a new account for Jane is inefficient compared to a simple renaming procedure. The question asks you to select "the best way" to ensure that Jane has exactly the same rights, group memberships, and permissions as Sally. This answer also does not recommend adding the appropriate group memberships.

D. **Incorrect:** SIDs must be unique in the system. By renaming Sally's user account to Jane, Jane automatically inherits Sally's SID. After the renaming process is complete, the "Sally user account" becomes the "Jane user account" and the Sally user account disappears from the SAM database.

70-067.03.01.003

John is a member of the following groups on your Windows NT 4.0 network: Everyone, Managers, Accounting, and Temporary.

He needs to access a file in the \LSAR folder on a member server with an NTFS partition. Permissions for the \LSAR folder are assigned as follows:

The "Everyone" group has read access, the "Managers" group has Full Control, the "Accounting" group has Change access, and the "Temporary" group has No Access.

What is John's effective permission for the \LSAR folder?

A. Read

B. Change

C. No Access

D. Full Control

70-067.03.01.003

John is a member of the following groups on your Windows NT 4.0 network: Everyone, Managers, Accounting, and Temporary.

He needs to access a file in the \LSAR folder on a member server with an NTFS partition. Permissions for the \LSAR folder are assigned as follows:

The "Everyone" group has read access, the "Managers" group has Full Control, the "Accounting" group has Change access, and the "Temporary" group has No Access.

What is John's effective permission for the \LSAR folder?

▶ **Correct Answer: C**

A. **Incorrect:** The No Access right always takes precedence over any other right.

B. **Incorrect:** The No Access right always takes precedence over any other right.

C. **Correct:** Regardless of any other right set on a folder, the No Access right always takes precedence. Therefore, since John is a member of the Temporary group and that group has been assigned the No Access right, John's effective permission is No Access.

D. **Incorrect:** The No Access right always takes precedence over any other right.

70-067.03.01.004

John is a member of the following groups on your Windows NT 4.0 network: Everyone, Managers, and Accounting.

He needs to control print jobs for a network printer.

The Everyone group has Print access, the Managers group has Full Control, and the Accounting group has Manage Documents permission.

What is John's effective permission for the printer?

A. Print

B. Change

C. No Access

D. Full Control

70-067.03.01.004

John is a member of the following groups on your Windows NT 4.0 network: Everyone, Managers, and Accounting.

He needs to control print jobs for a network printer.

The Everyone group has Print access, the Managers group has Full Control, and the Accounting group has Manage Documents permission.

What is John's effective permission for the printer?

▶ **Correct Answer: D**

A. **Incorrect:** As a member of the Everyone group, John is granted Print permission. However, he is also a member of the Manager group which imparts the Full Control permission to his account

B. **Incorrect:** The Change permission is not assigned to any group in which John is a member.

C. **Incorrect:** The No Access permission is not assigned to any group in which John is a member.

D. **Correct:** Since John is a member of the Manager group and the Manager group has been assigned Full Control to the network printer, John's effective rights are Full Control. Except for the No Access right, assignments are cumulative. In this case, as a member of the Everyone group, John is granted Print permission; as a member of the Accounting Group, John is granted Manage Documents permission; and as a member of the Manager group, he is given Full Control. Therefore, John's cumulative or effective right to the printer is Full Control.

70-067.03.01.005

You need to give all of the domains in the company access to a high performance color laser printer. Your company has a domain named ACCT, a domain named TECH, and a domain named MNGR.

The color laser printer is attached to the ACCT domain's primary domain controller. The ACCT domain trusts both the MNGR domain and the TECH domain. You create a local group on the ACCT domain's primary domain controller. This local group is given print permission to the laser printer.

How can all domains access the printer?

A. Make a local group for the members of both the TECH and MNGR domains, and add it to the ACCT domain's local group.

B. Make a global group for the members of both the TECH and MNGR domains, and add it to the ACCT domain's local group.

C. Make a separate global group for both the TECH and MNGR domains, and add both global groups to the ACCT domain's local group.

D. Make a global group for the members of the TECH domain and a global group for the members of the MNGR domain. Make the global group created in the MNGR domain a member of the global group created in the MNGR domain, and add it to the ACCT domain's local group.

70-067.03.01.006

Files in a shared directory are disappearing, but no one will admit to deleting files in the directory. How can you discover who is deleting the files? (Choose two.)

A. Log deletions in Performance Monitor.

B. Use Event Viewer to view the Security Log.

C. View the deleted file's properties in the Recycle Bin.

D. Use Windows NT Explorer to enable auditing of Delete events in the directory.

70-067.03.01.005

You need to give all of the domains in the company access to a high performance color laser printer. Your company has a domain named ACCT, a domain named TECH, and a domain named MNGR.

The color laser printer is attached to the ACCT domain's primary domain controller. The ACCT domain trusts both the MNGR domain and the TECH domain. You create a local group on the ACCT domain's primary domain controller. This local group is given print permission to the laser printer.

How can all domains access the printer?

▶ **Correct Answer: C**

A. **Incorrect:** A local group can contain user and global groups from its domain and all trusted domains. A local group cannot contain other local groups.

B. **Incorrect:** A global group can only contain users from within its domain. Therefore, you cannot add users from two domains to a single global group.

C. **Correct:** All domain users require access to a laser printer in the ACCT domain and the ACCT domain trusts the MNGR and TECH domains. Given this scenario, the best way to provide all domains access to this printer is by adding a global group from each domain to the local group with print permission in the ACCT domain. The assumption is that the global groups in the domains contain all users that require access to the printer. If the question had stated that all users should have access to the printer, then it would be more efficient to add the global Domain Users group from each domain to the local Users group in the ACCT domain.

D. **Incorrect:** A global group can only contain user accounts within its domain. Therefore, you cannot make a global group from one domain a member of a global group from another domain.

70-067.03.01.006

Files in a shared directory are disappearing, but no one will admit to deleting files in the directory. How can you discover who is deleting the files? (Choose two.)

▶ **Correct Answers: B and D**

A. **Incorrect:** Deletion logging is not an option in Performance Monitor.

B. **Correct:** The Event Viewer–Security log is where all audited events are recorded. Auditing must be enabled in User Manager or User Manager for Domains. Additionally, to audit file system activity like deleting files, the file system containing the share must be NTFS and the Success check box must be selected for File and Object Access in User Manager for Domains.

C. **Incorrect:** Files placed in the recycle bin do not show the name of the user who performed the deletion.

D. **Correct:** After auditing for File and Object Access is enabled in User Manager or User Manager for Domains, the specific directory or file on an NTFS partition must be selected before auditing will occur.

Further Reading

 Microsoft Windows NT Network Administration Training kit. Chapters 2–4 provide both a discussion of user and group management and exercises to reinforce your knowledge of user and group configuration.

 Microsoft Windows NT Server Concepts and Planning Manual. Chapter 1 sections: "Managing Windows NT Server Domains," "Managing Domains," and "Managing Domain Security Policies," describe both account policy and audit policy.

 Microsoft Windows NT Server Resource Kit. In the *Networking Guide,* review the section of Chapter 2 titled: "Controlling Access–User Rights." This chapter contains a useful table of the most common user rights, the groups assigned to these user rights by default, and user rights you may consider changing to increase system security.

O B J E C T I V E   3 . 2

Create and manage policies and profiles for various situations.

In Windows NT and Windows 9x, profiles define user environments. For example, a profile contains a user's desktop shortcuts and application configuration. Though there are similarities between the profiles used on a computer running Windows NT and a computer running Windows 9x, these profiles are not interchangeable. For the purpose of test preparation, this discussion focuses on the Windows NT profile.

You can configure two types of profiles in Windows NT, local and roaming. A local profile is local to the computer where it was created, and is stored under the \system_root\Profiles directory. As its name suggests, a roaming profile is located in a network accessible location.

Profiles are designed to provide two major categories of information, the system configuration, defined as HKEY_LOCAL_MACHINE (HKLM) in the Registry, and user specific settings. A user's settings travel throughout the network, while a system configuration is computer specific. A profile contains both a portion of the Registry (HKEY_CURRENT_USER, named ntuser.dat), and a profile directory structure. The directory structure stores information such as shortcuts and start menu options.

A System policy interacts with user profiles and Registry settings that are not part of a user's profile to provide centralized configuration and control of networked computers. A System policy provides you with more control of networked computers. It is also ideal for controlling parts of a customizable roaming profile, and enhancing network security.

System policy is implemented through a file containing Registry settings. When a user logs on the network, these Registry settings are applied to their local Registry. System policies can be implemented for specific users, groups, computers, or for all users. You create System policies with the System Policy Editor. To do so, you must run the System Policy Editor tool on Windows NT and create a system policy file for Windows NT client.

To successfully answer the questions for this objective, you need a firm understanding of several key terms. For definitions of these terms, refer to the Glossary in this book.

Key Terms

- Directory replication
- Local profile
- Mandatory profile
- Net Logon share
- Profile
- Registry
- Roaming profile
- System policy
- System Policy Editor

70-067.03.02.001

A network is composed of a single primary domain controller, two backup domain controllers, four member servers, and 112 Windows NT Workstation clients. Mandatory roaming profiles are assigned to every user in the domain.

What is the file extension of the mandatory user profile?

A. .ini

B. .req

C. .pro

D. .dat

E. .man

70-067.03.02.001

A network is composed of a single primary domain controller, two backup domain controllers, four member servers, and 112 Windows NT Workstation clients. Mandatory roaming profiles are assigned to every user in the domain.

What is the file extension of the mandatory user profile?

▶ **Correct Answer: E**

A. **Incorrect:** The .ini suffix is a common extension for Windows 3.*x* configuration files. They are still present in Windows 9*x* and Windows NT but are primarily used for backward compatibility with Win16-based applications.

B. **Incorrect:** This is not the correct extension.

C. **Incorrect:** This is not the correct extension.

D. **Incorrect:** This is the default extension of the ntuser.dat file. This file is mapped to Registry settings contained in the user's HKEY_CURRENT_USER subkey. The .dat extension allows the profile to be modified by the user; therefore, it is not mandatory.

E. **Correct:** The ntuser.dat file is renamed to ntuser.man to enforce the use of mandatory profiles. To deny logon, except if this file is accessible, rename the user profile path with the .man extension and specify this path in User Manager for Domains.

Further Reading

 Microsoft Windows NT Server 4.0 Enterprise Technologies Training Kit: Microsoft Windows NT Server in the Enterprise. Lesson 2 of Chapter 3, "Managing Enterprise Resources," will help you to see the relationship between profiles and policies, and to implement various profiles and policies in Windows NT.

 Microsoft Windows NT Technical Support Training kit. Chapter 4, "Managing System Policies," outlines how to implement a system policy, and explains its behavior once a user logs on to the network.

OBJECTIVE 3.3

Administer remote servers from various types of clients.

Windows NT Server can be administered from Windows 3.x, Windows for Workgroups, Windows 9x, or Windows NT clients. Objective 3.3 focuses on Windows NT Server administration from the two most common client operating systems, Windows 95 and Windows NT Workstation 4.0.

The remote server administration tools for Windows NT Workstation and Windows 9x are located under the \clients\srvtools directory on the Windows NT Server 4.0 installation CD-ROM. Two subdirectories below the srvtools directory, winnt and win95, are used to install the remote server tools on Windows NT Workstation or Windows 9x clients, respectively.

There are two different procedures for installing the remote administration tools on a Windows NT Workstation or a Windows 9x client. From the Windows NT Workstation command prompt, change to the \clients\srvtools\winnt directory, and run the setup.bat file. Setup.bat chooses the subdirectory below \client\srvtools\winnt, which contains compiled versions of the remote server tools. These compiled versions of the remote server administration tools are designed for Alpha, x86, PowerPC or MIPS-based computers running Windows NT Workstation. For a Windows 9x client: run the Control Panel–Add/Remove Programs program. From the Windows Setup tab, choose the Have Disk button and specify the \clients\srvtools\win95 directory on the Windows NT Server 4.0 installation CD-ROM.

To successfully answer the questions for this objective, you need a firm understanding of several key terms. For definitions of these terms, refer to the Glossary in this book.

Key Terms

- Directory share

- Dynamic Host Configuration Protocol (DHCP) Administrator

- Explorer interface extensions

- File and Print Services for NetWare (FPNW)

- Net Logon share

- NT File System (NTFS) permissions

- Object ownership

- Printer share

- Remote Access Service (RAS) Administrator

- Remoteboot Service Manager

- Remote server administration

- Share rights

- Windows Internet Naming Server (WINS) Administrator

70-067.03.03.001

Which tool allows a Windows NT Workstation 4.0 computer to administer the Remote Access Service on another Windows NT computer?

A. Rplmgr

B. Srvmgr

C. Rasadmin

D. Winsadmn

70-067.03.03.001

Which tool allows a Windows NT Workstation 4.0 computer to administer the Remote Access Service on another Windows NT computer?

▶ **Correct Answer: C**

    A. **Incorrect:** The Remote Boot Manager utility (rplmgr) is used to configure the remote boot service on a Windows NT Server.

    B. **Incorrect:** The Server Manager utility (srvmgr) is used to configure and manage Windows NT computers on the network.

    C. **Correct:** The Remote Access Administrator (rasadmin) is used to configure the remote access service on a Windows NT computer.

    D. **Incorrect:** The WINS Administrator (winsadmin) is used to configure the Windows Internet Naming Service on a Windows NT Server computer.

70-067.03.03.002

You need to administer permissions and configure user account properties on a Windows NT Server 4.0 Intel-based computer. From which operating systems can permissions be administered using resources that ship with the Windows NT Server 4.0 CD-ROM? (Choose three.)

A. Windows 95

B. Windows NT Server 4.0

C. Windows for Workgroups

D. OS/2 for LAN Manager 2.2c

E. Windows NT Workstation 4.0

F. MS-DOS with Microsoft Network Client

70-067.03.03.002

You need to administer permissions and configure user account properties on a Windows NT Server 4.0 Intel-based computer. From which operating systems can permissions be administered using resources that ship with the Windows NT Server 4.0 CD-ROM? (Choose three.)

▶ **Correct Answers: A, B, and E**

A. **Correct:** The Windows 95 tools located in the \clients\srvtools\win95 directory on the Windows NT Server 4.0 CD-ROM include Windows 95 Explorer extensions that allow you to administer permissions on a Windows NT Server 4.0. Additionally, the installation of the remote server administration tools includes User Manager for Domains, which allows you to configure users on a Windows NT Server.

B. **Correct:** The Windows NT Server 4.0 distribution CD-ROM contains the installation files and routine to set up Windows NT Server 4.0. After Windows NT Server 4.0 is installed, a Windows NT Server contains the tools necessary to manage itself and any other Windows NT Server on the network.

C. **Incorrect:** The Windows NT Server 3.5x CD-ROM contains the client installation tools to administer permissions and user accounts on a Windows NT Server. However, the Windows NT Server 4.0 CD-ROM does not contain remote server administration tools for Windows for Workgroups.

D. **Incorrect:** The Windows NT Server 4.0 distribution CD-ROM does not contain tools and utilities to allow an OS/2 for LAN Manager 2.2c server to remotely administer a Windows NT Server 4.0.

E. **Correct:** A Windows NT Workstation 4.0 can administer NTFS and printer permissions without the tools located below \clients\srvtools\winnt on the Windows NT 4.0 Server CD-ROM. However, the remote server administration tools are necessary for user account management (User Manager for Domains). The Windows NT Workstation 4.0 remote server administration routine installs User Manager for Domains on Windows NT 4.0 Workstation.

F. **Incorrect:** The Windows NT Server 4.0 distribution CD-ROM does not contain tools and utilities to allow an MS-DOS client to remotely administer a Windows NT Server 4.0.

70-067.03.03.003

Your network supports computers running Windows NT Server and Windows 95.

The required result is to use a Windows 95–based computer named WIN95TECHSRV to share folders on a Windows NT Server–based computer named NTS40BDC2.

The first optional result is to remotely manage file permissions from WIN95TECHSRV.

The second optional result is to use WIN95TECHSRV to add a new user account.

The proposed solution is to install the Windows NT Server client-based administration tools on WIN95TECHSRV and use Server Manager to share the necessary folders on NTS40BDC2. Use Explorer on WIN95TECHSRV to set permissions of files on NTS40BDC2. Use User Manager for Domains at WIN95TECHSRV to create the new user account.

What does the proposed solution provide?

A. The required result and all optional results.

B. The required result and one optional result.

C. The required result but none of the optional results.

D. The proposed solution does not provide the required result.

70-067.03.03.003

Your network supports computers running Windows NT Server and Windows 95.

The required result is to use a Windows 95–based computer named WIN95TECHSRV to share folders on a Windows NT Server–based computer named NTS40BDC2.

The first optional result is to remotely manage file permissions from WIN95TECHSRV.

The second optional result is to use WIN95TECHSRV to add a new user account.

The proposed solution is to install the Windows NT Server client-based administration tools on WIN95TECHSRV and use Server Manager to share the necessary folders on NTS40BDC2. Use Explorer on WIN95TECHSRV to set permissions of files on NTS40BDC2. Use User Manager for Domains at WIN95TECHSRV to create the new user account.

What does the proposed solution provide?

▶   **Correct Answer: A**

A. **Correct:** The required result is to share folders on Windows NT Server, NTS40BDC2, from the Windows 95 client, WIN95TECHSRV. The proposed solution, to install the remote server administration tools on the Windows 95 client and then use Server Manager on WIN95TECHSRV to share folders on NTS40BDC2, achieves the required result. The first optional result, to remotely manage file permissions from WIN95TECHSRV, is achieved through the Windows 95 Explorer interface extension installed with the remote server administration setup routine. The Explorer interface extension allows you to manage both printer and NTFS file objects on Windows NT computers. The second optional result, to use WIN95TECHSRV to add a new user account, is achieved through User Manager for Domains installed on WIN95TECHSRV through the remote server administration setup routine.

B. **Incorrect:** The required result and both optional results are achieved.

C. **Incorrect:** The required result and both optional results are achieved.

D. **Incorrect:** The required result is achieved.

70-067.03.03.004

Your network supports computers running Windows NT Server and Windows 95.

The required result is to use a Windows 95–based computer named WIN95TECHSRV to share folders on a Windows NT Server–based computer named NTS40BDC2.

The first optional result is to remotely manage file permissions from WIN95TECHSRV.

The second optional result is to use WIN95TECHSRV to add a new user account.

The proposed solution is to install the Windows NT Server client-based administration tools on WIN95TECHSRV, and use Server Manager to share the necessary folders on NTS40BDC2. Use Explorer on WIN95TECHSRV to set permissions of files on NTS40BDC2.

What does the proposed solution provide?

A. The required result and all optional results.

B. The required result and one optional result.

C. The required result but none of the optional results.

D. The proposed solution does not provide the required result.

70-067.03.03.004

Your network supports computers running Windows NT Server and Windows 95.

The required result is to use a Windows 95–based computer named WIN95TECHSRV to share folders on a Windows NT Server–based computer named NTS40BDC2.

The first optional result is to remotely manage file permissions from WIN95TECHSRV.

The second optional result is to use WIN95TECHSRV to add a new user account.

The proposed solution is to install the Windows NT Server client-based administration tools on WIN95TECHSRV, and use Server Manager to share the necessary folders on NTS40BDC2. Use Explorer on WIN95TECHSRV to set permissions of files on NTS40BDC2.

What does the proposed solution provide?

▶ **Correct Answer: B**

A. **Incorrect:** The required result and the first optional result are achieved. However, the second optional result, to use WIN95TECHSRV to add a new user account, is not achieved.

B. **Correct:** The required result is to share folders on the Windows NT Server, NTS40BDC2, from the Windows 95 client, WIN95TECHSRV. The proposed solution, to install the remote server administration tools on the Windows 95 client and then use Server Manager on WIN95TECHSRV to share folders on NTS40BDC2, achieves the required result. The first optional result, to remotely manage file permissions from WIN95TECHSRV, is achieved through the Windows 95 Explorer interface extension installed by the remote server administration setup routine. This extension allows you to manage both printer and NTFS file objects on Windows NT computers. The second optional result, to use WIN95TECHSRV to add a new user account, is not achieved since the proposed solution does not suggest running User Manager for Domains to add a new user account on the Windows NT Server.

C. **Incorrect:** The required result and one of the optional results are achieved.

D. **Incorrect:** The required result is achieved.

70-067.03.03.005

Your network supports computers running Windows NT Server and Windows 95.

The required result is to use a Windows 95–based computer named WIN95TECHSRV to share folders on a Windows NT Server–based computer named NTS40BDC2.

The first optional result is to remotely manage file permissions from WIN95TECHSRV.

The second optional result is to use WIN95TECHSRV to add a new user account.

The proposed solution is to install the Windows NT Server client-based administration tools on WIN95TECHSRV, and use Server Manager to share the necessary folders on NTS40BDC2.

What does the proposed solution provide?

A. The required result and all optional results.

B. The required result and one optional result.

C. The required result but none of the optional results.

D. The proposed solution does not provide the required result.

70-067.03.03.005

Your network supports computers running Windows NT Server and Windows 95.

The required result is to use a Windows 95–based computer named WIN95TECHSRV to share folders on a Windows NT Server–based computer named NTS40BDC2.

The first optional result is to remotely manage file permissions from WIN95TECHSRV.

The second optional result is to use WIN95TECHSRV to add a new user account.

The proposed solution is to install the Windows NT Server client-based administration tools on WIN95TECHSRV, and use Server Manager to share the necessary folders on NTS40BDC2.

What does the proposed solution provide?

▶ **Correct Answer: C**

A. **Incorrect:** Only the required result is achieved. The first optional result, to remotely manage file permissions from WIN95TECHSRV, and the second optional result, to use WIN95TECHSRV to add a new user account, is not achieved.

B. **Incorrect:** The required result is achieved, but none of the optional results are achieved.

C. **Correct:** The required result is to share folders on Windows NT Server, NTS40BDC2, from the Windows 95 client, WIN95TECHSRV. The proposed solution, to install the remote server administration tools on the Windows 95 client and then use Server Manager on WIN95TECHSRV to share folders on NTS40BDC2, achieves the required result. The first optional result, to remotely manage file permissions from WIN95TECHSRV, is not achieved because the proposed solution does not suggest running the Windows 95 Explorer interface to administer rights on Windows NT Server. The second optional result, to use WIN95TECHSRV to add a new user account is not achieved because the proposed solution does not include the use of User Manager for Domains.

D. **Incorrect:** The required result is achieved.

Further Reading

 Microsoft Windows NT Technical Support Training kit. Lesson 4 of Chapter 15, "Implementing Network Clients," includes practice steps for installing the remote server administration tools on both Windows NT 4.0 Workstation and Windows 95.

OBJECTIVE 3.4

Manage disk resources.

Disk and printer resources in Windows NT are made accessible to clients on the network through the Server and Browser services, which, together, make sharing possible. The Server service maintains any shared directories or printers on a Windows NT computer. The Browser service announces the presence of all shares on the network that are not hidden. In this way, a client can connect to the network and see all visible shares associated with a Windows NT computer.

This objective tests your ability to configure share rights and NTFS (local) permissions, and your knowledge of the characteristics of share rights (No Access, Read, Write, Full Control), and NTFS permissions. This objective also covers how to monitor user disk activity through auditing different files and directories.

To successfully answer the questions for this objective, you need a firm understanding of several key terms. For definitions of these terms, refer to the Glossary in this book.

Key Terms

- Change right
- Full Control right
- Hidden shares
- Net Share
- Net Use
- Net View
- No Access right
- Read right

70-067.03.04.001

A file named Ata_100.xls is copied from C:\Temp to D\:Der on a Windows NT Server 4.0 computer. Both drives are NTFS. The Users group has Read access to C:\Temp and Full Control to D\:Der.

Which permission does the User group have to Ata_100.xls after it is copied?

A. Read

B. None

C. No Access

D. Full Control

70-067.03.04.002

Who can set up auditing on a Windows NT 4.0 computer? (Choose two.)

A. Power Users

B. Administrators

C. Server Operators

D. Users with "manage auditing and security log" right

70-067.03.04.001

A file named Ata_100.xls is copied from C:\Temp to D\:Der on a Windows NT Server 4.0 computer. Both drives are NTFS. The Users group has Read access to C:\Temp and Full Control to D\:Der.

Which permission does the User group have to Ata_100.xls after it is copied?

▶ **Correct Answer: D**

A. **Incorrect:** The file Ata_100.xls is copied from one NTFS partition, C:\Temp, to another NTFS partition, D:\Der. The User group has Read access to C:\Temp and since files inherit the permissions assigned at the directory level, the Read access right is also applied to Ata_100.xls. After the file copy, however, Ata_100.xls inherits the rights of its new parent directory, D:\Der.

B. **Incorrect:** The file Ata_100.xls is copied from one NTFS partition to another so NTFS permissions will always be applied to the file. If the file was copied to a FAT partition, all rights would be lost and this answer would be correct.

C. **Incorrect:** The No Access right was not specifically applied to Ata_100.xls, or the new directory in which it was copied.

D. **Correct:** The file Ata_100.xls is copied from one NTFS partition, C:\Temp, to another NTFS partition, D:\Der. Since the file is copied from one partition to another, it inherits the rights of its new parent directory. Since the User group has Full Control of D:\Der, the Ata_100.xls file inherits this permission.

70-067.03.04.002

Who can set up auditing on a Windows NT 4.0 computer? (Choose two.)

▶ **Correct Answers: B and D**

A. **Incorrect:** Members of the Power Users group, which is created on a Windows NT Workstation or a Windows NT member server, do not have the ability to configure auditing.

B. **Correct:** Administrators are able to configure auditing on a Windows NT 4.0 computer.

C. **Incorrect:** Members of the Server Operators group are not granted the right to configure auditing on a Windows NT 4.0 computer.

D. **Correct:** Any user or group granted the User Right, "manage auditing and security log" can configure and manage auditing on a Windows NT computer.

70-067.03.04.003

Which group can administer security logs, but cannot set up audit policy?

A. Power Users

B. Administrators

C. Server Operators

D. Backup Operators

70-067.03.04.004

You are administering a Windows NT 4.0 network with five Windows NT 4.0 servers and twenty Windows 95 computers. You have problems with viruses infecting one of the servers' directories on an NTFS partition. Users run programs from this directory so you decide to assign a standard permission to this directory that will allow them to run programs but not infect the executable files.

Which standard permission should you assign to each executable file?

A. Read

B. Write

C. Delete

D. Execute

70-067.03.04.003

Which group can administer security logs, but cannot set up audit policy?

▶ **Correct Answer: C**

A. **Incorrect:** The Power User group, created on a Windows NT Workstation or a Windows NT Server member server, is not able to administer the Security logs or set up audit policy.

B. **Incorrect:** The Administrator group can both administer the Security logs and configure audit policy.

C. **Correct:** The Server Operator group can administer the Security logs, but cannot configure audit policy.

D. **Incorrect:** The Backup Operator group can neither administer the Security logs nor configure audit policy.

70-067.03.04.004

You are administering a Windows NT 4.0 network with five Windows NT 4.0 servers and twenty Windows 95 computers. You have problems with viruses infecting one of the servers' directories on an NTFS partition. Users run programs from this directory so you decide to assign a standard permission to this directory that will allow them to run programs but not infect the executable files.

Which standard permission should you assign to each executable file?

▶ **Correct Answer: A**

A. **Correct:** The Read standard NTFS right is the combination of the individual rights, read and execute. This standard right allows users to run programs, but they are not able to write to the program files. Viruses must be able to write to files in order to infect them.

B. **Incorrect:** The Write right is an individual right, not a standard right. With this right a virus may be able to infect executable files.

C. **Incorrect:** The Delete right is an individual right, not a standard right. This right alone will not allow users to run executable files.

D. **Incorrect:** The Execute right is an individual right, not a standard right. This right alone may not allow users to run programs.

70-067.03.04.005

A file named Playlist.doc is moved from the D:\Microsoft directory to the D:\Windowsnt directory on an NTFS partition. The Users group has Read permission for D:\Microsoft and Full Control permission for D:\Windowsnt.

Which permission does the Users group have to Playlist.doc after it is moved?

A. None

B. Read

C. No Access

D. Full Control

70-067.03.04.006

You share a directory with the share name app1 on an NTFS partition. What is the default permission given to the Everyone group when the share is created?

A. Read

B. Change

C. No Access

D. Full Control

70-067.03.04.005

A file named Playlist.doc is moved from the D:\Microsoft directory to the D:\Windowsnt directory on an NTFS partition. The Users group has Read permission for D:\Microsoft and Full Control permission for D:\Windowsnt.

Which permission does the Users group have to Playlist.doc after it is moved?

▶ **Correct Answer: B**

   A. **Incorrect:** The file, Playlist.doc is moved from one location to another location on the same NTFS partition. Therefore, NTFS rights are maintained. Rights are only stripped away from a file on an NTFS partition if it is moved to a FAT partition.

   B. **Correct:** The file Playlist.doc inherits the rights of its original parent directory, D:\Microsoft. The file is then moved to the D:\Windowsnt directory. Since Playlist.doc is moved to another location on the same partition, it maintains its original ACL. Therefore, the Users group has Read permission to this file.

   C. **Incorrect:** The No Access right is not explicitly assigned to the directory or the Playlist.doc file.

   D. **Incorrect:** The Playlist.doc is moved from one location to another on the same NTFS partition. Therefore, the file maintains its original ACL. As a result, the Users group has Full Control Permission to the D:\Windowsnt directory but only Read permission to the Playlist.doc file.

70-067.03.04.006

You share a directory with the share name app1 on an NTFS partition. What is the default permission given to the Everyone group when the share is created?

▶ **Correct Answer: D**

   A. **Incorrect:** When you share a directory, Windows NT does not restrict access to the share.

   B. **Incorrect:** The Change standard right is more restrictive than Full Control.

   C. **Incorrect:** The No Access standard right is the most restrictive setting available in Windows NT.

   D. **Correct:** Share rights and NTFS permissions always default to Full Control for the Everyone group. This is the most unrestricted setting available in Windows NT.

70-067.03.04.007

User DavidK is the owner of a file named Test.xls on the D: drive. He asks you to move the file. You and DavidK have Full Control permissions to this file.

The required result is to move Test.xls to a different folder on the same NTFS partition.

The first optional result is to preserve the file permissions of Test.xls.

The second optional result is to preserve the file ownership of Test.xls.

The proposed solution is to use Windows NT Explorer to move Test.xls to a target folder on the D: drive where you have Full Control permission.

What does the proposed solution provide?

A. The required result and all optional results.

B. The required result and one optional result.

C. The required result but none of the optional results.

D. The proposed solution does not provide the required result.

70-067.03.04.007

User DavidK is the owner of a file named Test.xls on the D: drive. He asks you to move the file. You and DavidK have Full Control permissions to this file.

The required result is to move Test.xls to a different folder on the same NTFS partition.

The first optional result is to preserve the file permissions of Test.xls.

The second optional result is to preserve the file ownership of Test.xls.

The proposed solution is to use Windows NT Explorer to move Test.xls to a target folder on the D: drive where you have Full Control permission.

What does the proposed solution provide?

▶ **Correct Answer: A**

A. **Correct:** You are asked to move Test.xls for DavidK. Since you have Full Control permissions to this file, you will have no trouble moving it to another directory where you have at least the Write individual permission. Since the proposed solution is to move the file to a target folder on the D: drive where you have Full Control permission, you will be able to move the file. Therefore, the required result, to move Test.xls to a different folder on the same NTFS partition, is achieved. The first optional result, to preserve the file permissions of Test.xls, is maintained since the file is moved to another location on the same NTFS partition. The second optional result, to preserve the file ownership of Test.xls, is achieved since you have Full Control permission to the file. If you are not given access to the file but you are an administrator or equivalent, you would have to take ownership of the file before moving the file.

B. **Incorrect:** The required result and both optional results are achieved.

C. **Incorrect:** The required result and both optional results are achieved.

D. **Incorrect:** The required result is achieved.

Further Reading

 Microsoft Windows NT Network Administration Training kit. Lesson 2 in Chapter 5 includes a comprehensive overview of sharing in a Windows NT network. Lessons 4 and 5 in Chapter 6, "Securing Network Resources with NTFS Permissions," provide an overview of implementing NTFS permissions in a Windows NT network. Lessons 2 and 3 in Chapter 9 "Auditing Resources and Events," provide a comprehensive overview of configuring and managing auditing in a Windows NT network.

 Microsoft Windows NT Server Concepts and Planning Manual. Chapter 4 contains a useful table that shows share rights and how they affect your ability to access resources. Chapter 4 also distinguishes between NTFS standard permissions and NTFS individual permissions, and explains how each are used. Chapter 9 provides a listing of file and object access events that can be monitored through the audit function.

Connectivity

Microsoft Windows NT was designed with networking in mind. The network components contained in the Windows NT architecture provide a robust platform for interoperability with other devices on the network. The term "connectivity" describes the various methods used to link network devices to one another, making this interoperability possible. So understanding connectivity will help you use a number of network technologies to build functional and robust networks that are suited to the needs of the client. (Windows NT supports many network connection services.)

The focus of this domain of objectives is on how to configure Windows NT Server to:

- Provide access to a NetWare server on a Microsoft network or migrate a NetWare server to a Windows NT Server.

- Provide Remote Access Service (RAS) to dial-in clients.

Tested Skills and Suggested Practices

The skills you need to successfully master the Connectivity Objective Domain on the exam include:

- Using a Windows NT Server to provide Microsoft clients with access to a NetWare server.

  - Practice 1: Install NWLink IPX/SPX and Gateway Services for NetWare (GSNW) on a system running Windows NT Server.

  - Practice 2: Study the basics of NetWare 3.*x* administration which includes: user setup and group creation using Syscon; implementing trustee assignments; creating a basic system login script; configuring a NetWare print queue, and mapping a drive.

  - Practice 3: Install a Novell NetWare 3.*x* server for the purpose of implementing GSNW on a Windows NT Server, and later for the purpose of performing a migration of Novell NetWare to a Windows NT Server.

- Practice 4: Study the hierarchical structure of a NetWare 4.x NetWare Directory Services (NDS) tree. You should be able to map a drive letter or an LPT port to a fully qualified NDS name.

- Practice 5: Understand the function of NetWare bindery services and NetWare directory services.

- Migrating a NetWare server to a system running Windows NT Server.

  - Practice 1: Install a NetWare 3.1x server in preparation for a migration to a system running Windows NT Server.

  - Practice 2: Run multiple, trial migrations of a NetWare 3.x server to a system running Windows NT Server using the Windows NT Server migration tool for NetWare. Once the procedure is running smoothly, perform an actual migration of a NetWare 3.x server to a Windows NT Server.

- Using RAS, configure a robust and secure method for clients to dial in to a Windows NT Server network.

  - Practice 1: Install RAS on a system running Windows NT Server. Configure it to support modem dial-in and clients running NetBEUI, IPX/SPX, and TCP/IP.

  - Practice 2: Configure MS-DOS, Windows 3.x or Windows for Workgroups, Windows 95, and Windows NT dial-out clients, and establish a Point to Point Protocol (PPP) connection with a Windows NT Server running RAS.

  - Practice 3: Read about the various methods of encryption and authentication used by RAS.

O B J E C T I V E   4 . 1

Configure Windows NT Server for interoperability with NetWare servers by using various tools.

In a network containing both Novell NetWare file servers and Windows NT Servers, clients are typically provided with access to file and print services on both network operating systems. Objective 4.1 discusses and tests the different ways to provide dual network operating system access. One way is to configure clients to support multiple network redirectors. One redirector provides services to a NetWare server while another redirector provides services to a Windows NT Server. This approach requires that you install and configure each client with both redirectors. It also requires that each client log on to both network operating systems.

Another, more efficient way, provided a client only requires limited access to a NetWare server, is to provide access to NetWare file and print services using Windows NT Server's Gateway Services for NetWare (GSNW). GSNW translates Novell's NetWare Core Protocol (NCP) to and from the Microsoft Server Message (SMB) Protocol. GSNW is only capable of providing limited access, because the gateway uses a single NetWare user connection to service all Microsoft network client requests. Servicing many Microsoft clients with one connection burdens the NetWare server and significantly increases processor utilization on a Windows NT Server running GSNW.

If GSNW does not provide the level of access required, and you don't wish to install additional redirectors on your Microsoft clients, you can migrate your NetWare servers to a system running Windows NT Server using the Migration Tool for NetWare. This utility allows you to easily transfer user and group accounts, volumes, directories, and files from a NetWare server to a computer running Windows NT Server.

To successfully answer the questions for this objective, you need a firm understanding of several key terms. For definitions of these terms, refer to the Glossary in this book.

Key Terms

- Attributes

- Bindery

- Client Services for NetWare (CSNW)

- File and Print Services for NetWare (FPNW)

- Gateway

- Gateway Services for NetWare (GSNW)

- Migration Tool for NetWare

- NetWare Core Protocol (NCP)

- NetWare Directory Services (NDS)

- Preferred server

- Print queue

- Redirector

- Server Message Block (SMB)

- Supervisor

- Trustee assignments

70-067.04.01.001

You need to add a Novell NetWare 4.11 server to a network that previously contained only Microsoft Windows clients and Windows NT 4.0 servers. The NetWare server will be used primarily to provide file and print services and network management services. You do not want to add NWLink to each client.

What can you install on the Windows NT Server–based computers to allow clients to connect to the NetWare server's directories and printers? (Choose two.)

A. FPNW

B. CSNW

C. GSNW

D. TCP/IP

E. NWLink

F. NetBEUI

70-067.04.01.001

You need to add a Novell NetWare 4.11 server to a network that previously contained only Microsoft Windows clients and Windows NT 4.0 servers. The NetWare server will be used primarily to provide file and print services and network management services. You do not want to add NWLink to each client.

What can you install on the Windows NT Server–based computers to allow clients to connect to the NetWare server's directories and printers? (Choose two.)

▶ **Correct Answers: C and E**

A. **Incorrect:** File and Print Services for NetWare (FPNW) is an add-on tool that allows a Windows NT Server to provide file and print services to native NetWare clients. The Windows NT Server appears to the NetWare clients as a NetWare 3.*x* file server.

B. **Incorrect:** Client Services for NetWare (CSNW) is the Windows NT Workstation NetWare redirector. CSNW allows a Windows NT Workstation to log on to NetWare servers and use their resources. The question asks what you can install on a Windows NT Server to allow clients to access the NetWare 4.11 server. CSNW cannot be installed on a Windows NT Server.

C. **Correct:** Gateway Services for NetWare (GSNW) is installed on a Windows NT Server to provide Microsoft clients with access to NetWare resources from a Windows NT Server logon. Clients using only the Microsoft network redirector can then access resources on the NetWare 4.11 server.

D. **Incorrect:** The TCP/IP protocol cannot be used to access NetWare file and print services.

E. **Correct:** NWLink IPX/SPX must be installed before, or during, the installation of GSNW. This protocol is required to log on to and access resources on NetWare 2.*x*, 3.*x*, and 4.*x* file servers. You don't have to add NWLink IPX/SPX to each client because the gateway translates incoming client SMB requests to NCP requests for a NetWare server regardless of the transport protocol(s) on the client.

F. **Incorrect:** The NetBEUI protocol cannot be used to access NetWare file and print services.

70-067.04.01.002

You want to migrate NetWare client information from a Novell NetWare 3.12 server to a computer running Windows NT Server 4.0 using the Windows NT Server Migration Tool for NetWare. What should you install on the Windows NT server before migrating if you want to preserve users' logon scripts?

A. GSNW

B. FPNW

C. CSNW

D. DSMN

70-067.04.01.003

Which accounts must you create before Microsoft clients can access NetWare servers through Gateway Services for NetWare? (Choose three.)

A. NTGATEWAY group account on the NetWare server.

B. NTGATEWAY local group account on the Windows NT server.

C. NetWare user account for each user that will access the NetWare server through the gateway.

D. Windows NT user account for each user that will access the NetWare server through the gateway.

70-067.04.01.002

You want to migrate NetWare client information from a Novell NetWare 3.12 server to a computer running Windows NT Server 4.0 using the Windows NT Server Migration Tool for NetWare. What should you install on the Windows NT server before migrating if you want to preserve users' logon scripts?

▶ **Correct Answer: B**

    A. **Incorrect:** GSNW is required to perform the migration of NetWare servers to a Windows NT Server but it does not allow you to migrate user logon scripts.

    B. **Correct:** Although FPNW is a Windows NT add-on product from Microsoft, it is required if you wish to migrate user logon scripts from NetWare servers to a Windows NT Server.

    C. **Incorrect:** CSNW is used to allow a Windows NT Workstation client to log on to NetWare servers but it does not play a role in migrating NetWare servers to a Windows NT Server.

    D. **Incorrect:** Directory Service Manager for NetWare (DSMN) is a Microsoft add-on tool that allows a Windows NT Server to integrate NetWare servers into Microsoft domains. This product does not play a role in a NetWare to Windows NT Server migration.

70-067.04.01.003

Which accounts must you create before Microsoft clients can access NetWare servers through Gateway Services for NetWare? (Choose three.)

▶ **Correct Answers: A, C, and D**

    A. **Correct:** The NTGATEWAY account must be created on the NetWare server or servers where resources will be accessed through GSNW. Additionally, the NetWare user account that will be used by GSNW must be added to this group.

    B. **Incorrect:** There is no need to create any groups on the Windows NT Server running GSNW in order to support the gateway service.

    C. **Correct:** A NetWare user account is used by GSNW to log on to NetWare servers where resources will be accessed. This account must be created on the NetWare servers before configuring GSNW on the Windows NT Server.

    D. **Correct:** The Windows NT Server running GSNW requires Microsoft clients to log on before they can access resources through the gateway. Resources available through the gateway are represented by Windows NT directory and printer shares. Share rights can be configured to control user access to these resources.

Further Reading

 "Explanation of Gateway Services for NetWare." This article provides a concise explanation of how GSNW interprets requests to NetWare servers from Microsoft clients and delivers responses from NetWare servers to Microsoft clients. You can find this article at the Microsoft Support Online Web site (http://support.microsoft.com/support/c.asp?FR=0) by selecting "Specific article ID number" under "I want to search by," entering **Q121394** in the "My question is" field, and then clicking the Find button.

 Microsoft Windows NT Server Network Supplement Manual. Chapter 14 provides detailed documentation of the Migration Tool and tables that show the relationships between NetWare functions and Windows NT Server functions as they relate to migration.

 Microsoft Windows NT Technical Support Training kit. Review Lessons 1 and 2 of Chapter 14 on two NetWare interoperability tools, GSNW and the Migration Tool for NetWare.

 "Supported 16-bit Utilities and NetWare-Aware Applications." This article provides you with a handy list of supported NetWare utilities when running CSNW on a Windows NT Workstation or GSNW on a Windows NT Server. The article can be accessed at the Microsoft Support Online Web site with the ID number **Q156429**.

Install and configure Remote Access Service (RAS).

Remote Access Service (RAS) provides clients with a method of accessing resources on a system running Windows NT Server by way of remote connections. RAS supports three types of remote access devices: modems (includes null modem cables), ISDN terminal adapters, and X.25 Packet Assembler Dissasemblers (PADs). Before any of these devices can be used for RAS, they must be installed and configured on the server

Using a VPN, the RAS server connects to a TCP/IP-based wide area network (WAN), such as the Internet, from the internal network. Remote connections are made over the WAN connection using the Point to Point Tunneling Protocol (PPTP).

Above a RAS hardware device or a VPN connection is a transport protocol. RAS supports NetBEUI, IPX/SPX, and TCP/IP transport protocols for remote connections. To support the transport protocols, like NetBEUI and application layer services like file and print services over dialup connections Windows NT RAS uses the Point to Point protocol (PPP). PPP handles framing rules and authentication for the RAS server.

Internal network security is robust in Windows NT. Like local clients, remote clients must log on to the network and are therefore controlled by internal network security settings. Additional security is built into RAS to make up for the inevitable lack of security in a remote connection.

The next step, once the RAS server is set up and security is established, is to configure clients to access the server. A system running Windows NT Server and RAS can support PPP clients, PPTP clients, and SLIP clients if properly configured.

To successfully answer the questions for this objective, you need a firm understanding of several key terms. For definitions of these terms, refer to the Glossary in this book.

Key Terms

- Challenge Handshake Authentication Protocol (CHAP)

- Encryption

- Integrated Service Digital Network (ISDN)

- Intermediary device

- Microsoft Challenge Handshake Authentication Protocol (MS-CHAP)

- Microsoft RAS protocol

- Packet assembler/dissassembler (PAD)

- Password Authentication Protocol (PAP)

- Point-to-Point Protocol (PPP)

- Point-to-Point Tunneling Protocol (PPTP)

- Point-to-Point Tunneling Protocol (PPTP) filtering

- Public switched telephone network (PSTN)

- Remote node

- RSA MD5

- RSA RC4

- Serial Line Internet Protocol (SLIP)

- Shiva Password Authentication Protocol (SPAP)

- Virtual Private Network (VPN)

- Windows Sockets

- X.25

70-067.04.02.001

Which network protocols can be used with a RAS connection? (Choose three.)

A. IPX/SPX

B. SNA

C. DECnet

D. TCP/IP

E. NetBEUI

F. AppleTalk

70-067.04.02.002

You are configuring a RAS server to allow remote Windows NT Workstation and Windows 95 clients to access the network using a dial-in connection. What is the highest authentication level you can use?

A. Allow any authentication including clear text.

B. Require encrypted authentication.

C. Require Microsoft encrypted authentication.

D. Require Virtual Private Network.

70-067.04.02.001

Which network protocols can be used with a RAS connection? (Choose three.)

▶ **Correct Answers: A, D, and E**

A. **Correct:** The IPX/SPX network protocol can be used by the RAS client and the RAS server. This transport protocol is typically used to access NetWare resources over a remote connection. However, Windows NT resources can also be accessed using IPX/SPX. IPX/SPX is also a routable protocol so resources across a router can be reached using this protocol.

B. **Incorrect:** The SNA protocol used for access to IBM hosts is not supported by RAS.

C. **Incorrect:** The DECnet protocol, often used in DEC-based networks, is not supported by RAS.

D. **Correct:** The TCP/IP protocol can be used by the RAS client and the RAS server. This transport protocol is typically used to access Internet-, intranet-, and TCP/IP-based host resources. TCP/IP is a routable protocol so resources across a router can be reached using this protocol.

E. **Correct:** The NetBEUI protocol can be used by the RAS client and the RAS server. This transport protocol is typically used for small networks where remote access is required. NetBEUI is the simplest and fastest protocol of those supported by RAS. Additionally, NetBEUI supports the NetBIOS gateway and the older Microsoft RAS protocol. NetBEUI is not a routable protocol. Therefore, it cannot be used to access resources across routers.

F. **Incorrect:** The AppleTalk protocol, used in Apple computer–based networks, is not supported by RAS.

70-067.04.02.002

You are configuring a RAS server to allow remote Windows NT Workstation and Windows 95 clients to access the network using a dial-in connection. What is the highest authentication level you can use?

▶ **Correct Answer: C**

A. **Incorrect:** The "Allow any authentication including clear text" option permits the client to use any of the supported client authentication methods requested by the server.

B. **Incorrect:** The "Require encrypted authentication" option means that a client can dial in to the RAS server using MS-CHAP, DES, or SPAP.

C. **Correct:** The "Accept only Microsoft encrypted authentication" means that the client must use MS-CHAP (RSA MD4) to establish a remote connection with the server.

D. **Incorrect:** This is not a valid option in Windows NT Server RAS.

70-067.04.02.003

Which network protocol should you configure your RAS server to use if remote clients need to access UNIX servers through RAS?

A. IPX/SPX

B. SNA

C. DECnet

D. TCP/IP

E. NetBEUI

F. AppleTalk

70-067.04.02.004

Which network protocol should you configure your RAS server to use if remote clients need to access NetWare servers through RAS?

A. IPX/SPX

B. SNA

C. DECnet

D. TCP/IP

E. NetBEUI

F. AppleTalk

70-067.04.02.003

Which network protocol should you configure your RAS server to use if remote clients need to access UNIX servers through RAS?

▶ **Correct Answer: D**

A. **Incorrect:** IPX/SPX is supported by RAS, but it is not supported on UNIX servers.

B. **Incorrect:** SNA is not supported by RAS.

C. **Incorrect:** DECnet is not supported by RAS.

D. **Correct:** TCP/IP is supported by RAS and is the native protocol used on UNIX hosts.

E. **Incorrect:** NetBEUI is supported by RAS, but it is not supported on UNIX servers.

F. **Incorrect:** AppleTalk is not supported by RAS.

70-067.04.02.004

Which network protocol should you configure your RAS server to use if remote clients need to access NetWare servers through RAS?

▶ **Correct Answer: A**

A. **Correct:** The IPX/SPX network protocol can be used by the RAS client and the RAS server. This transport protocol is typically used to access NetWare resources over a remote connection.

B. **Incorrect:** The SNA protocol used for access to IBM hosts is not supported by RAS.

C. **Incorrect:** The DECnet protocol, often used in DEC-based networks, is not supported by RAS.

D. **Incorrect:** The TCP/IP protocol can be used by the RAS client and the RAS server. This transport protocol is typically used to access Internet-, intranet-, and TCP/IP-based host resources, not NetWare servers.

E. **Incorrect:** The NetBEUI protocol can be used by the RAS client and the RAS server. This transport protocol is typically used for small networks where remote access is required. It cannot be used to access NetWare servers unless a Windows NT Server on the network is making NetWare resources available through GSNW. This, however, is not the best choice because IPX/SPX provides direct access to NetWare resources.

F. **Incorrect:** The AppleTalk protocol, used in Apple computer–based networks, is not supported by RAS.

70-067.04.02.005

You are configuring a RAS server to allow remote clients to access the network using dial-in connections. Most remote clients will be using Dial-Up Networking in Windows 95. Several OS/2 and Windows for Workgroups remote clients will also use RAS, but will use third-party software to establish the connection.

Which authentication level should you use to ensure a successful connection?

A. Allow any authentication including clear text.

B. Require encrypted authentication.

C. Require Microsoft encrypted authentication.

D. Require Virtual Private Network.

70-067.04.02.006

Which RAS connection protocol should you use if you want to support secure connections to your server over the Internet?

A. PPP

B. SLIP

C. PPTP

D. POP3

70-067.04.02.005

You are configuring a RAS server to allow remote clients to access the network using dial-in connections. Most remote clients will be using Dial-Up Networking in Windows 95. Several OS/2 and Windows for Workgroups remote clients will also use RAS, but will use third-party software to establish the connection.

Which authentication level should you use to ensure a successful connection?

▶ **Correct Answer: A**

A. **Correct:** Using the "Allow any authentication including clear text" option is the best choice. The Windows 95 clients should be configured to use MS-CHAP encrypted authentication. The OS/2 and Windows for Workgroups clients could use DES if they support this encryption level. However, since you are not told in the question whether the third-party software supports encryption, the best choice is to allow both CHAP and PAP for authentication.

B. **Incorrect:** In your testing, it is wise to choose "Require encrypted authentication" to increase security. If the OS/2 and Windows for Workgroups clients are able to connect using this setting, then the third-party client software supports an encryption scheme such as DES or SPAP. However, to ensure a successful connection, the "Allow any authentication including clear text" is your best choice.

C. **Incorrect:** The "Require Microsoft encrypted authentication" will allow the Windows 95 clients to connect. However, the Windows for Workgroups and OS/2 clients will not be able to connect to the RAS server.

D. **Incorrect:** This is not a valid option in Windows NT Server RAS.

70-067.04.02.006

Which RAS connection protocol should you use if you want to support secure connections to your server over the Internet?

▶ **Correct Answer: C**

A. **Incorrect:** PPP provides secure connections to a RAS server. However, this type of connection requires a dial-up device such as a modem, ISDN terminal adapter, or an X.25 PAD. Direct connections over the Internet are not supported.

B. **Incorrect:** SLIP is not supported on Windows NT Server RAS. A RAS client, however, can connect to a third-party SLIP server.

C. **Correct:** PPTP provides secure connections over WAN links using a VPN. The Internet can serve as the WAN link for this type of RAS remote communication.

D. **Incorrect:** POP3 is a protocol used for e-mail communications.

Further Reading

Microsoft Windows NT Server Network Supplement Manual. Read Chapter 5, "Understanding Remote Access Service" for an overview of dial-in and dial-out RAS. The graphics of an OSI model which shows where RAS components fit is also an excellent reference.

Microsoft Windows NT Server Network Supplement Manual. Review Chapter 11, "Point-To-Point Tunneling Protocol (PPTP)" for details of PPTP that are often missing from other documentation discussing this relatively new RAS feature.

Microsoft Windows NT Technical Support Training kit. To practice installing, configuring, and using RAS services, read Lessons 1, 3, and 4 of Chapter 12, "Implementing Remote Access Service."

"Remote Access Services Authentication Summary." This article provides a concise description of the authentication and encryption protocols used in RAS. Go to the Microsoft Support Online Web site (http://support.microsoft.com/support/c.asp?FR=0) and enter **Q136634** in the "My question is" field, select "Specific article ID number" for the type of search you want to perform, and click the Find button.

Monitoring and Optimization

The Monitoring and Optimization domain objective focuses on the Microsoft Windows NT services for network clients in terms of how to monitor the effects of these services upon your network and how to optimize your network when utilizing these services. Typically, a Windows NT Server provides application, directory, and file and print services. Each of these installed services, however, makes demands on hardware resources, and each service taxes the hardware resources in different ways.

To help determine exactly how hardware resources are being utilized during periods of peak server utilization and to optimize their use, Windows NT includes a powerful utility called Performance Monitor.

Performance Monitor allows you to record computer activity and establish a baseline. If you notice that server performance is degrading, you can compare the baseline data with new data to determine which hardware resource is being over-utilized. With this information you can determine how best to redistribute services or whether additional hardware resources are needed. Using Performance Monitor to identify such performance bottlenecks is an integral part of optimizing and maintaining a Windows network.

Tested Skills and Suggested Practices

The skills you need to successfully master the Monitoring and Optimization Objective Domain on the exam include:

- Taking a baseline measurement of Windows NT Server performance using disk performance counters. From the Windows NT command line, run Diskperf–y or Diskperf–ye (contains additional RAID array counters).

  - Practice 1: Create a chart of the common counters. To become familiar with data collection, read the explanation of these counters in Performance Monitor.

- Practice 2: Log the Memory, Processor, Disk, and Network objects shown in column 1 of the previous table. Configure the log interval for 600 seconds and log performance for three days. If possible, use a different computer to log the performance of the monitored Windows NT computer to avoid impacting the performance of the monitored computer.

- Practice 3: Isolate the periods of time when the server is most heavily utilized from the data collected in practice 2. Log server activity again, but this time only log server activity during the busiest times of the day. Log this activity for two weeks.

- Practice 4: Create a chart and a report of the logged data. If the performance is acceptable, use the data collected in practice 3 as your baseline of server performance.

- Identifying performance bottlenecks.

  - Practice 1: Create an alert condition from the baseline data collected in the previous practice skill. To trigger an alert, use the baseline data to set the counter at its threshold level.

  - Practice 2: Monitor the LogicalDisk object for the partition where users store their data, and for the partition used to spool print jobs on a file and print server.

  - Practice 3: Monitor all Windows NT computers for changes in baseline data. If performance is degrading, determine which hardware resource is creating the bottleneck. Upgrade the hardware resource, and continue monitoring the system for other bottlenecks.

OBJECTIVE 5.1

Monitor performance of various functions by using Performance Monitor.

Performance Monitor categorizes Windows NT resources by object. Three familiar objects are Memory, Processor, and Paging File. Objects contain counters, which measure given attributes of that object. For example, the Processor object counts the percentage of processing time (% Processor Time) and of interrupt time (Interupts/sec). When a computer has more than one example of the same object type, it is said to have multiple instances. In such cases, Performance Monitor counts each instance separately. For example, if your system has two CPUs then two instances of the Processor object will be counted.

Performance Monitor provides data in four different views and saves the data under the four filename extensions: the chart view (*.pmc), the log view (*.pml), the report view (*.pmr), and the alert view (*.pma). Each view can retrieve data from multiple Windows NT computers simultaneously, and display both real-time data (current activity) and logged data. A single view or the entire workspace can be saved for later use. A saved workspace contains all opened views and is given a filename extension of *.pmw. The list that follows describes the characteristics of each view.

To use this tool properly, it is important to understand what objects, instances, and counters are, the purpose of each of the four views contained in Performance Monitor, and how to navigate the Performance Monitor interface.

To successfully answer the questions for this objective, you need a firm understanding of several key terms. For definitions of these terms, refer to the Glossary in this book.

Key Terms

- Alert view

- Application server

- Baseline

- Bottleneck

- Chart view

- Counters

- Disk I/O

- Diskperf

- Instance

- Log view

- Objects

- Performance Monitor

- Report view

- Views

- Windows NT directory services

- Workspace

70-067.05.01.001

You want to use Performance Monitor to check on a Windows NT computer that has two hard disks, each containing a single NTFS partition.

The required result is to collect data that might identify a potential disk bottleneck on the remote client.

The first optional result is to set an alert to occur if the processor of the remote client becomes the bottleneck.

The second optional result is to reduce the impact of periodic alert monitoring (compared to the default value) at your computer.

The proposed solution is to enable disk counters for the client computer and use Performance Monitor from your computer to log Physical Disk: %Disk Time and Physical Disk: Avg. Disk Queue Length for each disk on the remote client. Set an alert to occur if the System: Processor Queue Length exceeds 3. Set the Alert Update Time Interval to 120.

What does the proposed solution provide?

A. The required result and all optional results.

B. The required result and one optional result.

C. The required result but none of the optional results.

D. The proposed solution does not provide the required result.

70-067.05.01.001

You want to use Performance Monitor to check on a Windows NT computer that has two hard disks, each containing a single NTFS partition.

The required result is to collect data that might identify a potential disk bottleneck on the remote client.

The first optional result is to set an alert to occur if the processor of the remote client becomes the bottleneck.

The second optional result is to reduce the impact of periodic alert monitoring (compared to the default value) at your computer.

The proposed solution is to enable disk counters for the client computer and use Performance Monitor from your computer to log Physical Disk: %Disk Time and Physical Disk: Avg. Disk Queue Length for each disk on the remote client. Set an alert to occur if the System: Processor Queue Length exceeds 3. Set the Alert Update Time Interval to 120.

What does the proposed solution provide?

▶ **Correct Answer: A**

A. **Correct:** The required result, to collect data that might identify a potential disk bottleneck on the remote client, is accomplished by the proposed solution. First, the disk counters are enabled on the remote client using the Diskperf–y command. After the remote client restarts, Performance Monitor is configured on your computer to log Physical Disk: %Disk Time and Physical Disk: Avg. Disk Queue Length for each disk drive. The %Disk Time counter indicates the amount of time that the disk drive is busy servicing read and write requests. If this is consistently close to 100 percent, it indicates that the disk drive is being over-utilized. The Avg. Disk Queue Length counter indicates the number of pending disk I/O requests for the disk drive. If this value is consistently over two, it indicates disk controller congestion. Monitoring these two counters will help you identify a potential disk bottleneck. Note, however, that disk congestion can be caused by low RAM causing a condition known as disk thrashing. In this case, RAM, and not the disk or disk controller, is the bottleneck. The first optional result, to set an alert to occur if the processor of the remote client becomes the bottleneck, is accomplished by the proposed solution. The proposed solution says that an alert should be set in Performance Monitor if the System: Processor Queue Length exceeds three. The Processor Queue Length indicates the number of threads that are ready to be executed and are waiting for processor time. Generally, a processor queue length that is consistently higher than two indicates a processor bottleneck. Further analysis of the individual processes making requests on the processor, by using the Task Manager or Performance Monitor, is required to determine the cause of the congestion. The second optional result, to reduce the impact of periodic alert monitoring (as compared to the default value) at your computer, is achieved by setting the Alert Update Time Interval to 120. The default Alert Update Time Interval is five seconds.

B. **Incorrect:** The required result and both optional results are achieved.

C. **Incorrect:** The required result and both optional results are achieved.

D. **Incorrect:** The required result is achieved.

70-067.05.01.002

Which utility must be run on Windows NT Server before Performance Monitor can be used to collect physical and logical disk data?

A. Ftdisk

B. Taskmgr

C. Diskperf

D. Dumpchk

70-067.05.01.003

How can you configure Windows NT Server so the system will notify you if disk space exceeds 80% of capacity?

A. Set an alert on Available Physical Memory in Task Manager.

B. Set an alert on the %Free Space counter in Performance Monitor.

C. Set an alert on the Free Disk Space option in Server Manager Alerter Service.

D. Set an alert on the Disk Space counter in the Server applet in Control Panel.

70-067.05.01.002

Which utility must be run on Windows NT Server before Performance Monitor can be used to collect physical and logical disk data?

▶ **Correct Answer: C**

    A. **Incorrect:** The ftdisk fault-tolerance disk driver is used in Windows NT implementations of RAID 1 and RAID 5. It is not run as the preliminary step to using Performance Monitor to collect physical and logical disk data.

    B. **Incorrect:** Taskmgr application can be accessed in a number of ways. For example, it can be launched from the properties of the Windows NT taskbar or from the CTRL+ALT+DEL Windows NT Security window. The Task Manager shows the running applications, processes, and performance information. It is not used to enable disk performance counters.

    C. **Correct:** The Diskperf Windows NT command is used at the Windows NT command line to enable disk performance counters in Performance Monitor. To enable disk performance counters, type **Diskperf–y** from the command line and then restart the computer. You can also enable additional disk counters for a RAID implementation using Diskperf–ye.

    D. **Incorrect:** The dumpchk utility is used to read a memory dump created after a system crash of Windows NT.

70-067.05.01.003

How can you configure Windows NT Server so the system will notify you if disk space exceeds 80% of capacity?

▶ **Correct Answer: B**

    A. **Incorrect:** It is not possible to set alerts using the Windows NT Task Manager. Therefore, Task Manager cannot be used to notify you of disk space utilization.

    B. **Correct:** Using the Performance Monitor, alert view, you can monitor each instance of the LogicalDisk: %Free Space counter. You can also monitor Total %Free Space on all LogicalDisk counters. The alert threshold can be configured to warn you if the %Free Space counter exceeds 80%.

    C. **Incorrect:** Server Manager is not used to set alert conditions. However, you can start and stop the Alerter service through the Computer menu–Services option. The Performance Monitor alert view is dependent on the Messenger Service to send alerts but it is not dependent on the Alerter service. The Alerter service is used to send general Windows NT alert messages to users or computer names configured through Server Manager.

    D. **Incorrect:** The Server program in Control Panel can be used to monitor users, shares, and files in use. It is also used to configure the Alerter service, not alerts.

70-067.05.01.004

What should you chart in Performance Monitor if you suspect excessive paging?

A. Memory: Page faults/sec

B. Thread: % Privileged Time

C. Processor: % Processor Time

D. Logical Disk: Disk Bytes/Transfer

70-067.05.01.004

What should you chart in Performance Monitor if you suspect excessive paging?

▶ **Correct Answer: A**

A. **Correct:** The Memory: Page Faults/sec counter is incremented when a process refers to a virtual memory page that is not in its working set (the physical memory visible to the program) in main memory. A Page Fault will not cause the page to be fetched from disk if that page is on the standby list, and hence already in main memory or if it is temporarily in use by another process. However, if this number is high, it does suggest at least some hard page faults. A better indicator of hard page faults is the Memory: Pages/sec counter. Hard page faults occur when the data a process requires is not found in its working set or elsewhere in physical memory, and must be retrieved from disk. Sustained hard page faults of over five per second are a clear indicator of a memory bottleneck and will lead to disk thrashing. Excessive paging appears as disk thrashing because the virtual memory manager must write program code in and out of physical memory to disk. While analyzing the Page Faults/sec counter isn't the best counter to measure hard page faults in practice, it is the best answer from the multiple-choice list provided.

B. **Incorrect:** The Thread: % Privileged Time is the percentage of elapsed time that an instance of a thread, or all threads in the system, spend executing code in privileged, or kernel mode. The time a thread spends in privileged mode is an indication of how the program is written and its function in the system.

C. **Incorrect:** The Processor: % Processor Time counter indicates how much a processor is utilized by non-idle threads in the system. Idle threads are low priority units of execution that keep the processor active when no other threads in the system require processor service. Though excessive paging can cause over-utilization of the processor, this relationship is indirect. The bottleneck in such a case is due to a lack of RAM, not an overloaded processor.

D. **Incorrect:** The Logical Disk: Disk Bytes/Transfer counter records the average number of bytes transferred to, or from, the disk during write or read operations. This counter indicates how fast data on a disk partition is moved to and from memory. If you suspect that disk I/O is your bottleneck, this value will be small while Avg. Disk Queue Length will be greater than two.

70-067.05.01.005

Which Performance Monitor view should you use to monitor the activity of a thread's counters over a weeklong period?

A. Log

B. Alert

C. Chart

D. Report

70-067.05.01.005

Which Performance Monitor view should you use to monitor the activity of a thread's counters over a weeklong period?

▶ **Correct Answer: A**

A. **Correct:** The Performance Monitor log view allows you to log information over a given period of time, such as a week. After logging a thread's counters for a week, the chart, report, and alert views can be used to analyze the thread's activity. Additionally, data can be exported into other tools such as a Microsoft Visual Basic application for further analysis.

B. **Incorrect:** The alert view can collect current activity or view logged data but it is not used for the purpose of initially collecting data for later analysis. Instead, it is typically used to monitor for significant events like processor over-utilization.

C. **Incorrect:** Like the alert view, the chart view can collect current activity and view logged data. The chart view provides a graphical interface of operating system data for optimizing the operating system and determining how hardware resources are being used.

D. **Incorrect:** The report view can also view both current and logged activity. It is designed to provide a textual view of data rather than the graphical view that is provided by the chart view. It is ideal for building summary reports of counter data.

Further Reading

Inside Windows NT, by Helen Custer and the second edition, by David Solomon, provide insight on how the Windows NT operating system was built and how it functions This book was originally written for Windows NT 3.1 and has been updated to investigate Windows NT 4.0 and, to a lessor extent, the Windows NT 5.0 operating system.

Microsoft Windows NT Server Concepts and Planning Manual. Chapter 8, "Monitoring Performance: Conceptual Overview and Running Performance Monitor," discusses using Performance Monitor with Windows NT Task Manager.

Microsoft Windows NT Server 4.0 Enterprise Technologies Training Kit: Supporting Windows NT Server in the Enterprise. Lessons 1 and 2 of Chapter 5, "Server Monitoring and Optimization," contain practice exercises to help you learn how to navigate in Performance Monitor.

OBJECTIVE 5.2

Identify performance bottlenecks.

A bottleneck occurs at the piece of hardware that takes the most time to execute a task, and sometimes the bottleneck results from inefficient use of a device. Slow hardware resources are another common cause of bottlenecks. Finally, improperly sized resources can create bottlenecks.

The four resources typically monitored when looking for bottlenecks are the processor, RAM, disk, and network adapter. The Performance Monitor objects used to oversee these resources include, but are not limited to: Memory, Processor, System, PhysicalDisk, LogicalDisk, Network Interface, Network Segment, TCP, UDP, NBT Connection, NWLink IPX.

To successfully answer the questions for this objective, you need a firm understanding of several key terms. For definitions of these terms, refer to the Glossary in this book.

Key Terms

- Available bytes

- Disk thrashing

- Interrupt

- Network Interface: Bytes Sent/sec

- Network Segment: % Network utilization

- Percent (%) Disk Time

- Pool Nonpaged Bytes

- Queue length

- Thread

- Virtual memory

70-067.05.02.001

You are using Performance Monitor to determine why a Windows NT Server computer is performing poorly, and you find that excessive paging is occurring. What should you do?

A. Install more RAM.

B. Upgrade the processor.

C. Install a faster hard disk.

D. Install a faster network interface card.

70-067.05.02.002

You are using Performance Monitor to determine why a Windows NT Server–based computer is performing poorly. Paging is not causing the problem, but you observe a sustained processor queue of more than two threads, even when the computer is not being accessed by many users.

What should you do?

A. Install more RAM.

B. Upgrade the processor.

C. Install a faster hard disk.

D. Install a faster network interface card.

70-067.05.02.001

You are using Performance Monitor to determine why a Windows NT Server computer is performing poorly, and you find that excessive paging is occurring. What should you do?

▶ **Correct Answer: A**

A. **Correct:** Excessive paging is usually caused by a low RAM condition. It is generally accepted that RAM is the resource with the greatest impact on system performance in Windows NT.

B. **Incorrect:** Excessive paging can lead to high processor utilization. However, the direct cause of excessive paging is usually a lack of RAM.

C. **Incorrect:** A faster hard disk will allow the virtual memory manager to page data faster. However, accessing data from a hard disk is approximately 100 times slower than accessing data from RAM. Therefore, adding RAM is a better choice since additional RAM will allow program code to remain in physical memory rather than being swapped to page files.

D. **Incorrect:** A faster network card may help if server access is slow. However, a faster network card will not solve an excessive paging problem.

70-067.05.02.002

You are using Performance Monitor to determine why a Windows NT Server–based computer is performing poorly. Paging is not causing the problem, but you observe a sustained processor queue of more than two threads, even when the computer is not being accessed by many users.

What should you do?

▶ **Correct Answer: B**

A. **Incorrect:** If the processor queue length is long, installing additional RAM may reduce some load placed on the processor by the virtual memory manager. However, the question states that excessive paging is not a problem on this computer.

B. **Correct:** The System: Processor Queue Length should consistently stay below two. Processor Queue Length is the instantaneous length of the processor queue in units of threads. All processors use a single queue in which threads wait for processor cycles. This length does not include the threads that are currently executing. A sustained processor queue length greater than two generally indicates processor congestion. Adding or upgrading a processor will remedy this problem. If it does not solve the problem, consider redistributing processes to other Windows NT computers on the network. Note that the Processor Queue Length counter registers 0 unless you are also monitoring a thread counter.

C. **Incorrect:** A faster hard disk may exacerbate a Processor Queue Length problem. Disk I/O will execute more efficiently and add more requests to the processor queue.

D. **Incorrect:** A faster network card may exacerbate a Processor Queue Length problem. Network I/O will execute more efficiently and add more requests to the processor queue.

70-067.05.02.003

You are using Performance Monitor to determine why a Windows NT Server–based computer is performing poorly. Paging is not causing a problem, but you discover sustained disk use and persistently long disk queues.

What should you do?

A. Install more RAM.

B. Upgrade the processor.

C. Install a faster hard disk and controller.

D. Install a faster network interface card.

70-067.05.02.004

Which tool can you use to identify potential bottlenecks on a Windows NT Server–based computer?

A. CrashDump

B. Server Manager

C. Performance Monitor

D. Windows NT Diagnostics

70-067.05.02.003

You are using Performance Monitor to determine why a Windows NT Server–based computer is performing poorly. Paging is not causing a problem, but you discover sustained disk use and persistently long disk queues.

What should you do?

▶ **Correct Answer: C**

   A. **Incorrect:** If Memory: Page Faults/sec are low but disk thrashing does appear to be a problem, installing more RAM will not help since the Virtual Memory Manager is not over-utilizing the disk drives.

   B. **Incorrect:** Since the problem appears to be sustained disk use and persistently long disk queues, it is unlikely that adding or upgrading the processors will solve this problem. The problem is disk I/O, not the availability of the processor.

   C. **Correct:** Installing faster disk technology is likely to solve poor disk I/O: a problem often associated with sustained disk use and persistently long disk queues. If disk I/O continues to be a problem after upgrading the disk drives and controller, consider implementing RAID 0, 5, or 10. Remember that RAID 0 is not fault-tolerant.

   D. **Incorrect:** Installing a faster network interface card will not solve a disk I/O problem.

70-067.05.02.004

Which tool can you use to identify potential bottlenecks on a Windows NT Server–based computer?

▶ **Correct Answer: C**

   A. **Incorrect:** If the Windows NT operating system fails, it writes a file called CrashDump to the page file contained on the boot partition. CrashDump is not a tool but a function in Windows NT.

   B. **Incorrect:** Server Manager is a Windows NT Administrative tool used to view and administer domains, workgroups, and computers. It is not used to identify bottlenecks in Windows NT.

   C. **Correct:** Performance Monitor is a Windows NT Administrative tool used to identify bottlenecks in Windows NT.

   D. **Incorrect:** Windows NT Diagnostics is a troubleshooting tool used to determine how hardware resources are configured to work with Windows NT. Information in Windows NT Diagnostics can be viewed but not modified.

Further Reading

 "Optimizing Windows NT for Performance." This article was written for Windows NT 3.51 but many of the bottleneck detection counters are applicable to Windows NT 4.0. Read this article to learn more about bottleneck detection using specific object:counter combinations. You can find this article at the Microsoft Support Online Web site (http://support.microsoft.com/support/c.asp?FR=0) by selecting "Specific article ID number" under "I want to search by," entering **Q146005** in the "My question is" field, and then clicking on the Find button.

 Microsoft Windows NT Server 4.0 Enterprise Technologies Training Kit: Supporting Windows NT Server in the Enterprise. Lessons 3–6 in Chapter 5, "Server Monitoring and Optimization," review how to monitor and optimize a file and print server, an application server, and a domain controller.

Troubleshooting

Troubleshooting is the process of isolating the source of a system error and correcting it. At first glance this may sound like a simple process. However, effective troubleshooting requires tenacity, creativity, and a thorough technical understanding of the system needing your attention. Troubleshooting is a critical part of Windows NT network management and is therefore a major part of Microsoft's Windows NT certification exams.

Tested Skills and Suggested Practices

The skills you need to successfully master the Troubleshooting Objective Domain on the exam include:

- Running and troubleshooting multiple installations of Windows NT Server and Windows NT Workstation.

    - Practice 1: Watch and write down what happens at each phase of the installation process.

    - Practice 2: Read some of the entries on the Windows NT Hardware Compatibility List (HCL) found on Microsoft's Web site. Read about preinstallation preparation for some of the hardware listed in the HCL.

- Running the Windows NT Server boot process after an installation of Windows NT Server is completed.

    - Practice1: Watch and write down what happens at each phase of the boot process.

    - Practice 2: If your computer can dual-boot, boot it in another operating system. Then, rename essential boot files like Ntldr on an x86 computer to determine what happens the next time Windows NT starts. Write down the results of your experiment. Make sure to change the essential boot files back to their original names.

- Installing and configuring services, applications, devices (including printers), and device drivers.

  - Practice 1: After installing a new network adapter, configure the adapter device driver to use different resources than are configured for the new adapter. Attempt to create a device driver conflict. Reconfigure the hardware to work properly with your computer.

  - Practice 2: Work in the Windows NT Diagnostics program to identify how resources are being used in the computer.

  - Practice 3: Create a printer in Windows NT and configure a printing device on the network that is serviced by that printer. Relocate the spooler directory to another drive on the Windows NT computer which services the printing device. Restrict printer permissions and then try to send a print job to the printing device from a restricted user account.

  - Practice 4: Install Windows 95 printer drivers on a Windows NT Server so that a Windows 95 client can conveniently add a printer using the Windows NT print server.

- Troubleshooting RAS on a Windows NT Server and on a client.

  - Practice 1: Enable PPP logging in the registry. Change protocol settings on the Windows NT RAS server so as to create a protocol mismatch on the client and the server. Dial to the server from the RAS client and observe the error that occurs on the client and the error generated in the ppp.log file on the RAS server.

  - Practice 2: Enable device.log in the registry. Change the modem driver used by the RAS server so that it is different than the modem attached to the dial-in port. Attempt to connect to the RAS server. After the connection fails, review the device.log file.

- Troubleshooting both GSNW and an attempted migration of a NetWare server to a Windows NT server.

  - Practice 1: Remove the gateway account from the NTGateway group on the NetWare server. Stop and start GSNW. Attempt to create shared resources that point to a NetWare file and print server.

  - Practice 2: Run trial migrations of a NetWare server to a Windows NT Server. Read the migration logs to see the types of errors generated.

- Configuring and managing resource access and NTFS permissions on a Windows NT Server.

  - Practice 1: Create a directory share that is more than eight characters long. Then, attempt to connect to the share from an MS-DOS client and observe the error.

  - Practice 2: Restrict access to a shared directory and a shared printer and attempt to connect to these resources from a client without access to these shares.

  - Practice 3: Configure NTFS permissions on a share created in practice 2. Restrict access so that a user given share rights is given the No Access NTFS permission to a file within the shared directory. Then attempt to access the file from a client logged on as the user with the No Access NTFS permission.

- Maintaining the proper operation of your disaster recovery methods.

  - Practice 1: Run a tape backup procedure with files open on the Windows NT Server. Review the backup.log file to determine which files did not back up. Run a restore procedure with files open on the server. Review restore.log to determine which files were not restored.

  - Practice 2: Unload your tape device driver and try to run NTBackup. Isolate the error and fix the error.

  - Practice 3: On a Windows NT Server test system, shut down the server and remove a drive from a mirror set. Restart the server and observe indications of an orphaned mirror set in Disk Administrator. If you remove the system partition that is part of a mirror set, modify a Windows NT boot disk so that the operating system starts from the remaining drive of the mirror set. Shut down the server and reinstall the missing drive. Start the server, run Disk Administrator, and remirror the orphaned drive.

  - Practice 4: On a Windows NT Server test system, shut down the server and remove a drive from a RAID 5 array. Start Windows NT Server and observe Windows NT Disk Administrator to see how the incomplete array appears. Shut down the server and reinstall the missing drive. Start the server, run Disk Administrator, and regenerate the array.

OBJECTIVE   6 . 1

Choose the appropriate course of action to take to resolve installation failures.

Even before attempting an installation of Windows NT, you should verify that the computer equipment that will run Windows NT is on the Hardware Compatibility List (HCL). While Windows NT can run on hardware that is not on the HCL, Microsoft does not support it. A computer that is not able to run Windows NT is likely to show a fatal STOP message during installation. To check your computer hardware against the HCL, visit http://www. microsoft.com and search for HCL.

After checking your hardware against the HCL, determine the hardware configuration of your adapters. Common hardware resources include IRQ, I/O port, port setting, DMA, and cable type. If you don't know the type of hardware installed in the computer or the configuration of the computer's hardware, run the NTHQ hardware detection utility. NTHQ is located under \support\hqtool in the Windows NT CD-ROM directory. This tool obtains hardware information in a text file that you can review after it runs.

The installation process runs in two discrete phases; the first phase is the character-based setup and the second phase is the graphical-based setup. During the character-based phase, the installation routine gathers essential information on the system architecture in order to determine the current configuration and which device drivers must be installed. This phase also decides if the installation process can continue, and where on the existing fixed disks to install Windows NT.

These detection routines and the information you provide during phase 1 are used to construct a "mini" version of Windows NT. After reboot, phase 2 begins. First device drivers load and initialize and the "mini" version of Windows NT starts. Then a graphical installation wizard appears to help you complete the installation process.

To successfully answer the questions for this objective, you need a firm understanding of several key terms. For definitions of these terms, refer to the Glossary in this book.

Key Terms

- NT Hardware Qualifier (NTHQ)

- STOP message

70-067.06.01.001

You install a new video card in a Pentium-based computer running Windows NT Server. After restarting the server, the screen remains black. Subsequent restarts have the same result.

What should you do to solve this problem?

A. Start the server using the VGA mode option and reconfigure the video device.

B. Start the server using the Last Known Good Configuration and reconfigure the video device.

C. Start the server using the Setup disks and use the Emergency Repair Disk to reset the system.

D. Start the server from an MS-DOS boot floppy, reformat the hard drive, and reinstall the operating system.

70-067.06.01.002

What should you do if you receive a STOP message while installing Windows NT Server on a new computer?

A. Use Fdisk to check for and set the system partition.

B. Check for partition table corruption using DiskProbe.

C. Restart using the setup disks, and repair with the Emergency Repair Disk.

D. Check the computer hardware for compatibility with Windows NT Server in the HCL.

E. Restart using the Last Known Good Configuration, and run Windows NT Diagnostics.

70-067.06.01.001

You install a new video card in a Pentium-based computer running Windows NT Server. After restarting the server, the screen remains black. Subsequent restarts have the same result.

What should you do to solve this problem?

▶ **Correct Answer: A**

A. **Correct:** If after installing a new video card, the monitor is unreadable or black, this indicates that the previous video adapter driver is not compatible with the new video adapter. By choosing [VGA Mode] from the boot loader, you are starting Windows NT with the /basevideo switch. This switch causes Windows NT to load a 640-x-480 resolution and 16-color standard VGA adapter. Most VGA adapters can support this setting so Windows NT will start and the display will be readable. At this point, the correct adapter driver can be loaded.

B. **Incorrect:** The question states that hardware was replaced, not that a device driver was improperly configured or installed. Therefore, running the Last Known Good Configuration will not solve the problem.

C. **Incorrect:** Using the ERD will not solve the problem since the device driver for the video adapter is not corrupted. It is simply the wrong device driver for the new hardware.

D. **Incorrect:** While reformatting the drive and reinstalling Windows NT will solve the problem, it is not the most efficient solution to the problem.

70-067.06.01.002

What should you do if you receive a STOP message while installing Windows NT Server on a new computer?

▶ **Correct Answer: D**

A. **Incorrect:** If the installation of Windows NT was able to start, then a system partition is active and Windows NT will locate it early in the installation process. The system partition will contain the initial boot files necessary to start Windows NT.

B. **Incorrect:** If the partition table is corrupted, the Windows NT Resource Kit utility, DiskProbe, can be used. However, this tool is used after Windows NT is installed.

C. **Incorrect:** The ERD is created at the end of the installation process. Because Windows NT cannot be installed, this procedure will not remedy the problem.

D. **Correct:** If the installation process fails, it is likely that a hardware component in the computer is malfunctioning, improperly configured, or is not compatible with Windows NT. Check the HCL on the Microsoft Web site. The HCL lists compatible hardware and any special settings or firmware updates required for compatibility with Windows NT.

E. **Incorrect:** The Last Known Good Configuration is not available until after Windows NT is installed.

70-067.06.01.003

You install an additional large capacity SCSI hard disk in a computer running Windows NT Server. After the installation, the POST test fails when you power on the computer.

What should you do to solve this problem?

A. Use Fdisk to check for and set the system partition.

B. Check for partition table corruption using DiskProbe.

C. Check for improper termination and other hardware-related problems.

D. Start the server using the VGA Mode option and reconfigure the SCSI device.

E. Restart using the Last Known Good Configuration and run Windows NT Diagnostics.

70-067.06.01.003

You install an additional large capacity SCSI hard disk in a computer running Windows NT Server. After the installation, the POST test fails when you power on the computer.

What should you do to solve this problem?

▶ **Correct Answer: C**

A. **Incorrect:** The failure occurs during the POST routine and the question states that a disk was just installed. Therefore, involving operating system utilities like Fdisk will not solve the problem.

B. **Incorrect:** The failure occurs during the POST routine and the question states that a disk was just installed. Therefore, involving operating system utilities like DiskProbe will not solve the problem.

C. **Correct:** Since the computer is failing during the power on self test (POST) routine, the problem must be in the hardware configuration of the computer. At this point in the process, there is no operating system involvement. Since a SCSI hard disk was just installed, it is likely that the drive termination is incorrect. In a SCSI chain, there must be termination at both ends of the chain.

D. **Incorrect:** The VGA Mode does not appear until after the POST test is complete. Also, the VGA Mode option is used to solve video adapter driver problems, not disk hardware configuration problems.

E. **Incorrect:** The Last Known Good Configuration option does not appear until after the POST test is complete. Also, the Last Known Good Configuration is used to remove all software configuration changes made since the last successful local logon to the computer.

70-067.06.01.004

You add a new IDE hard disk to a computer running Windows NT Server. You are able to create a FAT volume on the new hard disk, but you cannot access the drive. Disk Administrator displays the volume as Unknown.

What should you do to solve this problem? (Choose two.)

A. Check for viruses.

B. Repair the Master File Table.

C. Repartition and reformat the drive.

D. Assign appropriate permissions for the drive.

E. Start the server with the startup disks and repair using the ERD.

70-067.06.01.004

You add a new IDE hard disk to a computer running Windows NT Server. You are able to create a FAT volume on the new hard disk, but you cannot access the drive. Disk Administrator displays the volume as Unknown.

What should you do to solve this problem? (Choose two.)

▶ **Correct Answers: A and C**

A. **Correct:** If Disk Administrator displays a formatted drive as unknown, this indicates that the partition on the drive is damaged, perhaps by a virus. Corruption problems can also occur if you dual-boot Windows 95 and you use the Windows 95 version of Fdisk. To avoid problems with Fdisk, delete the Windows 95 version, make sure that you have the MS-DOS–based version, and run Fdisk only when you start MS-DOS.

B. **Incorrect:** The Master File Table is involved in the boot process. Since Windows NT starts and you are attempting to manipulate the installed IDE drive through Disk Administrator, this suggests that the start was proper and therefore the MFT is not involved.

C. **Correct:** By repartitioning this drive in Disk Administrator or by using the MS-DOS version of Fdisk, you prepare the drive for reformatting. After formatting the new partition, the drive should function properly. If it is still not available, run a virus detection program to determine if the drive is infected with a virus. If it is not infected, the drive may require a low-level format, be improperly configured, or be defective.

D. **Incorrect:** This error can occur with an NTFS partition if local permissions have been improperly configured. However, the question states that this error is occurring on a FAT partition. Local permissions do not apply to the FAT file system. For more information see *Windows NT Workstation Resource Guide* Chapter 21, "Troubleshooting Startup and Disk Problems."

E. **Incorrect:** Windows NT starts properly so there is no need to run an emergency repair procedure. The Windows NT setup disks (startup disks) and the ERD are only required if Windows NT does not boot due to a corrupted Registry or due to corrupted operating system files on the system or boot partition.

Further Reading

 Microsoft Windows NT Server Concepts and Planning Manual. In Chapter 7, "Protecting Data," the section titled, "System Diagnosis, Recovery, and Repair" teaches how to determine which troubleshooting approach is most likely to resolve a Windows NT problem.

 Microsoft Windows NT Server Resource Kit. Chapter 7, "Disk, File System, and Backup Utilities" is an excellent disk troubleshooting reference which discusses four powerful low-level disk utilities available with the kit.

 "Windows NT 4. 0 Setup Troubleshooting Guide." To locate this article, go to www.microsoft.com and click the Support link at the top of the page. Once the Microsoft Support Online Web page appears, select "Specific article ID number" under "I want to search by," and enter **Q126690** in the "My question is" field. Click the Find button.

OBJECTIVE 6.2

Choose the appropriate course of action to take to resolve boot failures.

Like the installation process, the Windows NT startup process occurs in discrete, observable phases. To troubleshoot the system, you must know the names and functions of the files required to run the Windows NT boot sequence (phase 1 of the startup process), what happens in each subsequent phase of the startup process, and what procedures should be followed to remedy errors.

To successfully answer the questions for this objective, you need a firm understanding of several key terms. For definitions of these terms, refer to the Glossary in this book.

Key Terms

- *.pal

- Boot.ini

- Boot.ini switches

- Bootsect.dos

- Boot sequence

- Device drivers

- Emergency Repair Disk (ERD)

- Kernel Initialize

- Kernel Load

- Last Known Good Configuration

- Ntbootdd.sys

- Ntdetect.com

- Ntldr

- Ntoskrnl.exe

- Osloader

- Session Manager

- Startup process

- Win32 subsystem

70-067.06.02.001

You have a new Pentium-based Windows NT Server computer to install on your network. When the server is started, you get the message:

"Error loading operating system."

What should you do to solve this problem?

A. Use MSD to check for IRQ conflicts.

B. Check the ARC path in the Boot.ini to verify the path to the boot partition.

C. Use the debug version of Ntdetect to identify the faulty component.

D. Use the Last Known Good Configuration and run Windows NT Diagnostics.

70-067.06.02.001

You have a new Pentium-based Windows NT Server computer to install on your network. When the server is started, you get the message:

"Error loading operating system."

What should you do to solve this problem?

▶ **Correct Answer: B**

A. **Incorrect:** Microsoft Diagnostics (MSD) cannot be started since the operating system will not start. While you could start the operating system from a bootable floppy diskette and run MSD, it is unlikely that the error is caused by an IRQ conflict since an IRQ conflict usually appears after the operating system is loaded.

B. **Correct:** When you start Windows NT from a hard disk on and *x*86-based computer, the system BIOS code identifies the boot disk (usually disk 0), and reads the Master Boot Record. The code in the Master Boot Record searches for a system partition on the hard disk. If the startup process stops and the screen displays the error message, "Error loading operating system," this means that the system partition was found, but it could not find the operating system boot partition or the operating system root directory. Adjust the ARC path in Boot.ini so the operating system can be found.

C. **Incorrect:** The checked version of Ntdetect is used if you suspect that Ntdetect is not identifying hardware properly. The "Error loading operating system" message is not related to the function of Ntdetect since the boot loader must start and Windows NT must be selected before Ntdetect will load.

D. **Incorrect:** The Last Known Good Configuration is not available until control is passed to the Windows NT kernel. Since the operating system cannot be located, the kernel cannot load.

70-067.06.02.002

You have a new Pentium-based Windows NT Server to install on your network. The POST test completes successfully, but then startup simply stops.

What should you do to solve this problem?

A. Use MSD to check for IRQ conflicts.

B. Use Fdisk to check for and set the system partition.

C. Use the debug version of Ntdetect to identify the faulty component.

D. Use the Last Known Good Configuration and run Windows NT Diagnostics.

70-067.06.02.002

You have a new Pentium-based Windows NT Server to install on your network. The POST test completes successfully, but then startup simply stops.

What should you do to solve this problem?

▶ **Correct Answer: B**

A. **Incorrect:** Microsoft Diagnostics (MSD) cannot be started since the operating system will not start. While you could start the operating system from a bootable floppy diskette and run MSD, it is unlikely that the error is caused by an IRQ conflict.

B. **Correct:** When you start Windows NT from a hard disk on an *x*86-based computer, the system BIOS code identifies the boot disk (usually disk 0), and reads the Master Boot Record. The code in the Master Boot Record searches for a system partition on the hard disk. If it can't find the system partition, the startup process stops. It is possible that there is no system partition, it is not active, or the wrong partition is active. Use the MS-DOS version of Fdisk to review and modify the partition information.

C. **Incorrect:** The checked version of Ntdetect is used if you suspect that Ntdetect is not identifying hardware properly. A blank screen after the POST routine is not related to the function of Ntdetect since the boot loader must start and Windows NT must be selected before Ntdetect will load.

D. **Incorrect:** The Last Known Good Configuration is not available until control is passed to the Windows NT kernel. Since the operating system cannot be located, the kernel cannot load.

70-067.06.02.003

You have a new Pentium-based Windows NT Server computer that you are trying to install on your network. When the server is started, you get a blue screen with this error message:

STOP 0x0000007B INACCESSIBLE_BOOT_DEVICE.

What should you do to solve this problem?

A. Use DiskProbe to check for partition table corruption.

B. Make sure there are no checksum errors in the CMOS settings.

C. Use the debug version of Ntdetect to identify the faulty component.

D. Restart using the Last Know Good Configuration and run Windows NT Diagnostics.

70-067.06.02.003

You have a new Pentium-based Windows NT Server computer that you are trying to install on your network. When the server is started, you get a blue screen with this error message:

> STOP 0x0000007B INACCESSIBLE_BOOT_DEVICE.

What should you do to solve this problem?

▶ **Correct: Answer: A**

A. **Correct:** Several known viruses can cause problems with the master boot record even if it is located on an NTFS volume. The damage to the boot sector can cause the computer to stop responding after displaying a blue screen with the message: STOP 0x0000007B INACCESSIBLE_BOOT_DEVICE. The Windows NT Resource Kit utility, DiskProbe, can be used to identify and repair this problem.

B. **Incorrect:** The computer uses the CMOS checksum to determine if any CMOS values have been changed by something other than the CMOS Setup program. If the checksum is incorrect, the computer will not start. Therefore, "STOP 0x0000007B INACCESSIBLE_BOOT_DEVICE" will not appear.

C. **Incorrect:** The checked version of Ntdetect is used if you suspect that Ntdetect is not identifying hardware properly. The "STOP 0x0000007B INACCESSIBLE_BOOT_DEVICE" message is more likely to be related to a hardware incompatibility that causes the installation to fail, or to a corrupted MBR.

D. **Incorrect:** The Last Known Good Configuration is used to recover from configuration errors. The "STOP 0x0000007B INACCESSIBLE_BOOT_DEVICE" message is more likely to be related to a hardware incompatibility that causes the installation to fail, or to a corrupted MBR.

70-067.06.02.004

You have a new Pentium-based Windows NT Server computer to install on your network. When the server is started, a STOP message appears on a blue screen shortly after the NTDETECT V4.0 Checking Hardware phase of startup begins.

What should you do to solve this problem?

A. Check for partition table corruption using DiskProbe.

B. Make sure there are no checksum errors in the CMOS settings.

C. Use the debug version of Ntdetect to identify the faulty component.

D. Restart using the Last Know Good Configuration and run Windows NT Diagnostics.

70-067.06.02.004

You have a new Pentium-based Windows NT Server computer to install on your network. When the server is started, a STOP message appears on a blue screen shortly after the NTDETECT V4.0 Checking Hardware phase of startup begins.

What should you do to solve this problem?

► **Correct Answer: C**

A. **Incorrect:** The Windows NT startup files were found on the system partition because Ntdetect was called by the Ntldr. Therefore, you can assume that the boot sector on the system disk is operational.

B. **Incorrect:** The computer uses the CMOS checksum to determine if any CMOS values have been changed by something other than the CMOS Setup program. If the checksum is incorrect, the computer will not start. Ntldr and the Ntdetect program would never load in this case.

C. **Correct:** Since the error occurred around the time that Ntdetect was checking the computer's hardware, it is likely that the hardware detection routine is misidentifying hardware. Use the checked version of Ntdetect (Ntdetect.chk) located on the Windows NT installation CD to observe what hardware the program detects.

D. **Incorrect:** The Last Known Good Configuration is not available until control is passed to the Windows NT kernel. Since the failure occurred during the hardware detection phase, it is likely that control was not passed back to Ntldr so that it could load the kernel.

70-067.06.02.005

You are converting an existing NetWare 3.*x* server to a Windows NT Server. The Windows NT Server operating system is successfully installed, but the initial attempt to start Windows NT Server fails. The failure occurs shortly after the NT boot loader program began loading files.

The Ntldr program loads several files, then produces a Fatal System Error: 0x0000006b with a message that Process 1 Process Initialization failed. Following this message is a hexadecimal dump and system lockup.

What should you do to solve this problem?

A. Check for boot sector corruption using DiskProbe.

B. Use the debug version of Ntdetect to identify the faulty component.

C. Check the computer hardware for compatibility with Windows NT Server in the HCL.

D. Restart using the Last Known Good Configuration, and run Windows NT Diagnostics.

70-067.06.02.005

You are converting an existing NetWare 3.*x* server to a Windows NT Server. The Windows NT Server operating system is successfully installed, but the initial attempt to start Windows NT Server fails. The failure occurs shortly after the NT boot loader program began loading files.

The Ntldr program loads several files, then produces a Fatal System Error: 0x0000006b with a message that Process 1 Process Initialization failed. Following this message is a hexadecimal dump and system lockup.

What should you do to solve this problem?

▶ **Correct Answer: C**

A. **Incorrect:** Since Ntldr was found, this indicates that the boot sector is operational.

B. **Incorrect:** The checked version of Ntdetect is used if you suspect that Ntdetect is not identifying hardware properly. Although this may help you determine where the failure is occurring, it is more likely that the hardware installed in the computer is not compatible with Windows NT.

C. **Correct:** This error is often caused because Windows NT is not compatible with all ESDI disks with more than 1024 cylinders. Windows NT installation proceeds normally until the first startup after installation. The Windows NT Boot Loader will load various files and then produce a Fatal System Error: 0x0000006b with the message that Phase 1 Process Initialization Failed. You don't need to know this detail in order to troubleshoot; however, it is important to recognize that STOP messages occurring on the first startup of Windows NT installation are usually caused by a hardware incompatibility with the operating system.

D. **Incorrect:** The Last Known Good Configuration isn't created until the first successful logon after installation. This type of failure does not indicate that a recovery using the Last Known Good Configuration is possible.

70-067.06.02.006

A Windows NT Server is experiencing failures that you can correct using an Emergency Repair Disk. You locate a recently updated ERD but are unable to find the setup boot disks used to start the server.

How can you create the setup disks without performing the entire installation again?

A. Run Winnt.exe or Winnt32.exe using the /b switch.

B. Run Winnt.exe or Winnt32.exe using the /x switch.

C. Run Winnt.exe or Winnt32.exe using the /s switch.

D. Run Winnt.exe or Winnt32.exe using the /ox switch.

70-067.06.02.006

A Windows NT Server is experiencing failures that you can correct using an Emergency Repair Disk. You locate a recently updated ERD but are unable to find the setup boot disks used to start the server.

How can you create the setup disks without performing the entire installation again?

▶ **Correct Answer: D**

    A. **Incorrect:** The question states that you need to create setup disks to run the repair process and that you do not want to reinstall Windows NT to solve the problem. However, the /b switch does not create setup disks. Instead, it provides for a floppyless installation of Windows NT.

    B. **Incorrect:** The question states that you need to create setup disks to run the repair process. However, /x switch prevents the Windows NT installation process from creating setup disks. This is only used when you already have setup disks.

    C. **Incorrect:** The /s switch helps automate the installation process by providing the installation routine with the source directory of the Windows NT distribution files. This switch is not used to create Windows NT setup disks.

    D. **Correct:** The /ox switch is used to create setup boot floppies. After they are created, the setup routine should begin by starting the computer with setup disk 1 inserted in the computer. During the installation process, you choose "R" to run an emergency repair procedure. For more information on these installation switches, review Domain Objective 2.

Further Reading

 Microsoft Windows NT Technical Support Training kit. Chapter 17, "The Windows NT Boot Process," provides a comprehensive discussion of the boot process, and how to troubleshoot it. It also contains exercises on how to use the Last Known Good Configuration, create a Windows NT fault-tolerance boot diskette, and run an Emergency Repair.

 Microsoft Windows NT Workstation Resource Guide. Review Chapter 19 and 21 on the startup process and how to troubleshoot it.

 Microsoft Windows NT Workstation Resource Guide. Review Chapter 38, "Windows NT Executive STOP Messages" for a description of the kinds of STOP, STATUS, and hardware malfunction messages.

OBJECTIVE   6 . 3

Choose the appropriate course of action to take to resolve configuration errors.

Configuration errors can usually be traced to network components, device drivers, or services. For example, if you reconfigure two domain controllers to run different protocols they will not be able to communicate with each other. A network component, in this case a protocol mismatch, is the cause of the configuration error. Protocol configuration in Windows NT is rarely a trivial administrative task. The more configurable a protocol is, the more vulnerable it is to configuration errors. This is why it is more common to encounter configuration errors in TCP/IP and IPX/SPX than in NetBEUI.

To successfully answer the questions for this objective, you need a firm understanding of several key terms. For definitions of these terms, refer to the Glossary in this book.

Key Terms

- Dynamic Host Configuration Protocol (DHCP)

- External network number

- Host name resolution

- Internal network number

- IP address

- IPX/SPX frame type

- Last Known Good Configuration

- NetBIOS name resolution

- Subnet mask

- VGA mode

70-067.06.03.001

A Windows NT server is having trouble communicating using TCP/IP. The server is a Pentium-based computer with a single network interface card. The network interface card is configured to use both TCP/IP and NetBEUI.

Communications using NetBEUI works fine, but the server will not communicate using TCP/IP. When you PING the server's IP address at the server's command prompt, a "Request timed out" message appears.

What should you do to solve this problem?

A. Replace the network interface card.

B. Reconfigure TCP/IP in the Control Panel–Network program.

C. Add an entry for the server's IP address in the LMHOSTS file.

D. Manually add a second frame type to the network interface card.

70-067.06.03.001

A Windows NT server is having trouble communicating using TCP/IP. The server is a Pentium-based computer with a single network interface card. The network interface card is configured to use both TCP/IP and NetBEUI.

Communications using NetBEUI works fine, but the server will not communicate using TCP/IP. When you PING the server's IP address at the server's command prompt, a "Request timed out" message appears.

What should you do to solve this problem?

▶ **Correct Answer: B**

   A. **Incorrect:** The question states that communications using the NetBEUI protocol works fine. Therefore, you can assume that the network adapter is operating properly.

   B. **Correct:** If you run the PING utility and you receive the "Request timed out" message, it is probably caused by an incorrectly configured IP address or subnet mask. From the Network program in Control Panel, you can reconfigure the TCP/IP protocol configuration to solve this problem.

   C. **Incorrect:** Since you are pinging the server's IP address, NetBIOS name resolution is not necessary. Therefore, adding an entry to the LMHOSTS file will not resolve this problem.

   D. **Incorrect:** Frame type is not relevant to the configuration of the TCP/IP protocol in Windows NT.

70-067.06.03.002

You add a second network interface card to your Windows NT Server. The new network interface card is configured to use both TCP/IP and NWLink IPX/SPX. IPX/SPX is configured to use the Ethernet 802.2 frame type. Both networks are configured for the 802.2 frame type.

TCP/IP is configured identically to the same existing network interface card except for the IP address. NWLink was configured identically to the existing network interface card. Both adapters are able to communicate using TCP/IP, but problems occur when using NWLink.

What should you do to solve the problems with NWLink communications?

A. Assign the new network interface card the 802.3 frame type.

B. Assign the new network interface card the same IRQ as the existing network interface card's IRQ.

C. Assign the new network interface card an internal network number that is different from the existing network interface card's internal network number.

D. Assign the new network interface card an external network number that is different from the existing network interface card's external network number.

70-067.06.03.002

You add a second network interface card to your Windows NT Server. The new network interface card is configured to use both TCP/IP and NWLink IPX/SPX. IPX/SPX is configured to use the Ethernet 802.2 frame type. Both networks are configured for the 802.2 frame type.

TCP/IP is configured identically to the same existing network interface card except for the IP address. NWLink was configured identically to the existing network interface card. Both adapters are able to communicate using TCP/IP, but problems occur when using NWLink.

What should you do to solve the problems with NWLink communications?

▶ **Correct Answer: C**

A. **Incorrect:** Since the new network is using the 802.2 frame type, setting the IPX/SPX frame type to 802.3 will compound the problem.

B. **Incorrect:** You are told in the question that TCP/IP is working properly on both network adapters, therefore, you can assume that the network adapters are functioning properly.

C. **Correct:** Windows NT does not autodetect the internal network number. You must manually set a unique, nonzero, internal network number if you bind NWLink to multiple network adapters. Otherwise the computer will not be able to process NWLink IPX/SPX protocol traffic.

D. **Incorrect:** Windows NT can autodetect the external network number used for each network, if the value for this number is set to 0.

70-067.06.03.003

The UPS device attached to a Windows NT server shuts off during Windows NT startup. What should you do to solve this problem?

A. Replace the serial cable.

B. Switch the UPS interface voltage.

C. Change the COM port that the UPS uses.

D. Edit the Registry settings for the UPS device.

E. Add the /noserialmice switch to the Boot. ini file.

70-067.06.03.004

You add a driver to your Windows NT–based computer, and you suspect it is causing a boot failure. How can you recover?

A. Use the Rdisk utility.

B. Use the Drwtsn32 utility.

C. Reinstall Windows NT Server.

D. Reboot and select the Last Known Good Configuration.

70-067.06.03.003

The UPS device attached to a Windows NT server shuts off during Windows NT startup. What should you do to solve this problem?

▶ **Correct Answer: E**

A. **Incorrect:** Since the UPS is shutting off you can assume that it is receiving a signal from the computer through the serial cable.

B. **Incorrect:** The UPS will not react to power loss properly with an incorrect interface voltage but the UPS will not shut down as a result of this incorrect configuration.

C. **Incorrect:** Because the UPS is shutting off, you can assume that it is able to communicate with the computer through the COM port that receives a signal from the computer.

D. **Incorrect:** It is unlikely that UPS Registry settings will have any effect on a UPS shutdown on startup. The question indicates that the UPS is getting a signal from the computer before Windows NT is fully initialized.

E. **Correct:** During startup on an *x*86-based computer, Windows NT sends a detection signal to each port in order to recognize hardware attached to that port. Some UPS units use serial connections to monitor the server and respond to a detection signal by turning off. If this happens, using the /noserialmice switch in the Boot.ini file will prevent the system from sending this signal to the COM port connected to the UPS.

70-067.06.03.004

You add a driver to your Windows NT–based computer, and you suspect it is causing a boot failure. How can you recover?

▶ **Correct Answer: D**

A. **Incorrect:** The Rdisk utility is used to update or create emergency repair information. You are told in the question that the addition of a new driver may be causing an observed boot failure. Therefore, running the Rdisk utility will not resolve this problem.

B. **Incorrect:** The Drwatsn32 (Dr. Watson) utility is used to collect information on general protection failures. It is not used to recover from improper driver installations.

C. **Incorrect:** Although it is possible that reinstalling Windows NT Server will solve this boot failure, it is not the most efficient way to solve this problem.

D. **Correct:** The Last Known Good Configuration is designed to solve device driver configuration errors that lead to boot failures and other operating system errors. Running the Last Known Good Configuration restores the system to the last successful local system logon.

70-067.06.03.005

You change the display type on your Windows NT–based computer, and now the screen is unreadable. How can you recover without losing configuration changes that were applied during your last Windows NT session?

A. Use the CrashDump utility.

B. Reinstall Windows NT Server.

C. Reboot and select VGA mode at the boot menu.

D. Reboot and select the Last Known Good Configuration.

70-067.06.03.005

You change the display type on your Windows NT–based computer, and now the screen is unreadable. How can you recover without losing configuration changes that were applied during your last Windows NT session?

▶ **Correct Answer: C**

A. **Incorrect:** The CrashDump utility collects a memory dump for later analysis. The question states that you changed your display type and the screen is unreadable, not that the system crashed.

B. **Incorrect:** By reinstalling Windows NT you could lose your configuration changes. Even if an upgrade is selected instead of a full installation, this is not the most efficient way to solve the display problem.

C. **Correct:** If after changing the video adapter settings, the monitor is unreadable or black, this indicates that the video adapter driver settings are not compatible with the video adapter or monitor. By choosing the VGA Mode option from the boot loader after the computer is restarted, you are running Windows NT with the /basevideo switch. This switch causes Windows NT to load a 640-x-480 resolution and 16-color standard VGA adapter. Most VGA adapters can support this setting so Windows NT will start and the display will be readable. Then the incorrect adapter driver configuration can be adjusted and the system can be restarted to load the correct adapter driver configuration.

D. **Incorrect:** The Last Known Good Configuration option will solve this problem, but you will lose all configuration changes since the last successful Windows NT startup and local logon.

Further Reading

 Microsoft Windows NT Server 4.0 Resource Kit. In Chapter 8 of the *Resource Guide*, the section titled, "Troubleshooting Using HKEY_LOCAL_MACHINE" explains how the Registry stores and maintains data for services and device drivers. It also explains how to use the Registry to troubleshoot device driver and service errors.

Choose the appropriate course of action to take to resolve printer problems.

Although network printing is relatively easy to configure in Windows NT, it is a complex process involving many application components. Resolving printer problems first requires that you determine the point in the printing process where the error is occurring. For example, if a print job isn't producing output, but you can send a print job and see the job processing on the Windows NT print server, the problem is occurring somewhere between the print server and the printer. To prepare for the exam, familiarize yourself with the following list of seven stages that define the printing process:

1. Administrator creates a printer and a printer share on the print server.

2. Client connects to the share.

3. Client creates a print job.

4. Client sends the print job to the print share on the print server.

5. Print server receives spools, and, when necessary, modifies the print job.

6. Print server sends the job to the print device.

7. Print device interprets the job and produces output.

To successfully answer the questions for this objective, you need a firm understanding of several key terms. For definitions of these terms, refer to the Glossary in this book.

Key Terms

- Add Printer Wizard

- Line Printer Daemon (LPD)

- Line Printer Remote (LPR)

- Spooler

70-067.06.04.001

You are having problems sending print jobs from a Windows NT Server to a printer attached to a UNIX server. Other Windows NT computers are successfully sending print jobs to the UNIX server. TCP/IP and NetBEUI are installed on the Windows NT Server computer.

What should you install on the Windows NT Server computer to solve this problem?

A. LPR

B. LPD

C. DLC

D. SNA

70-067.06.04.002

You are having problems sending print jobs from UNIX computers to a new Windows NT Server acting as a print server. TCP/IP is installed on the Windows NT Server computer. What should you install on the Windows NT Server computer to solve this problem?

A. LPR

B. LPD

C. DLC

D. SNA

70-067.06.04.001

You are having problems sending print jobs from a Windows NT Server to a printer attached to a UNIX server. Other Windows NT computers are successfully sending print jobs to the UNIX server. TCP/IP and NetBEUI are installed on the Windows NT Server computer.

What should you install on the Windows NT Server computer to solve this problem?

▶ **Correct Answer: A**

    A. **Correct:** LPR lets a client send a document to a TCP/IP print server. The client, in this case the Windows NT Server, runs LPR and the service (or daemon) running on the UNIX computer is named LPD. Windows NT includes the LPR.EXE utility, which sends print jobs to an LPD service running on another computer.

    B. **Incorrect:** The LPD service allows a Windows NT Server to function as a print server. However, the question states that print jobs need to be sent directly from your computer to the UNIX print server. Therefore, installing the LPD service is not necessary.

    C. **Incorrect:** DLC is used to allow a Windows NT Server to act as the print server for an HP Direct-Connect network printer. It is also the protocol used to access IBM hosts over an SNA network.

    D. **Incorrect:** SNA is the network service that allows access to IBM hosts running on an SNA network.

70-067.06.04.002

You are having problems sending print jobs from UNIX computers to a new Windows NT Server acting as a print server. TCP/IP is installed on the Windows NT Server computer. What should you install on the Windows NT Server computer to solve this problem?

▶ **Correct Answer: B**

    A. **Incorrect:** LPR lets a client send a document to a TCP/IP print server. The question asks what you should install on the Windows NT Server computer to allow a UNIX computer print to it. The LPR utility runs on the UNIX computer to allow it to print to remote TCP/IP print servers.

    B. **Correct:** The LPD service is installed when Windows NT Printing Services is installed from the Control Panel–Network program. Once the LPD service is installed and the TCP/IP printer is configured in Windows NT Server, the UNIX computer can send a print job to it using the LPR utility.

    C. **Incorrect:** DLC allows a Windows NT Server to act as the print server for an HP Direct-Connect network printer. It is also the protocol used to access IBM hosts over an SNA network.

    D. **Incorrect:** SNA is the network service that allows access to IBM hosts running on an SNA network.

70-067.06.04.003

You are having trouble defining an HP network printer on a Windows NT Server computer. The printer is attached directly to the network cable, and is located on the same Ethernet segment as the Windows NT Server. However, you are unable to locate the option to install the printer port.

What should you install on the Windows NT Server computer to solve this problem?

A. DLC

B. LPD

C. DecNet

D. NetBEUI

E. Proper print driver

70-067.06.04.004

While troubleshooting a network printing problem, you discover that the partition on which Windows NT Server stores the spool directory has run out of free disk space. How can you change the location of the spool directory?

A. Edit the Server Properties in Printers.

B. Modify Print properties in Disk Administrator.

C. Create a Shortcut from the spooler directory to the new location.

D. Drag the present spool file directory to another location in Explorer.

70-067.06.04.003

You are having trouble defining an HP network printer on a Windows NT Server computer. The printer is attached directly to the network cable, and is located on the same Ethernet segment as the Windows NT Server. However, you are unable to locate the option to install the printer port.

What should you install on the Windows NT Server computer to solve this problem?

▶ **Correct Answer: A**

   A. **Correct:** DLC is used to allow a Windows NT Server to act as the print server for an HP Direct-Connect network printer. After you install the DLC protocol using the Control Panel–Network program, the Hewlett-Packard Network Port option will appear as an available print monitor.

   B. **Incorrect:** TCP/IP Printing Services install the LPR port monitor which delivers print jobs to RFC1179-compliant LPD servers. These may be network-attached print devices or print server computers (if the print server runs Windows NT, the job goes to its LPD service). By default, Hewlett-Packard Direct-Connect printers are configured for the DLC protocol.

   C. **Incorrect:** The DecNet port monitor delivers jobs to DEC network-attached print devices.

   D. **Incorrect:** The NetBEUI protocol is not designed to provide services to direct connect network printers.

   E. **Incorrect:** Although the correct printer driver is important for delivering print jobs to printing devices, it is not installed until after the printer is created on the print server.

70-067.06.04.004

While troubleshooting a network printing problem, you discover that the partition on which Windows NT Server stores the spool directory has run out of free disk space. How can you change the location of the spool directory?

▶ **Correct Answer: A**

   A. **Correct:** You can point the spooler directory to a different partition and directory through the Registry or through the Printers window on the print server. From the Printers window, choose the File menu–Server Properties option. Next select the Advanced tab and change the Spool Folder directory setting.

   B. **Incorrect:** The Windows NT Disk Administrator is not used to modify printer properties.

   C. **Incorrect:** This function is not possible in Windows NT.

   D. **Incorrect:** Moving the spooler directory would cause the spooler service to fail the next time it was started because the service has not been reconfigured to the new location.

Further Reading

 Microsoft Windows NT Network Administration Training kit. For a review of printer troubleshooting problems and their solutions, as well as an additional reading list, see Lesson 4 in Chapter 8, "Administering a Network Print Server."

OBJECTIVE 6.5

Choose the appropriate course of action to take to resolve RAS problems.

The Windows NT Remote Access Server (RAS) includes a number of log files that can be used to resolve connection problems for RAS and other clients. For the exam, familiarize yourself with these files and, where applicable, practice using them to resolve connection problems. The following list targets the most common errors encountered when using RAS:

- PPP connection errors occur.

- RAS server error events occur in Windows NT.

- Modem device initialization and connection errors occur.

- Client validation fails.

- A client connection fails when using TCP/IP to connect to the RAS server but dynamic IP addressing is configured.

- Your modem is not listed in the Modem.inf file.

- Your users complain that they have to manually log on to SLIP servers.

To successfully answer the questions for this objective, you need a firm understanding of several key terms. For definitions of these terms, refer to the Glossary in this book.

Key Terms

- Callback

- Device.log

- Modem.inf

- Multilink

- Pad.inf

- PPP logging

- Remote Access Server Administrator (RAS Admin)

70-067.06.05.001

Remote users are having trouble authenticating over PPP. Since you have not found any configuration errors while troubleshooting the problem, more information is needed to determine the problem's source.

What should you do to gain more information on RAS PPP connections?

A. Edit the Registry to enable PPP logging.

B. Use the RAS Admin utility to view port status.

C. Chart the RAS port connections in Performance Monitor.

D. Check the RAS logging check box in RAS configuration.

E. Use the Dial-Up Monitor program in Control Panel to monitor PPP activity.

70-067.06.05.001

Remote users are having trouble authenticating over PPP. Since you have not found any configuration errors while troubleshooting the problem, more information is needed to determine the problem's source.

What should you do to gain more information on RAS PPP connections?

▶ **Correct Answer: A**

    A. **Correct:** When PPP logging is enabled in the Registry and the Remote Access Server service is restarted, a Ppp.log file is created in the winnt_root\system32\ras directory. This text file can be reviewed after a failed PPP connection to troubleshoot the failure.

    B. **Incorrect:** You are told in the question that RAS clients are having trouble authenticating to the remote access server. You can use the RAS Admin utility to view port status. Using the RAS Admin utility you see that users connect for a moment while authentication is attempted and then they are disconnected. Therefore, the port status function only confirms that a connection problem exists, but it can't be used to troubleshoot a PPP connection error.

    C. **Incorrect:** The RAS port object in Performance Monitor can help you monitor and optimize RAS, but it will not help you troubleshoot a PPP connection problem.

    D. **Incorrect:** There is no RAS logging check box in the Remote Access Service configuration dialog boxes. Instead various RAS logging functions are enabled through the Registry.

    E. **Incorrect:** The Dial-Up Monitor program allows you to watch Windows NT RAS client status information but it does not allow you to troubleshoot RAS server connection problems.

70-067.06.05.002

What should you do if the RAS server service fails to start?

A. Edit the Registry to enable PPP logging.

B. Use Event Viewer to check the system log.

C. Restart using the setup disks, and repair with ERD.

D. Chart the RAS port connections in Performance Monitor.

E. Use the RAS Admin utility to view the status of RAS ports.

70-067.06.05.002

What should you do if the RAS server service fails to start?

▶ **Correct Answer: B**

A. **Incorrect:** PPP logging is designed to log PPP authentication errors and will function only after the RAS service starts.

B. **Correct:** The Event Viewer–System log provides descriptive information on service startup failures. Viewing this log will help you troubleshoot a RAS service startup failure because it allows you to view the changes that have occurred since RAS was last functioning properly.

C. **Incorrect:** Using setup disks and ERD could solve a RAS service startup failure, but it is not the most efficient approach to solving a service failure. Before an emergency repair is run, the reason for the error should be determined.

D. **Incorrect:** If the RAS service cannot start, there will be no RAS port data available in Performance Monitor.

E. **Incorrect:** The RAS Admin utility will not be able to run because the RAS service did not start.

70-067.06.05.003

The Network Configuration of a RAS server is set to use TCP/IP as the Dial-out Protocol and to allow remote users that use TCP/IP. The encryption setting is configured as "Allow any authentication including clear text." Remote users connecting through the RAS server are not able to access file and print services on NetWare servers.

What should you do to solve this problem?

A. Enable Multilink.

B. Configure TCP/IP to use DHCP.

C. Enable IPX as a dial-out protocol.

D. Require Microsoft encrypted authentication.

E. Enable the IPX option under Server Settings.

F. Disable the TCP/IP option under Server Settings.

70-067.06.05.003

The Network Configuration of a RAS server is set to use TCP/IP as the Dial-out Protocol and to allow remote users that use TCP/IP. The encryption setting is configured as "Allow any authentication including clear text." Remote users connecting through the RAS server are not able to access file and print services on NetWare servers.

What should you do to solve this problem?

▶ **Correct Answer: E**

A. **Incorrect:** The Multilink function allows RAS clients to connect to the server using multiple dial-in devices. This can effectively increase the bandwidth of the remote connection. This function is not related to NetWare server access.

B. **Incorrect:** Novell NetWare 3.x and 4.x do not allow file and print service access over TCP/IP. Therefore configuring DHCP for dynamic IP configuration delivery is not relevant to file and print server access to NetWare servers.

C. **Incorrect:** the problem is related to configuration settings on the Windows NT RAS server, not the RAS client. Therefore, enabling IPX as a dial-out protocol has no effect on the IPX/SPX dial-in function of the RAS server.

D. **Incorrect:** Remote users are able to access the RAS server and network services excluding NetWare file and print services. Therefore, you can assume that Microsoft encrypted authentication is not related to the NetWare access problem presented in the question.

E. **Correct:** Enabling the IPX option under Server Settings in the Network Configuration dialog box allows the RAS server to provide IPX/SPX services to RAS clients. RAS clients will then be able to access NetWare file and print services, provided that they can log on to the NetWare server.

F. **Incorrect:** A RAS server and RAS clients can support multiple protocols over PPP connections. Therefore, both IPX/SPX and TCP/IP can be active at the same time.

70-067.06.05.004

You want to log on to a remote computer using RAS, but an error occurs. You suspect that there may be a problem with your script.

Which file contains a log of data passed between RAS, the modem, and the remote device?

A. Serial.log

B. Device.log

C. Modem.log

D. System.log

70-067.06.05.005

You suspect that a RAS performance problem exists. What can provide real-time information about active users and current connections to your Windows NT Server–based computer?

A. Ppp.log

B. Modem.inf

C. Event Viewer

D. RAS Admin

70-067.06.05.004

You want to log on to a remote computer using RAS, but an error occurs. You suspect that there may be a problem with your script.

Which file contains a log of data passed between RAS, the modem, and the remote device?

▶ **Correct Answer: B**

    A. **Incorrect:** Serial.log is not a valid log file in RAS.

    B. **Correct:** The device.log file is used to diagnose modem initialization problems. This file logs all communications between the remote and local modem until PPP authentication begins.

    C. **Incorrect:** Modem.log is not a valid log file in RAS.

    D. **Incorrect:** System.log is not a valid log file in RAS.

70-067.06.05.005

You suspect that a RAS performance problem exists. What can provide real-time information about active users and current connections to your Windows NT Server–based computer?

▶ **Correct Answer: D**

    A. **Incorrect:** PPP logging will allow you to troubleshoot authentication errors after they have occurred. It does not allow you to perform real-time monitoring.

    B. **Incorrect:** The modem.inf file provides initialization strings to modems so that they can be used by the remote access server. This file does not provide any real-time monitoring capability.

    C. **Incorrect:** The Event Viewer logs remote access events in the system log. This information is not designed for real-time viewing.

    D. **Correct:** The RAS Admin allows you to monitor live connections provided by the remote access server.

Further Reading

 Microsoft Windows NT Server Networking Supplement Manual. Chapter 8, "Maintenance and Troubleshooting" includes a list of steps to take when troubleshooting and discusses the log files used for resolving RAS connection problems. Chapter 10, "Logging On To Remote Computers Using RAS Terminal and Scripts" explains how to use scripts to automate the connection process.

OBJECTIVE   6.6

Choose the appropriate course of action to take to resolve connectivity problems.

For the purpose of the Windows NT Server exam 70-067, troubleshooting connectivity focuses only on Gateway Services for NetWare (GSNW) and the Migration Tool for NetWare. However, the troubleshooting methods used are generally applicable to other types of connectivity in Windows NT Server.

Both GSNW and the Migration Tool for NetWare require that a Windows NT Server communicate with at least one NetWare server over the network. This communication is achieved using the IPX/SPX protocol. Therefore, the troubleshooting procedures discussed in objective 6.3 for IPX/SPX apply here as well.

Above the transport protocol is the GSNW application layer. The following list shows common errors with GSNW.

- The GSNW service will not start.

- GSNW cannot establish a connection with the NetWare server.

- Microsoft client users are unable to access a volume, directory, or printer on a NetWare server through GSNW.

- Microsoft client users are unable to run 16-bit NetWare administrative applications.

The following list shows common errors in the implementation and use of the Migration Tool for NetWare.

- The Migration Tool for NetWare will not function on the Windows NT Server.

- The Migration Tool cannot migrate NetWare to a member server.

- The Migration Tool cannot migrate trustee assignments to a Windows NT Server from a NetWare server.

- The Migration Tool for NetWare migrates NetWare-specific user account information including grace logons, limited concurrent connections, and station restrictions, but cannot migrate logon scripts.

To successfully answer the questions for this objective, you need a firm understanding of several key terms. For definitions of these terms, refer to the Glossary in this book.

Key Terms

- Gateway Services for NetWare (GSNW)

- Migration Tool for NetWare

- Trustee assignments

70-067.06.06.001

You add a Windows NT 4.0 Server to an Ethernet network that previously contained only NetWare servers and NetWare clients. The network uses IPX/SPX over 10BaseT Ethernet. The Windows NT server recognizes clients using the 802.3 frame type but is unable to recognize clients using the 802.2 frame type.

What can you do to solve this problem without installing a second network interface card in the Windows NT server?

A. Install GSNW on the Windows NT server.

B. Configure both frame types for the Windows NT server.

C. Configure the Windows NT Server to autodetect the frame type.

D. Configure a virtual network interface card for the Windows NT server, and specify the 802.2 frame type.

70-067.06.06.001

You add a Windows NT 4.0 Server to an Ethernet network that previously contained only NetWare servers and NetWare clients. The network uses IPX/SPX over 10BaseT Ethernet. The Windows NT server recognizes clients using the 802.3 frame type but is unable to recognize clients using the 802.2 frame type.

What can you do to solve this problem without installing a second network interface card in the Windows NT server?

▶ **Correct Answer: B**

A. **Incorrect:** GSNW is an application service. The question states that your server must be able to communicate with clients running both the IPX/SPX 802.3 and 802.2 frame types. This is a transport protocol issue, not an application service issue.

B. **Correct:** A Windows NT Server can support multiple frame types for IPX/SPX. Therefore, by configuring it for both 802.2 and 802.3, both client types will be recognized and can be serviced by the Windows NT Server. To reduce network utilization, all clients using IPX/SPX should be configured to use a single frame type.

C. **Incorrect:** Through the frame type autodetection process, the Windows NT Server will recognize the first frame type it finds, at which point any additional frame types that the server must support have to be added by configuring the NWLink IPX/SPX protocol through the Control Panel–Network program.

D. **Incorrect:** This is not a feature in Windows NT Server.

70-067.06.06.002

You install GSNW on a Windows NT Server so that a Windows NT Workstation client can access files on a NetWare server. Clients are able to access files stored on two of the NetWare volumes through the gateway, but are not able to access the third volume. Clients need access to all three NetWare volumes.

What can you do to solve this problem?

A. Install NWLink on the Windows NT server.

B. Create the NTGateway group on the NetWare server.

C. Map a shared drive on the Windows NT server for the NetWare volume.

D. Configure File and Print Services for NetWare on the Windows NT server.

70-067.06.06.003

A user attempts to use dial-up networking to connect to a RAS server, but the process fails. How can you grant dial-in permission for this user account? (Choose two.)

A. Disk Administrator

B. Remote Access Admin

C. User Manager for Domains

D. Network Client Administrator

70-067.06.06.002

You install GSNW on a Windows NT Server so that a Windows NT Workstation client can access files on a NetWare server. Clients are able to access files stored on two of the NetWare volumes through the gateway, but are not able to access the third volume. Clients need access to all three NetWare volumes.

What can you do to solve this problem?

▶ **Correct Answer: C**

    A. **Incorrect:** The question indicates that GSNW is already installed on a Windows NT Server. GSNW will not install on the server unless NWLink IPX/SPX is installed first.

    B. **Incorrect:** Because clients are using the gateway to access volumes contained on the NetWare server, the NetWare gateway account must already be a member of the NTGateway group on the NetWare server.

    C. **Correct:** All resources available through GSNW must first be shared through GSNW. Currently, two volumes on the NetWare server are available to the clients. To make the inaccessible volume available to the clients, it must first be shared through GSNW.

    D. **Incorrect:** It is not necessary to install and configure File and Print Services for NetWare to make NetWare resources available through GSNW.

70-067.06.06.003

A user attempts to use dial-up networking to connect to a RAS server, but the process fails. How can you grant dial-in permission for this user account? (Choose two.)

▶ **Correct Answers: B and C**

    A. **Incorrect:** The Windows NT Disk Administrator is used to configure and manage disk drives in Windows NT; it cannot be used to provide a user account with dial-in permission to the RAS server.

    B. **Correct:** The Remote Access Admin utility is used to provide a single interface for managing remote access connections, including granting users dial-in permission to the RAS server.

    C. **Correct:** User Manager for Domains is used to configure users and groups in Windows NT, including granting users dial-in permission to the RAS server.

    D. **Incorrect:** The Network Client Administrator is used to perform various network-client installation tasks; it cannot be used to provide a user account with dial-in permission to the RAS server.

Further Reading

 Microsoft Windows NT Server Networking Supplement Manual. Chapters 13 and 14 explore troubleshooting tips for GSNW and Migration Tool For NetWare.

Choose the appropriate course of action to take to resolve resource access problems and permission problems.

File system access on a computer using Windows NT is implemented in two ways: through shares and through local permissions. These access methods can conflict with each other and are often the cause of problems. If you recall from Objective 3, the most important rule to remember about share rights and local permissions is that the most restrictive set of rights applies. Taken individually, rights assignments are cumulative. The only exception to this rule is the explicit assignment of No Access, which always takes precedence over any other right assigned to a resource for a user or group. The following list will help you understand the reasons for access restriction associated with share rights, local permissions, and other file system characteristics.

- A user cannot access a resource when connecting to a shared directory over the network but can access the resource when logging on locally.

  Share rights are restricting the user. Share rights only apply when a connection is made over the network.

- A user can neither access a resource when connecting to a shared directory over the network nor locally.

  NTFS local permissions are restricting the user's access to the directory or file.

- A user can access a file resource by logging on over the network and locally, but the resource cannot be modified regardless of logon location.

  Another user or process is accessing the file.

  The file's attribute is set to read-only.

  The NTFS local permission is set to Read.

To successfully answer the questions for this objective, you need a firm understanding of several key terms. For definitions of these terms, refer to the Glossary in this book.

Key Terms

- Attributes
- Effective rights
- No Access right
- Share rights

70-067.06.07.001

A user on a Windows NT 4.0 network needs access to a file on a Windows NT Server 4.0 Intel-based computer with NTFS partitions. The user is a member of the Editors, Power Users, and Administrators groups.

The Editors group has No Access permission to the file, and the Power Users and Administrators groups have Full Control permissions. The user is unable to access the file.

Which two solutions will allow the user to access the file? (Choose two.)

A. Assign the Read permission to the Editors group.

B. Remove the Editors group from the user's profile.

C. Remove the Administrators group from the user's profile.

D. Change the access level of the Power Users group to Read access.

70-067.06.07.001

A user on a Windows NT 4.0 network needs access to a file on a Windows NT Server 4.0 Intel-based computer with NTFS partitions. The user is a member of the Editors, Power Users, and Administrators groups.

The Editors group has No Access permission to the file, and the Power Users and Administrators groups have Full Control permissions. The user is unable to access the file.

Which two solutions will allow the user to access the file? (Choose two.)

▶ **Correct Answers: A and B**

    A. **Correct:** The No Access permission is an explicit permission that always overrides any other permission a user may have to a resource. Therefore, by changing the Editors group right from No Access to Read, the user's effective rights to the resource is Full Control.

    B. **Correct:** If the user is no longer a member of the Editors group, the No Access right will not apply to him. Therefore, the user's effective right to the resource is Full Control.

    C. **Incorrect:** The Administrators group has Full Control to the resource but the user is also a member of another group with Full Control to this resource, the Power Users group. Therefore, removing the user from the Administrators group has no effect on the user's effective rights to the resource. The access restriction is present in the Editors group. This group has been assigned the No Access permission to the resource and the user is a member of this group.

    D. **Incorrect:** Changing the access level of the Power Users group to Read permission has no effect on the user's effective rights. The user is a member of the Editors group that has been assigned the No Access permission. This permission overrides any other rights assigned to the user for the resource.

70-067.06.07.002

You are the administrator of a Windows NT 4.0 network. You add User1 to the Accounting group and assign permissions for a file on the accounting server. User1, however, is not able to access the file.

Which steps might solve this problem? (Choose two.)

A. Search in Explorer for the file and click on it.

B. Add the user to the Administrators group because its members have Full Access to all resources.

C. Check membership in other groups and make sure no one has No Access to the file.

D. Have the user log off and then back on in order to update the user's group membership list.

70-067.06.07.002

You are the administrator of a Windows NT 4.0 network. You add User1 to the Accounting group and assign permissions for a file on the accounting server. User1, however, is not able to access the file.

Which steps might solve this problem? (Choose two.)

▶ **Correct Answers: C and D**

A. **Incorrect:** Finding the file in the Explorer interface will not resolve this rights issue.

B. **Incorrect:** Because the Administrators group members are also affected by the No Access right, if a user is a member of another group that has been assigned the No Access right to the resource, she will not be able to access the resource. Note that a member of the Administrators group can take ownership of files and obtain access in this way. However, this event can be audited.

C. **Correct:** The user may be a member of another group that has been assigned the No Access right. This right overrides any other rights assignment given to the user for the resource.

D. **Correct:** Before rights can take effect for a user, the user must log off the system. This is because the user's access token must be recreated to reflect the new rights assignment.

Further Reading

 Microsoft Windows NT Network Administration Training kit. Review Lesson 7 in Chapter 6, "Securing Network Resources with NTFS Permissions."

O B J E C T I V E   6 . 8

Choose the appropriate course of action to take to resolve fault-tolerance failures.

Windows NT Backup, software level RAID implementations (RAID 1 and RAID 5), and the UPS Service are the most common fault-tolerance features in Windows NT. When any of these features fail, the server usually continues to run. However, resolving these failures is important for protecting the server from a catastrophic failure in the future.

To successfully answer the questions for this objective, you need a firm understanding of several key terms. For definitions of these terms, refer to the Glossary in this book.

Key Terms

- Active partition

- ARC path

- Backup.log

- Mirror set

- Software level RAID

- Stripe set with parity

- UPS Service

- Windows NT Backup

- Windows NT fault-tolerance boot disk

70-067.06.08.001

The primary hard disk in your Windows NT Server has failed. Because the disk was part of a mirror set, the server is able to function normally despite the failure. However, the failed hard disk must be replaced in order to maintain fault tolerance for the server.

What should you do first to recover from the failed disk?

A. Break the mirror set.

B. Regenerate the data.

C. Create an Emergency Repair Disk.

D. Restart the server using the fault-tolerance boot disk.

70-067.06.08.001

The primary hard disk in your Windows NT Server has failed. Because the disk was part of a mirror set, the server is able to function normally despite the failure. However, the failed hard disk must be replaced in order to maintain fault tolerance for the server.

What should you do first to recover from the failed disk?

▶ **Correct Answer: A**

 A. **Correct:** The failed drive in the mirror set will be orphaned in Windows NT Disk Administrator so the first step to recovery is to break the mirror set.

 B. **Incorrect:** Data regeneration applies to a RAID 5 (Disk Striping with Parity) array, not a RAID 1 (mirror) array.

 C. **Incorrect:** The ERD is not used to recover from a failed drive in a mirror set.

 D. **Incorrect:** You may have to restart the computer using a Windows NT fault-tolerance boot disk if you need to replace a mirrored system disk that has failed. However, the first step in the process is always to break the mirror set.

70-067.06.08.002

The primary hard disk on your company's Intel-based Windows NT 4.0 server fails. The failed drive contains mission-critical data on its two NTFS partitions. The disk is part of a mirrored set. The server functions normally until it is powered down to replace the failed hard disk.

After the server is powered down, all attempts to restart are unsuccessful. When an untested fault-tolerance boot disk is tried, this error message is displayed:

> "OS loader V4. 00.
>
> Windows NT could not start because of a computer disk hardware configuration problem.
>
> Could not read from the selected boot disk. Check boot path and disk hardware.
>
> Please check the Windows NT documentation about hardware disk configuration and your hardware reference manuals for additional information."

How can you solve this problem?

A. Change the computer's boot drive BIOS setting.

B. Modify the boot.ini file on the fault-tolerance boot disk.

C. Start with the Windows NT setup disks and repair using the ERD.

D. Boot with an MS-DOS boot disk and copy the contents of the secondary drive to the new primary disk drive.

70-067.06.08.002

The primary hard disk on your company's Intel-based Windows NT 4.0 server fails. The failed drive contains mission-critical data on its two NTFS partitions. The disk is part of a mirrored set. The server functions normally until it is powered down to replace the failed hard disk.

After the server is powered down, all attempts to restart are unsuccessful. When an untested fault-tolerance boot disk is tried, this error message is displayed:

"OS loader V4. 00.

Windows NT could not start because of a computer disk hardware configuration problem.

Could not read from the selected boot disk. Check boot path and disk hardware.

Please check the Windows NT documentation about hardware disk configuration and your hardware reference manuals for additional information."

How can you solve this problem?

▶ **Correct Answer: B**

A. **Incorrect:** The computer attempted to boot from the fault-tolerance boot disk since this error message was generated by the Ntldr on the fault-tolerance boot disk. Therefore, adjusting the computer's boot drive BIOS setting will have no effect.

B. **Correct:** The question states that the fault-tolerance boot disk was not tested on this computer previously. This suggests that the ARC name path in the Boot.ini file does not point to the boot partition containing the operating system. Therefore, modifying the Boot.ini file may allow the operating system to start by using the fault-tolerance boot disk.

C. **Incorrect:** The ERD will not allow the fault-tolerance boot diskette to find the Windows NT operating system because any file modifications performed by the ERD are to the hard disks in the computer, not the diskette acting as the fault-tolerance boot disk.

D. **Incorrect:** The question states that all of the data is contained on two NTFS partitions. Therefore, starting the computer with an MS-DOS diskette will not make the NTFS partitions accessible. NTFS is only accessible when Windows NT is running.

70-067.06.08.003

The hard disk in your Windows NT Server fails. Because the disk is part of a stripe set with parity, the server is able to function despite the failure. However, server performance is suffering due to a lack of free disk space, so you need to install a new hard disk and make it part of the stripe set.

What should you do first after the new hard disk is physically installed?

A. Break the stripe set.

B. Regenerate the data.

C. Create an Emergency Repair Disk.

D. Restart the server using the fault-tolerance boot disk.

70-067.06.08.004

A Windows NT Server computer has two hard disks, each with a single NTFS partition. Disk duplexing is implemented to provide fault tolerance. The primary disk uses a SCSI controller, while the secondary disk uses an IDE controller. A fault-tolerance boot disk is created, but it cannot be used to reboot the computer after a primary disk crash due to invalid ARC paths in the boot.ini file.

Which ARC path values should you modify so the disk can be used to recover from a primary hard disk crash? (Choose two.)

A. Disk

B. Multi

C. Rdisk

D. Partition

70-067.06.08.003

The hard disk in your Windows NT Server fails. Because the disk is part of a stripe set with parity, the server is able to function despite the failure. However, server performance is suffering due to a lack of free disk space, so you need to install a new hard disk and make it part of the stripe set.

What should you do first after the new hard disk is physically installed?

▶ **Correct Answer: B**

    A. **Incorrect:** Breaking the stripe set in Disk Administrator will destroy all of the data contained on the disks.

    B. **Correct:** From Disk Administrator, select the stripe set with parity and the new drive, then select Regenerate from the Fault-Tolerance menu to return the stripe set with parity to normal working order.

    C. **Incorrect:** The ERD is not relevant to returning a drive array to normal working order.

    D. **Incorrect:** If the new drive is properly configured, the server will function properly without a fault-tolerance boot disk.

70-067.06.08.004

A Windows NT Server computer has two hard disks, each with a single NTFS partition. Disk duplexing is implemented to provide fault tolerance. The primary disk uses a SCSI controller, while the secondary disk uses an IDE controller. A fault-tolerance boot disk is created, but it cannot be used to reboot the computer after a primary disk crash due to invalid ARC paths in the boot.ini file.

Which ARC path values should you modify so the disk can be used to recover from a primary hard disk crash? (Choose two.)

▶ **Correct Answers: B and C**

    A. **Incorrect:** The question states that there are two drives in the computer and they are duplexed. The primary partition is a SCSI controller with the BIOS enabled. You know the BIOS is enabled because the computer starts from this drive. In this case, the disk parameter is not used.

    B. **Correct:** The multi parameter is used to specify non-SCSI controllers or SCSI controllers with the BIOS enabled. Therefore, modifying this parameter to point to the IDE controller is the first step.

    C. **Correct:** The rdisk parameter is used to specify drives connected to non-SCSI disk drives, or SCSI disk drives connected to controllers with the BIOS enabled. Therefore, modifying this parameter to point to the second drive is the second step.

    D. **Incorrect:** There is no need to change the partition value since the question states that there is a single partition on each disk.

Further Reading

 Microsoft Windows NT Technical Support Training kit. Review Lesson 2 in Chapter 7, "Managing Fault Tolerance." This lesson provides excellent figures to explain the process of recovering from failures in a RAID 1 or RAID 5 array. The ARC pathname used in Boot.ini is also explained.

 "Steps to Recover A Failed Mirrored System/Boot Partition." Go to www.microsoft.com and click the Support link at the top of the page. On the Microsoft Support Online Web page, select "Specific article ID number" under "I want to search by" and enter **Q120227** in the "My question is" field. Click the Find button. This article presents two ways to recover from a failed drive in a mirror set that is implemented for the system partition.

APPENDIX

The Microsoft Certified Professional Program

The Microsoft Certified Professional (MCP) program is designed to comprehensively assess and maintain software-related skills. Microsoft has developed several certifications to provide industry recognition of a candidate's knowledge and proficiency with Microsoft products and technologies. This appendix provides suggestions to help you prepare for an MCP exam, and describes the process for taking the exam. The appendix also contains an overview of the benefits associated with certification, and gives you an example of the exam track you might take for MCSE certification.

Preparing for an MCP Exam

This section contains tips and information to help you prepare for a Microsoft Certified Professional certification exam. Besides study and test-taking tips, this section provides information on how and where to register, test fees, and what to expect upon arrival at the testing center.

Studying for an Exam

The best way to prepare for a Microsoft Certified Professional exam is to study, learn, and master the technology or operating system on which you will be tested. The Readiness Review can help complete your understanding of the software or technology by assessing your practical knowledge and helping you focus on additional areas of study. For example, if you are pursuing the Microsoft Certified Systems Engineer (MCSE) certification, you must learn and use the tested Microsoft operating system. You can then use the Readiness Review to understand the skills that test your knowledge of the operating system, perform suggested practices with the operating system, and ascertain additional areas where you should focus your study by using the electronic assessment.

▶ **To prepare for any certification exam**

1. Identify the objectives for the exam.

   The Readiness Review lists and describes the objectives you will be tested on during the exam.

2. Assess your current mastery of those objectives.

   The Readiness Review electronic assessment tool is a great way to test your grasp of the objectives.

3. Practice the job skills for the objectives you have not mastered and read more information about the subjects tested in each of these objectives.

   You can take the electronic assessment multiple times until you feel comfortable with the subject material.

Your Practical Experience

MCP exams test the specific skills needed on the job. Since in the real world you are rarely called upon to recite a list of facts, the exams go beyond testing your knowledge of a product or terminology. Instead, you are asked to *apply* your knowledge to a situation, analyze a technical problem, and decide on the best solution. Your hands-on experience with the software and technology will greatly enhance your performance on the exam.

Test Registration and Fees

You can schedule your exam up to six weeks in advance, or as late as one working day before the exam date. Sylvan Prometric and Virtual University Enterprises (VUE) administer all the Microsoft Certified Professional exams. To take an exam at an authorized Prometric Testing Center, in the United States call Sylvan at 800-755-EXAM (3926). To register online, or for more registration information, visit Sylvan's Web site at http://www.slspro.com. For information about taking exams at a VUE testing center, visit the VUE information page at http://www.vue.com, or call 888-837-8616 in the United States. When you register, you will need the following information:

- Unique identification number (This is usually your Social Security or Social Insurance number. The testing center also assigns an identification number, which provides another way to distinguish your identity and test records.)

- Mailing address and phone number

- E-mail address

- Organization or company name

- Method of payment (Payment must be made in advance, usually with a credit card or check.)

Testing fees vary from country to country, but in the United States and many other countries the exams cost approximately $100 (U.S.). Contact the testing vendor for exact pricing. Prices are subject to change, and in some countries, additional taxes may be applied.

When you schedule the exam, you will be provided with instructions regarding the appointment, cancellation procedures, identification requirements, and information about the testing center location.

Taking an Exam

If this is your first Microsoft certification exam, you may find the following information helpful upon arrival at the testing center.

Arriving at Testing Center

When you arrive at the testing center, you will be asked to sign a log book, and show two forms of identification, including one photo identification (such as a driver's license or company security identification). Before you may take the exam, you will be asked to sign a Non-Disclosure Agreement and a Testing Center Regulations form, which explains the rules you will be expected to comply with during the test. Upon leaving the exam room at the end of the test, you will again sign the log book.

Exam Details

Before you begin the exam, the test administrator will provide detailed instructions about how to complete the exam, and how to use the testing computer or software. Because the exams are timed, if you have any questions, ask the exam administrator before the exam begins. Consider arriving 10 to 15 minutes early so you will have time to relax and ask questions before the exam begins. Some exams may include additional materials or exhibits (such as diagrams). If any exhibits are required for your exam, the test administrator will provide you with them before you begin the exam and collect them from you at the end of the exam.

The exams are all closed book. You may not use a laptop computer or have any notes or printed material with you during the exam session. You will be provided with a set amount of blank paper for use during the exam. All paper will be collected from you at the end of the exam.

The Exam Tutorial

The test administrator will show you to your test computer and will handle any preparations necessary to start the testing tool and display the exam on the computer. Before you begin your exam, you can take the exam tutorial which is designed to familiarize you with computer-administered tests by offering questions similar to those on the exam. Taking the tutorial does not affect your allotted time for the exam.

Exam Length and Available Time

The number of questions on each exam varies, as does the amount of time allotted for each exam. Generally, certification exams consist of 50 to 70 questions and take approximately 90 minutes to complete. Specific information about the number of exam questions and available time will be provided to you when you register.

Tips for Taking the Exam

Since the testing software lets you move forward and backward through the exam, answer the easy questions first. Then go back and spend the remaining time on the harder questions.

When answering the multiple-choice questions, eliminate the obviously incorrect answers first. There are no trick questions on the test, so the correct answer will always be among the list of possible answers.

Answer all the questions before you quit the exam. An unanswered question is scored as an incorrect answer. If you are unsure of the answer, make an educated guess.

Your Rights as a Test Taker

As an exam candidate, you are entitled to the best support and environment possible for your exam. In particular, you are entitled to a quiet, uncluttered test environment and knowledgeable and professional test administrators. You should not hesitate to ask the administrator any questions before the exam begins, and you should also be given time to take the online testing tutorial. Before leaving, you should be given the opportunity to submit comments about the testing center, staff, or about the test itself.

Getting Your Exam Results

After you have completed an exam, you will immediately receive your score online and be given a printed Examination Score Report which also breaks down the results by section. Passing scores on the different certification exams vary. You do not need to send these scores to Microsoft. The test center automatically forwards them to Microsoft within five working days, and if you pass the exam, Microsoft sends a confirmation to you within two to four weeks.

If you do not pass a certification exam, you may call the testing vendor to schedule a time to retake the exam. Before re-examination, you should review the appropriate sections of the Readiness Review, and focus additional study on the topic areas where your exam results could be improved. Please note that you must pay the full registration fee again each time you retake an exam.

About the Exams

Microsoft Certified Professional exams follow recognized standards for validity and reliability. They are developed by technical experts who receive input from job-function and technology experts.

How MCP Exams Are Developed

To ensure the validity and reliability of the certification exams, Microsoft adheres to a rigorous exam-development process that includes an analysis of the tasks performed in specific job functions. Microsoft then translates the job tasks into a comprehensive set of objectives which measure knowledge, problem-solving abilities, and skill level. The objectives are prioritized and then reviewed by technical experts to create the certification exam questions. (These objectives are also the basis for developing the Readiness Review series.) Technical and job function experts review the exam objectives and questions several times before releasing the final exam.

Computer-Adaptive Testing

Microsoft is developing more effective ways to determine who meets the criteria for certification by introducing innovative testing technologies. One of these testing technologies is computer-adaptive testing (CAT). This testing method is currently available on a few certification exams, and may not be available for the exam you are currently studying. When taking this exam, all test takers start with an easy-to-moderate question. Those who answer the question correctly get a more difficult follow-up question. If that question is answered correctly, the difficulty of subsequent questions also increases. Conversely, if the second question is answered incorrectly, the following questions will be easier. This process continues until the testing system determines the test taker's ability.

With this system, everyone may answer the same percentage of questions correctly, but because the high-ability people can answer more difficult questions correctly, they will receive a higher score. To learn more about computer-adaptive testing and other testing innovations visit http://www.microsoft.com/mcp.

If You Have a Concern about the Exam Content

Microsoft Certified Professional exams are developed by technical and testing experts, with input and participation from job-function and technology experts. Microsoft ensures that the exams adhere to recognized standards for validity and reliability. Candidates generally consider them to be relevant and fair. If you feel that an exam question is inappropriate or if you believe the correct answer shown to be incorrect, write or call Microsoft at the e-mail address or phone number listed for the Microsoft Certified Professional Program in the "References" section of this appendix.

Although Microsoft and the exam administrators are unable to respond to individual questions and issues raised by candidates, all input from candidates is thoroughly researched and taken into consideration during development of subsequent versions of the exams. Microsoft is committed to ensuring the quality of these exams, and your input is a valuable resource.

Overview of the MCP Program

Becoming a Microsoft Certified Professional is the best way to show employers, clients, and colleagues that you have the knowledge and skills required by the industry. Microsoft's certification program is one of the industry's most comprehensive programs for assessing and maintaining software-related skills, and the MCP designation is recognized by technical managers worldwide as a mark of competence.

Certification Programs

Microsoft offers a variety of certifications so you can choose the one that meets your job needs and career goals. The MCP program focuses on measuring a candidate's ability to perform a specific job function, such as one performed by a systems engineer or a Solution Developer. Successful completion of the certification requirements indicates your expertise in the field. Microsoft certifications include:

- Microsoft Certified Systems Engineer (MCSE)

- Microsoft Certified Systems Engineer + Internet (MCSE + I)

- Microsoft Certified Professional (MCP)

- Microsoft Certified Professional + Internet (MCP + I)

- Microsoft Certified Professional + Site Building

- Microsoft Certified Solution Developer (MCSD)

Microsoft Certified Systems Engineer (MCSE)

Microsoft Certified Systems Engineers have a high level of expertise with Microsoft Windows NT and the Microsoft BackOffice integrated family of server software, and can plan, implement, maintain, and support information systems with these products.

MCSEs are required to pass four operating system exams and two elective exams. The Implementing and Supporting Microsoft Windows NT Server 4.0 exam earns core credit toward this certification.

MCSE Exam Requirements

You can select a Microsoft Windows NT 3.51 or Microsoft Windows NT 4.0 track for the MCSE certification. From within the track you have selected, you must pass four core operating system exams, and then pass two elective exams. Visit the Microsoft Certified Professional Web site for details about current exam requirements, exam alternatives, and retired exams. This roadmap outlines the path an MCSE candidate would pursue for Windows NT 4.0.

Microsoft Windows NT 4.0 Core Exams

You must pass four core exams and two elective exams. You must choose to test on Windows 95, Windows NT Workstation 4.0, or Windows 98 for one of the core exams. The core exams are as follows:

Exam 70-067: Implementing and Supporting Microsoft Windows NT Server 4.0

Exam 70-068: Implementing and Supporting Microsoft Windows NT Server 4.0 in the Enterprise

Exam 70-064: Implementing and Supporting Microsoft Windows 95, or exam 70-073: Microsoft Windows NT Workstation 4.0, or exam 70-098: Implementing and Supporting Microsoft Windows 98

Exam 70-058: Networking Essentials

MCSE Electives

The elective exams you choose are the same for all Windows NT tracks. You must choose two exams from the following list.

Exam 70-013: Implementing and Supporting Microsoft SNA Server 3.0, or exam 70-085: Implementing and Supporting Microsoft SNA Server 4.0 (If both SNA Server exams are passed, only one qualifies as an MCSE elective.)

Exam 70-018: Implementing and Supporting Microsoft Systems Management Server 1.2, or exam 70-086: Implementing and Supporting Microsoft Systems Management Server 2.0 (If both SMS exams are passed, only one qualifies as an MCSE elective.)

Exam 70-021: Microsoft SQL Server 4.2 Database Implementation, or exam 70-027: Implementing a Database Design on Microsoft SQL Server 6.5, or exam 70-029: Implementing a Database Design on Microsoft SQL Server 7.0 (If more than one SQL Server exam is passed, only one qualifies as an MCSE elective. Also note that exam 70-021 is scheduled to be retired in 1999.)

Exam 70-022: Microsoft SQL Server 4.2 Database Administration for Microsoft Windows NT, exam 70-026: System Administration for Microsoft SQL Server 6.5, or exam 70-028: System Administration for Microsoft SQL Server 7.0 (If more than one exam is passed from this group, only one would qualify as an MCSE elective. Also note that exam 70-022 is scheduled to be retired in 1999.)

Exam 70-053: Internetworking Microsoft TCP/IP on Microsoft Windows NT (3.5-3.51), or exam 70-059: Internetworking with Microsoft TCP/IP on Microsoft Windows NT 4.0 (If both exams are passed, only one would qualify as an MCSE elective.)

Exam 70-056: Implementing and Supporting Web Sites Using Microsoft Site Server 3.0

Exam 70-076: Implementing and Supporting Microsoft Exchange Server 5, or exam 70-081: Implementing and Supporting Microsoft Exchange Server 5.5 (If more than one of these exams is passed, only one would qualify as an MCSE elective.)

Exam 70-077: Implementing and Supporting Microsoft Internet Information Server 3.0 and Microsoft Index Server 1.1, or exam 70-087: Implementing and Supporting Microsoft Internet Information Server 4.0 (If both exams are passed, only one would qualify as an MCSE elective.)

Exam 70-078: Implementing and Supporting Microsoft Proxy Server 1.0, or exam 70-088: Implementing and Supporting Microsoft Proxy Server 2.0 (If both exams are passed, only one would qualify as an MCSE elective.)

Exam 70-079: Implementing and Supporting Microsoft Internet Explorer 4.0 by Using the Internet Explorer Administration Kit

Note that certification requirements may change. In addition, some retired certification exams may qualify for credit towards current certification programs. For the latest details on core and elective exams, go to http://www.microsoft.com/mcp and review the appropriate certification.

Novell, Banyan, and Sun Exemptions

The Microsoft Certified Professional program grants credit for the networking exam requirement for candidates who are certified as Novell CNEs, Master CNEs, or CNIs, Banyan CBSs or CBEs, or Sun Certified Network Administrators for Solaris 2.5 or 2.6. Go to the Microsoft Certified Professional Web site at http://www.microsoft.com/mcp for current information and details.

Other Certification Programs

In addition to the MCSE certification, Microsoft has created other certification programs that focus on specific job functions and career goals.

Microsoft Certified Systems Engineer + Internet (MCSE + I)

An individual with the MCSE + Internet credential is qualified to enhance, deploy, and manage sophisticated intranet and Internet solutions that include a browser, proxy server, host servers, database, and messaging and commerce components.

Microsoft Certified Systems Engineers with a specialty in the Internet are required to pass seven operating system exams and two elective exams.

Microsoft Certified Professional (MCP)

Microsoft Certified Professionals have demonstrated in-depth knowledge of at least one Microsoft product. An MCP has passed a minimum of one Microsoft operating system exam, and may pass additional Microsoft Certified Professional exams to further qualify his or her skills in a particular area of specialization. A Microsoft Certified Professional has extensive knowledge about specific products but has not completed a job-function certification. The MCP credential provides a solid background for other Microsoft certifications.

Microsoft Certified Professional + Internet (MCP + I)

A person receiving the Microsoft Certified Professional + Internet certification is qualified to plan security, install and configure server products, manage server resources, extend servers to run CGI scripts or ISAPI scripts, monitor and analyze performance, and troubleshoot problems.

Microsoft Certified Professional + Site Building

Microsoft has recently created a certification designed for Web site developers. Individuals with the Microsoft Certified Professional + Site Building credential are qualified to plan, build, maintain, and manage Web sites using Microsoft technologies and products. The credential is appropriate for people who manage sophisticated, interactive Web sites that include database connectivity, multimedia, and searchable content. Microsoft Certified Professionals with a specialty in site building are required to pass two exams that measure technical proficiency and expertise.

Microsoft Certified Solution Developer (MCSD)

The Microsoft Certified Solution Developer credential is the premium certification for professionals who design and develop custom business solutions with Microsoft development tools, technologies, and platforms. The MCSD certification exams test the candidate's ability to build Web-based, distributed, and commerce applications by using Microsoft's products, such as Microsoft SQL Server, Microsoft Visual Studio, and Microsoft Transaction Server.

Certification Benefits

Obtaining Microsoft certification has many advantages. Industry professionals recognize Microsoft Certified Professionals for their knowledge and proficiency with Microsoft products and technologies. Microsoft helps to establish the program's recognition by promoting the expertise of MCPs within the industry. By becoming a Microsoft Certified Professional, you will join a worldwide community of technical professionals who have validated their expertise with Microsoft products.

In addition, you will have access to technical and product information directly from Microsoft through a secured area of the MCP Web Site. You will be invited to

Microsoft conferences, technical training sessions, and special events. MCPs also receive *Microsoft Certified Professional Magazine,* a career and professional development magazine.

Your organization will receive benefits when you obtain your certification. Research shows that Microsoft certification provides organizations with increased customer satisfaction and decreased support costs through improved service, increased productivity, and greater technical self-sufficiency. It also gives companies a reliable benchmark for hiring, promoting, and career planning.

Skills 2000 Program

Microsoft launched the Skills 2000 initiative to address the gap between the number of open jobs in the computing industry and the lack of skilled professionals to fill them. The program, launched in 1997, builds upon the success of Microsoft's training and certification programs to reach a broader segment of the work force. Many of today's computing professionals consider the current skills gap to be their primary business challenge.

Skills 2000 aims to significantly reduce the skills gap by reaching out to individuals currently in the computing work force, as well as those interested in developing a career in information technology. The program focuses on finding and placing skilled professionals in the job market today with Microsoft Solution Provider organizations. Microsoft will also facilitate internships between MSPs and students developing IT skills. In addition, Skills 2000 targets academic instructors at high schools, colleges and universities by offering free technical training to teachers and professors who are educating the work force of tomorrow.

For more information about the Skills 2000 initiative, visit the Skills 2000 site at http://www.microsoft.com/skills2000. This site includes information about starting a career in Information Technology (IT), IT-related articles, and a career aptitude tool.

Volunteer Technical Contributors

To volunteer for participation in one or more of the exam development phases, please sign up using the Technical Contributors online form on the MCP Web site: http://www.microsoft.com/mcp/examinfo/certsd.htm.

References

To find out more about Microsoft certification materials and programs, to register with an exam administrator, or to get other useful resources, check the following references. For Microsoft references outside the United States or Canada, contact your local Microsoft office.

Microsoft Certified Professional Program

To find information about Microsoft certification exams and information to help you prepare for any specific exam, go to http://www.microsoft.com/mcp, send e-mail to mcp@msprograms.com, or call 800-636-7544.

The MCP online magazine provides information for and about Microsoft Certified Professionals. The magazine is also a good source for exam tips. You can view the online magazine at http://www.mcpmag.com.

Microsoft Developer Network (MSDN)

The MSDN subscription center is your official source for software development kits, device driver kits, operating systems, and information about developing applications for Microsoft Windows and Windows NT. You can visit MSDN at http://www.microsoft.com/msdn or call 800-759-5474.

Microsoft Press

Microsoft Press offers comprehensive learning and training resources to help you get the most from Microsoft technology. For information about books published by Microsoft Press, go to http://mspress.microsoft.com, or call 800-MSPRESS.

Microsoft Press ResourceLink

Microsoft Press ResourceLink is an online information resource for IT professionals who deploy, manage, or support Microsoft products and technologies. ResourceLink gives you access to the latest technical updates, tools, and utilities from Microsoft, and is the most complete source of technical information about Microsoft technologies available anywhere. You can reach ResourceLink at http//mspress.microsoft.com/reslink.

Microsoft TechNet IT Home

Microsoft TechNet IT Home is a resource designed for IT professionals. You can find information on current IT topics, resources, and reference material at http://www.microsoft.com/ithome.

Microsoft Training and Certification Web Site

You can find lists of various study aids for the certification exams at http://www.microsoft.com/train_cert.

Self Test Software

Self Test Software provides the Readiness Review online assessment. For an additional fee, Self Test Software will provide test questions for this exam and other certification exams. For further information go to http://www.stsware.com/microsts.htm.

Sylvan Prometric Testing Centers

To register to take a Microsoft Certified Professional exam at any of the Sylvan Prometric testing centers around the world, go online at http://www.slspro.com. In the United States, you can call 800-755-EXAM.

Virtual University Enterprises (VUE)

You can register for a certification exam with VUE by using online registration, registering in person at a VUE testing center, or by calling 888-837-8616 in the United States. Visit http://www.vue.com/ms for testing sites, available examinations, and other registration numbers.

Glossary

*.pal Files used on an ACP-based RISC computer that are involved in the Windows NT startup process.

8.3 format A short file name standard where a file contains up to eight characters followed by a period and then a three-character extension. Windows NT Server automatically translates long names of files and folders to 8.3 names for compatibility with MS-DOS applications.

A

access control entry (ACE) An entry in an access control list (ACL) which defines the protection or auditing to be applied to a file or other object for a specific user or group of users.

access control list (ACL) The part of a security descriptor that enumerates both the protections to accessing a resource and the auditing of a resource. The owner of an object has discretionary access control of the object, and can change the object's ACL to allow or disallow others access to the object. ACLs are ordered lists of access control entries (ACEs).

access token An object that uniquely identifies a user who has logged on. An access token is attached to all of the user's processes and contains: the user's security ID (SID); the SIDs of any groups to which the user belongs; any permissions that the user has been granted; the default owner of any objects that the user's processes create, and the default access control list (ACL) to be applied to any objects that the user's processes create.

account policy Controls the way passwords must be used by all user accounts of a domain or of an individual computer. Specifics include minimum password length, how often a user must change his or her password, and how often users can reuse old passwords.

active partition This is the volume that contains a flag instructing the operating system to start from this partition.

Add Printer Wizard A Windows NT and Windows 9x tool used to install and add printer drivers for local or network printing.

Advanced RISC Computing Specifications (ARC) pathname A generic method of identifying devices and paths to hardware resources. Windows NT uses this naming convention to locate the Windows NT boot partition upon startup.

alert view One of four ways to analyze data provided by Performance Monitor. This view of data allows you to determine when monitored resources have exceeded the threshold values you have configured in Performance Monitor.

answer file The file used to automate the Windows NT installation process. The default name for this file in Windows NT is unattend.txt.

application server A computer on the network that provides specific program services, other than file and print services, to users. Common programs accessed in this way include database and e-mail services.

attributes Information that indicates whether a file is a read-only, hidden, system, or compressed file, and that indicates whether the file has been changed since the last backup copy was made.

auditing Provides reporting capabilities to any directory, file, or other object on the system. Only NTFS provides auditing of its directories and files. The owner of an object has discretionary access control of the object and can change the object's access settings to allow or disallow access by other individuals to the object.

available bytes This indicates the amount of available physical memory. It will normally be low, since the Windows NT Disk Cache Manager uses extra memory for caching and then returns it when requests for memory are made. However, a value consistently below 4 MB on a Windows NT Server indicates that excessive paging is occurring.

avg. disk bytes/transfer The average number of bytes transferred to or from the disk during write or read operations. The larger the transfer size, the more efficient the system is running.

B

backup.log An ASCII text file created by the Windows NT Backup program when a backup is running. This file can be reviewed to determine the results of the backup session and to troubleshoot backup problems.

baseline Data that represents the normal operation of a network server. This data can be used to determine when a server requires additional resources or reconfiguration.

base memory address The starting address of an area in RAM that is used by hardware to temporarily store data collected through I/O operations.

Bindery A Novell database of user accounts and groups maintained on a Novell NetWare server.

binding A process that establishes the communication channel between a protocol driver (such as TCP/IP) and a network adapter.

Boot.ini The Windows NT boot manager configuration file read by the Windows NT loader. This text file stores the timeout value, the default operating system, and the ARC paths to installed operating systems.

Boot.ini switches Configuration options that can be included inside the boot menu to change the behavior of the operating system on startup.

BOOTP relay agent Software that forwards requests from local DHCP clients to the remote DHCP server and subsequently returns DHCP server responses back to the DHCP clients.

Bootsect.dos A file on a Windows NT computer that stores the previous operating system's boot partition. The Ntldr file can read this file to start the previous operating system.

boot sequence The process that a computer runs through to load and initialize an operating system.

bottleneck A hardware resource that consumes the most time during a task's execution.

built-in users and built-in groups Objects created by Windows NT for user account administration that cannot be deleted.

C

callback A feature common in many remote node and remote control packages that allows a remote client to connect to a server, authenticate username and password, disconnect from the server, and re-establish communications when the server reconnects with the client. This is achieved in RAS using the Call Back Control Protocol (CBCP), which negotiates this process with a remote client.

case preserving The process by which information is stored on the system by the case initially entered. For example, User Manager stores usernames in whichever case they were initially entered. However, when logging on to the system the usernames TOM and tom are equivalent.

case sensitive Text that is entered in a specific case and is always referred to in that case. For example, a case-sensitive file on an NTFS partition named "file.txt" is different from a file stored on the same partition with the name "FILE.txt."

case-sensitive file naming To meet POSIX requirements, NTFS provides a case-sensitive file and directory naming convention. This means two files with the same name, but different cases, stored on an NTFS partition are distinct files. For example, HELLO.TXT and hello.txt are different files to a POSIX application and the Windows NT file system.

Challenge Handshake Authentication Protocol (CHAP) A method used by Microsoft RAS to negotiate the most secure form of encrypted authentication supported by both server and client.

Change right This right provides the same access as the Read right plus the ability to modify files, subdirectories, and attributes. Users can also delete and create subdirectories and files.

chart view One of four ways to analyze data provided by Performance Monitor. This view of data allows you to graphically analyze server data in real time or through an archive compiled by Performance Monitor logging.

client network drivers The files required by workstation NICs to access the network.

Client Services for NetWare (CSNW) The network redirector that enables a Windows NT Workstation to make direct connections to file and printer resources on NetWare severs running NetWare 2.*x* or later.

Complex Instructions Set Computing (CISC) processor The CISC CPU is used in Intel-based computer platforms. CISC is also referred to as *x*86 or Intel-based processors.

computer name A unique name of up to 15 uppercase characters that identifies a computer to the network. The name cannot be the same as any other computer or domain name in the network.

Convert.exe A Windows NT utility that allows for a one-way partition conversion from FAT to NTFS in Windows NT.

counters Tools that measure given attributes of a Performance Monitor object.

D

Data Link Control (DLC) DLC is not designed to be a primary protocol for network use between personal computers. DLC provides applications with direct access to the data-link layer. The DLC protocol is primarily used for two tasks, accessing IBM mainframes that are usually running 3270 applications, and printing to Hewlett-Packard printers connected directly to the network.

device drivers Software that provides an interface between the operating system and hardware installed in the computer.

device.log This file collects all information passed between RAS, the modem, and the remote device, including errors reported by the remote device. Review this file to troubleshoot hardware-related RAS connection problems. The Device.log file is created only after logging is enabled in the Registry. After logging is enabled, the Device.log file is stored in the systemroot\SYSTEM32\RAS directory.

Devices applet The Control Panel application used to stop, start, or change the startup behavior of any installed device driver on the local computer running Windows NT.

directory replication Also called Directory Replicator service. The copying of a master set of directories from a server (*export* server) to specified servers or workstations (*import* computers) in the same or other domains. Replication simplifies the task of maintaining identical sets of directories and files on multiple computers, because only a single master copy of the data is maintained. Files are replicated when they are added to an export directory, and each time a change is saved to one of the exported files.

Directory Replicator service Replicates directories, and the files in those directories, between computers.

directory share A representation of a directory resource on a Microsoft network. Users can connect to this resource and work with files and subdirectories below it.

Disk Administrator The Windows NT utility used to configure disk drives.

Disk Administrator Orphan A member of a mirror set or a stripe set with parity that has failed. Common causes for failure are disk power loss or a disk head crash. When a drive fails, the fault-tolerance driver (ftdisk) determines that it can no longer use the orphaned member and directs all new reads and writes to the remaining members of the fault-tolerance volume.

Disk Administrator Regenerate This option is used after a new disk is installed to replace a failed drive that is part of a RAID 5 array. The regenerate option informs the fault-tolerance disk driver to recreate the stripe set with parity to the new drive.

disk array A collection of disks typically connected to a SCSI controller that can support a RAID configuration.

disk bytes/sec This is the rate bytes are transferred to or from the disk during write or read operations. The higher the average, the more efficient the system is running.

disk controller A hardware adapter designed to support disk drives. The hardware adapter usually connects to a computer's system bus through an ISA, EISA, or PCI connection. The disk drives connect through a channel or channels contained on the disk controller. All disk I/O operations use the card to communicate with the computer.

disk duplexing When drives are connected to two disk controllers or two channels on a single disk controller it is considered disk duplexing. This configuration is used to provide data redundancy across disk controllers or multiple channels.

disk input/output (I/O) The process of sending data to and from fixed or removable drives for computer processing.

Diskperf A Windows NT command used to enable disk performance counters in Performance Monitor.

disk thrashing Excessive writing of pages in physical memory to and from disk.

Domain Name System (DNS) Sometimes referred to as the BIND service in BSD. UNIX DNS offers a static, hierarchical name service for TCP/IP hosts.

domain synchronization To replicate the domain database from the primary domain controller (PDC) to one or more backup domain controllers (BDCs) in the domain. Typically, this is accomplished automatically by the system, but can be invoked manually by an administrator through the Server Manager application.

Dynamic Host Configuration Protocol (DHCP) A protocol that offers dynamic configuration of IP addresses and related information. DHCP provides safe, reliable, and simple TCP/IP network configuration, prevents address conflicts, and helps conserve the use of IP addresses through centralized management of address allocation.

Note when troubleshooting that if a TCP/IP computer is configured to receive its IP address configuration from a DHCP server but a DHCP server can't be found, TCP/IP will not initialize on the client. An error message will display on the client and the computer will not be able to use TCP/IP to communicate on the network.

Dynamic Host Configuration Protocol (DHCP) Administrator Allows for the management of the DHCP running on a Windows NT Server.

E

effective rights In a Novell network, this is defined as the combination of trustee assignments and the inherited rights mask. The intersection of these two access control mechanisms determines the actual access rights, known as effective rights, a user or group has to a particular directory or file.

Emergency Repair Disk (ERD) This diskette is created either during Windows NT installation or after the installation using the Rdisk.exe program. Using the ERD and the Windows NT setup diskettes, it is possible to recover from various Windows NT system failures.

encryption The process of making information indecipherable to protect it from unauthorized viewing or use, especially during transmission or when it is stored on a transportable magnetic medium.

Explorer interface extensions Additional functions added to Windows 9x so that it is capable of managing permissions for file and printer objects located on a Windows NT computer.

export directory The path to which subdirectories and the files in those subdirectories are automatically exported from an export server.

extended partition Created from free space on a hard disk, an extended partition can be subpartitioned into zero or more logical drives. Only one of the four partitions allowed per physical disk can be an extended partition. A primary partition does not have to be present to create an extended partition.

external network number The IPX network number uniquely defines the physical network segment in which IPX/SPX is running, just as a network ID in a TCP/IP network uniquely defines the network segment in which it is running. The IPX network number is assigned to each configured frame type and adapter combination. A client with an incorrect network number will be unable to communicate with other clients with the correct network number.

F

fault tolerance This feature ensures data integrity when hardware failures occur. In Windows NT, the FTDISK.SYS driver provides fault tolerance. In Disk Administrator, fault tolerance is provided using mirror sets and stripe sets with parity.

File Allocation Table (FAT) A table or list maintained by some operating systems to keep track of the status of various segments of disk space used for file storage. Also referred to as the FAT file system.

file and object access control The part of the Windows NT security subsystem that protects files, directories, and other objects from unauthorized access.

file and print server A server that provides directory creation, file storage, and print services to clients on the network. A Windows NT Server configured as a file and print server is usually but not always a domain controller.

File and Print Services for NetWare (FPNW) A Windows NT Server component that enables a computer running Windows NT Server to provide file and print services directly to native NetWare clients. To the native NetWare client, the Windows NT Server appears to be a Novell NetWare 3.x file and print server.

file system In an operating system, the overall structure in which files are named, stored, and organized. NTFS and FAT are the file systems typically installed in Windows NT.

floppyless installation An installation of Windows NT that does not require the three Windows NT setup diskettes.

frame In synchronous communication, a package of information transmitted as a single unit from one device to another.

Full Control right This right provides the same access as the Change right plus the ability to change NTFS file and subdirectory permissions and to take ownership of files on NTFS partitions.

G

gateway Software and, in some cases, hardware that translates between different transport protocols (for example, IPX and IP) or data formats (for example, NCP and SMB) and is generally added to a network primarily for its translation ability.

Gateway Services for NetWare (GSNW) A Windows NT service which enables a computer running Windows NT Server to connect to NetWare servers. Creating a gateway enables computers running only Microsoft client software to access NetWare resources through the gateway.

global group For Windows NT Server, a group that can be used in its own domain, member servers and workstations of the domain, and trusting domains. This group can be granted rights and permissions and can become a member of local groups.

H

Hardware Abstraction Layer (HAL) Software provided by the hardware manufacturer that hides, or abstracts, hardware differences from higher layers of the operating system. Through the interface provided by the HAL, different types of hardware look alike to the other layers of the operating system. This allows Windows NT to be portable from one hardware platform to another. The HAL also provides routines that allow a single device driver to support the same device on all platforms.

Hardware Compatibility List (HCL) The Windows NT Hardware Compatibility List lists the devices supported by Windows NT. The latest version of the HCL can be downloaded from the Microsoft Web Page (microsoft.com) on the Internet.

hidden shares Any directory that is given a sharing name with a dollar sign at the end. This dollar sign creates a resource that does not appear in the browse list of available resources. Therefore, users must know about this resource before a connection can be made.

hive A section of the Registry that appears as a file on your hard disk. These files represent discrete groups of keys, subkeys, and values that are rooted at the top of the Registry hierarchy. Each hive is contained in a single file and a .log file, which are in the Systemroot\System32\Config or the Systemroot\Profiles\Username folder. By default, most of these files (Default, SAM, Security, and System) are stored in the Systemroot\System32\Config folder.

host name resolution The process of determining the IP address of a computer given the computer's IP name. This function is provided either through a DNS (Domain Name Server) or through a HOSTS file.

HOSTS file A local text file that maps host names to IP addresses. In Windows NT, this file is stored in the \<*winnt_root*>\System32\Drivers\Etc directory.

hot fixing or sector sparing If bad disk sectors are found during hard disk I/O, the fault-tolerance driver attempts to move the data to a good sector and map out the bad sector. If the mapping by the fault-tolerance driver is successful, then the file system is not informed of the problem. Otherwise the file system's I/O request completes with a known error code and the file system has the option of mapping (sparing) the sector itself.

I

import directory The path to which imported subdirectories, and the files in those subdirectories, will be stored on an import computer.

input/output (I/O) addresses Reserved registers within a special area of memory in an Intel-based computer which is used by the operating system to send instructions to installed hardware like a network adapter or a modem.

instance When a monitored computer has more than one example of the same object type. Performance Monitor displays the multiple examples, or instances, of that object.

Integrated Service Digital Network (ISDN) A type of telephone line used to enhance WAN speeds. This type of connection can transmit at speeds of 64 or 128 kilobits per second, as opposed to standard phone lines, which typically transmit at only 9600 bits per second (bps). This type of phone line must be installed at both the server site and the remote site. Both sites also require a dial-up device that supports this type of connection, such as an ISDN terminal adapter.

Integrated Service Digital Network (ISDN) adapter A device that connects to a digital phone line to enhance connection speeds. Standard ISDN connections can transmit at speeds of 64 or 128 kilobits per second. An ISDN line must be installed by the telephone company at both the server site and the remote site.

intermediary device A security host or switch, such as a modem pool switch that is located between the remote access client and the remote access server. Using Microsoft RAS, clients must authenticate to this device before they are allowed to log on through a RAS server.

internal network number This network number is used to uniquely identify the IPX internal network to the computer for internal routing. You must manually set a unique, nonzero, internal network number on a Windows NT computer. If you run multiple frame types on a single network adapter, bind NWLink to multiple network adapters, or run

an application that uses the NetWare Service Advertising Protocol (SAP), such as SQL Server or SNA Server.

Internet This is the global network of networks. This is the largest single network in the world whose underlying protocol suite is TCP/IP.

interrupt An asynchronous operating system condition which disrupts a processor's normal execution and transfers control to an interrupt handler. This request for service from the processor can be made by both the software and hardware devices. When software issues a request for service, it calls an interrupt service routine (ISR). When hardware issues a request, it signals an interrupt request (IRQ) line.

interrupts/sec This is the number of interrupts the processor is servicing from applications or from hardware devices.

intranet In Windows NT, an intranet is a collection of two or more private networks, or private inter-enterprise TCP/IP networks.

IP address This number uniquely identifies a TCP/IP computer, also called an IP host, to the network. Each computer on the network running TCP/IP must be assigned a unique and valid IP address for its network segment. If a duplicate IP address is assigned to two Windows NT computers, the computer that starts second will not be able to communicate using TCP/IP. Both Windows NT computers will display a "duplicate IP address detected" pop-up error message and log an event to their respective application logs.

IPX/SPX frame type The IPX/SPX protocol supports multiple frame types, 802.2, 802.3, Ethernet II, Ethernet SNAP, and ArcNet. Frame types describe how data is packaged for transport on the network. Two computers must be configured for the same frame type in order to communicate with each other using IPX/SPX. For example, a Windows 95 computer configured for 802.3 is unable to communicate with a Novell NetWare server configured for 802.2. Windows NT Server and Novell NetWare can support multiple frame types. However, supporting multiple frame types isn't recommended since it increases network traffic. To determine the configuration of IPX/SPX, including the frame type being used, run the ipxroute utility.

K

kernel initialize The phase in the Windows NT startup sequence when the operating system starts essential device drivers. The screen is painted blue when this phase begins.

kernel load The phase in the Windows NT startup sequence when the operating system loads essential device drivers. The screen is black when this phase begins.

L

Last Known Good Configuration The most recent control set (system configuration) that correctly started the system and resulted in a successful startup. The control set is saved as the LKG control set in the Registry when you successfully log on to a Windows NT computer.

license logging service The service that support the License Manager for both per-server and per-seat licensing modes.

License Manager An application in Windows NT Server that is used to configure licensing for Windows NT and the applications that are designed to use it.

Line Printer Daemon (LPD) This is the TCP/IP printing service that receives print jobs on the print server.

Line Printer Remote (LPR) This is a port monitor that sends the print job to the TCP/IP printing device. It is installed when the TCP/IP protocol is added to the print server. The LPD and LPR work together to receive and send print jobs to TCP/IP printing device.

LMHOSTS file A local text file that maps computer names to IP addresses of Windows NT networking computers outside the local subnet. In Windows NT, this file is stored in the \<*winnt_root*>\System32\ Drivers\Etc directory.

local group For Windows NT Workstation, a group that can be granted permissions and rights only for its own workstation. This workstation can contain user accounts from its own computer, and, if the workstation participates in a domain, user accounts and global groups both from its own domain and from trusted domains.

For Windows NT Server, a group that can be granted permissions and rights only for the domain controllers of its own domain. However, it can contain user accounts and global groups both from its own domain, and from trusted domains.

local permissions Permissions set on the directories and files residing on an NTFS formatted partition. Rights assigned in this way apply to both users working at the computer itself and, if the directory or a parent directory is shared, to users accessing these files over the network.

local printing devices Printing devices attached to physical ports (LPT*x* or COM*x*).

local profile User configuration settings that are specific to a computer. A user who accesses this type of configuration information on a specific computer can gain access to that information only while logged on that computer.

local security Using NTFS, permissions (local security) can be set on files and directories. These permissions specify which groups and users have access to certain files and directories and what level of access is permitted. NTFS file and directory permissions apply both to users working at the computer where the file is stored and to users accessing the file over the network.

Lockout After The number of incorrect logon attempts that will cause an account to be locked. The range is 1 to 999.

Lockout Duration Select Forever to cause locked accounts to remain locked until an administrator unlocks them. Accounts are unlocked from the User Properties dialog box in User Manager or User Manager for Domains. Select Duration and type a number to cause accounts to remain locked for the specified number of minutes.

LogicalDisk One of two disk objects listed in Performance Monitor. LogicalDisk represents the individual partition on the computer. For example, if your computer supports C:, D:, and E: drives, there will be three instances of the LogicalDisk object, one for each partition. Even if the partition exists on a single physical drive, there will still be three instances of LogicalDisk.

logical port A network connection to a remote print server, *compuername**printername*.

logon script A file that can be assigned to user accounts. Typically a batch program, a logon script runs automatically every time the user logs on. It can be used to configure a user's working environment at every logon, and it allows an administrator to affect a user's environment without managing all aspects of it. A logon script can be assigned to one or more user accounts.

logon validation or authentication The procedure taken by the server to test whether a user name and password combination is acceptable for accessing the system. The Net Logon service is responsible for providing this service to Windows NT Server domain controllers.

log view One of four ways to analyze data provided by Performance Monitor. This view allows you to collect data for analysis in the chart, report, or alert view. You can also analyze data collected through this view in external applications such as Microsoft Excel.

long file name (LFN) This term represents a folder or file name that is longer than the 8.3 format. Windows NT supports LFNs up to 255 characters.

M

mandatory profile A mandatory profile is a preconfigured roaming profile that the user cannot change. Usually, a mandatory profile is assigned to a person or group of people who require both a common interface and a standard configuration.

maximum password age The period of time a password can be used before the system requires the user to change it.

member server A computer that runs Windows NT Server but is not a primary domain controller (PDC) or backup domain controller (BDC) of a Windows NT domain. Member servers do not receive copies of the directory database. Also called a stand-alone server.

Microsoft Challenge Handshake Authentication Protocol (MS-CHAP) This protocol is used to provide encrypted authentication to Windows 9*x* and Windows NT 4.0 RAS clients. It is a variant of CHAP that does not require a plain text version of the password on the authenticating server. Instead, the challenge response is calculated with a hashed version of the password and a challenge from the RAS server

Microsoft Networking Software that runs above the transport protocol and allows a client to log on to another computer running a server service such as the Windows NT Server service or a Windows 9x computer running File and Printer Sharing for Microsoft Networks.

Microsoft RAS protocol A method of negotiating a connection with a RAS server that supports older RAS clients such as Windows NT 3.1, Windows for Workgroups, and RAS 1.1a (used in MS-DOS and Windows 3.1).

Migration Tool for NetWare Included with Windows NT, it enables you to easily transfer user and group accounts, volumes, directories, folders, and files from a NetWare server to a computer running Windows NT Server.

minimum password age The period of time a password must be used before the user is allowed to change it.

minimum password length The fewest characters a password can contain.

mirror set A fully redundant or shadow copy of data. Mirror sets provide an identical twin of a selected disk; all data written to the primary disk is also written to the shadow or mirror disk. Mirror sets provide fault tolerance.

modem Abbreviation for modulator/demodulator. A communications device that enables a computer to transmit information over a standard telephone line.

modem.inf A file that lists all modems supported by Remote Access Services along with the command and response strings each modem needs for correct operation.

multi-homed computer A computer containing more than one NIC connected to two or more network segments or that has been configured with multiple IP addresses for a single network adapter. Multi-homed computers with more than one NIC can be used for routing packets from one network to another.

Multilink (Multilink dialing) A RAS feature which combines multiple physical links into a logical bundle. This aggregate link increases your bandwidth. RAS performs this function over PPP using multiple ISDN, X.25, or modem lines. The feature is available only if multiple WAN adapters are available on the computer.

Multi-Protocol Router (MPR) The MPR is used in Windows NT Server to allow a multi-homed server to route IPX/SPX and TCP/IP packets from one network segment to another.

N

NetBEUI A network protocol usually used in small, department-size local area networks with from 1 to 200 clients. It can use Token Ring source routing as its only method of routing. However, this protocol is not designed for use in routed networks.

NetBIOS name resolution A client unable to communicate with a WINS server will not be able to resolve NetBIOS computer names for clients located on remote network segments. If an LMHOSTS file is in use, they will be able to resolve IP addresses for computer names specified in this file.

NetLogon service Provides users with a single access point to a domain's PDC and all BDCs. Additionally, it synchronizes changes to the directory database stored on the PDC to all domain controllers.

Net Logon share The location on a Windows NT Server that stores user logon files such as logon scripts. This location is created during installation.

Net Share This command is issued at the Windows NT command line. It is used to make a directory or printer available on the network. The same effect can be achieved through the Explorer interface or through Server Manager.

Net Use This command is issued at the Windows NT command line. It is designed to connect a client to a network resource.

Net View This command is issued at the Windows NT command line. It is used to see a listing of all visible shares available on a particular computer.

NetWare Core Protocol (NCP) Rules which define how workstations request services from the server, and how servers interpret and respond to those requests. Requests are typically for file, print, or account manipulation. Protocol used by Novell NetWare Servers to service all incoming requests. This is the native protocol used by NetWare clients and servers.

NetWare Directory Services (NDS) A Novell NetWare service that enables the location of resources on a NetWare network through a unified, single, hierarchical tree structure. This hierarchical structure is made up of components like organizational units and leaf objects. NetWare clients use a single logon to the NDS to access resources on multiple NetWare servers.

network adapter An expansion card or other device used to connect a computer to a local area network (LAN). Synonymous with network card, network adapter card, adapter card, and network interface card (NIC).

network adapter driver Operating system software that provides an interface to send and receive instructions between a specific network adapter and the operating system and installed protocols.

Network Basic Input/Output System (NetBIOS) An application programming interface (API) that can be used by applications on a local area network. This API provides applications with a uniform set of commands for requesting the lower-level services required to conduct sessions between nodes on a network, and to transmit information back and forth.

Network Client Administrator Operating system software that provides an interface to send and receive instructions between a specific network adapter and the operating system and installed protocols.

network interface: bytes sent/sec This is the number of bytes sent using the local network adapter card. If this number is high, but access to the server using this segment is slow, consider segmenting the network or reducing the number or protocols in use on the segment.

network interface printing device A printing device that is directly connected to the network. For example, a Hewlett-Packard network-connected printer.

Network Segment: % Network Utilization This is the percentage of the network bandwidth in use for the local network segment. This can be used to monitor the effect of different network operations on the network, such as user logon validation or domain account synchronization. If network utilization is high, consider segmenting the network, reducing the number of protocols in use, distributing servers so they are connected to the segment they service the most, or consider creating a high-speed network backbone for the servers.

network share A location on a network drive that is accessible from workstations on the network.

No Access right Any user or group given this right will be unable to access the share regardless of any other right to the share that they are given.

Novell NetWare Novell Corporation's network operating system. NetWare is typically used for file and print services and less commonly for application services.

Ntbootdd.sys The device driver used to access devices attached to a SCSI hard disk whose adapter is not using the SCSI controller's BIOS.

Ntdetect.com The file on an x86-based computer that passes information on a computer's hardware configuration to Ntldr.

NT File System (NTFS) A file system designed for use specifically within the Windows NT operating system. It supports file system recovery, extremely large storage media, long filenames, and various features required to support the POSIX subsystem. It also supports object-oriented applications by treating all files as objects with user-defined and system-defined attributes.

NT File System (NTFS) permissions Rules associated with a file or directory object on an NTFS partition that regulates which users can have what type of access to the object.

NT Hardware Qualifier (NTHQ) A utility included on the Windows NT Server CD-ROM that is used to determine the hardware components on your system. To determine the computer's hardware configuration, this utility should be run prior to the installation of Windows NT.

Ntldr The operating system loader on an *x*86-based computer. This file must be located in the root directory of the system partition.

Ntoskrnl.exe The Windows NT operating system kernel.

NWLink Internet Protocol Exchange/Sequenced Packet Exchange (NWLink IPX/SPX) A standard network protocol that supports routing and can support NetWare client/server applications where NetWare-aware, Sockets-based applications communicate with IPX\SPX Sockets-based applications.

O

object ownership In Windows NT, every file and directory on an NTFS partition is assigned an owner account, which controls how permissions are set on the file or directory and who can grant permissions to others.

objects The way in which counters are categorized for monitoring in the Performance Monitor tool.

Osloader The operating system loader on a RISC-based computer. This file performs all of the functions that are provided on an *x*86-based computer by Ntldr, Ntdetect.com, and Bootsect.dos. By default, this file is located in the \Os\Winnt40 directory on the system partition.

P

packet assembler/dissassembler (PAD) A connection used in X.25 networks. An X.25 adapter can be used in place of modems when provided with a compatible COM driver.

Pad.inf This RAS file is used on X.25 networks to automate the logon process to X.25 providers instead of using the manual RAS Terminal screen.

page file A reserved area or areas on fixed disks that the virtual memory manager uses to swap program code to and from physical memory.

pages/sec This is the number of requested pages that are not immediately available in RAM, and thus must be accessed from disk, or be written to disk to make room in RAM for other pages. If the Pages/sec value exceeds 5 for extended periods, the system bottleneck may be memory.

partition Also known as a volume, a partition is a portion of a physical disk that appears and functions as though it were a physically separate unit.

pass-through authentication When the user account must be authenticated, but the computer being used for the logon is not a domain controller in the domain where the user account is defined, nor is it the computer where the user account is defined, the local computer passes the logon information to a domain controller (directly or indirectly) where the user account is defined. The NetLogon service is responsible for providing this service to Windows NT Server domain controllers.

Password Authentication Protocol (PAP) A type of authentication that uses clear-text passwords. The least sophisticated authentication protocol.

password uniqueness The number of new passwords that must be used by a user account before an old password can be reused.

percent (%) Disk Time This indicates the amount of time a disk drive is busy servicing read and write requests. If this value is consistently between 90 and 100 percent, the disk is over-utilized. Monitoring individual processes will help determine which process or processes are making the majority of disk requests.

percent (%) Privileged Time This measures the time the processor spends performing operating system services. A high value here indicates that the processor is busy with critical operating system tasks.

percent (%) Processor Time This measures the amount of time the processor is busy. Analyze processor utilization to determine what is causing the processor activity. This is accomplished by monitoring individual processes. If the system has multiple processors, then monitor the System: % Total Processor Time counter.

percent (%) User Time This measures the time the processor spends performing user services, such as running a word processor. Because threads running in privileged processor time are a higher priority than threads running in user time, the % User Time number is influenced by the % Privileged Time.

Performance Monitor A Windows NT administrative tool that allows you to monitor, analyze, and optimize a Windows NT computer.

per-seat licensing Clients are licensed to connect to all servers and applications in the network that are configured for this type of licensing.

per-server licensing The server is licensed to allow a specific number of maximum client connections, also called concurrent server connection licensing. This is ideal for single-server networks.

PhyscialDisk One of two objects in Performance Monitor. The PhysicalDisk object lists each instance of fixed or removable drives in the computer. For example, if your computer contains two fixed disk drives, there will be two instances of the PhysicalDisk object. In a RAID implementation, the PhysicalDisk object will provide you with details on each fixed disk, even if the RAID implementation spans multiple physical disks.

physical port Hardware connection to a printing device; for example, a parallel or serial port.

Point-to-Point Protocol (PPP) A set of industry-standard framing and authentication protocols, which as part of the Windows NT RAS Server works to ensure interoperability with third-party remote access software. This protocol negotiates configuration parameters for multiple layers of the OSI model.

Point-to-Point Tunneling Protocol (PPTP) This protocol is a new networking technology that supports multiprotocol virtual private networks (VPNs), enabling remote users to access corporate networks securely across the Internet by dialing into an Internet service provider (ISP) or by connecting directly to the Internet.

Point-to-Point Tunneling Protocol (PPTP) filtering Provides a form of security for a private network by configuring an adapter on the computer to block all packets except PPTP packets.

policy file Registry settings maintained in a file that together define the computer resources available to a group of users or an individual. Windows NT and Windows 9x support policy files that are created specifically for their operating system.

Pool Nonpaged Bytes This is the amount of RAM held in the nonpaged pool system. This memory space is allocated to operating system components as they accomplish their tasks. If the Pool Nonpaged Bytes value steadily increases without a corresponding increase in activity on the server, this may indicate that a running process has a memory leak, and should be monitored closely.

Portable Operating System Interface (POSIX) Institute of Electrical and Electronics Engineers (IEEE) standard that defines a set of operating system services. Programs that adhere to the POSIX standard can be easily ported from one system to another.

Ports applet The Control Panel application used to add, remove, and configure serial port drivers.

Power On Self Test (POST) When you start a computer, it runs through the POST routine, which determines the amount of physical memory present, and whether the needed hardware components (such as the keyboard) are present.

Once the computer has run through this routine, each adapter card with a BIOS runs its own hardware test. The computer and adapter card manufacturers determine what appears on the screen during these procedures.

PPP logging The process creating a point-to-point protocol (PPP) log file (PPP.LOG) to help diagnose connectivity problems between a PPP server and a PPP client when one of the computers is a Windows NT Remote Access Service client. PPP logging must be enabled through the Registry, and the log file is stored in the systemroot\SYSTEM32\RAS directory.

preferred server A term defined by Novell that describes a NetWare server that is used by a requester to log on to the NetWare network.

print device The hardware device that produces printer output.

printer Software interface between the application and the printing device.

printer pool Multiple printing devices pointing to a single printer.

printer router (WINSPOOL.DRV) Locates the requested printer, copies printer drivers to local computers and passes print jobs from local to remote spoolers.

printer share A representation of a printing resource on a Microsoft network. Users can connect to this resource and send print jobs to it.

print monitor Closest software component to the physical port on a printer. It controls printer data streams to the printing device. It provides error messages and end-of-job notification and monitors the printer device status.

print queue A NetWare directory that holds print jobs before they are sent to the print device on a Novell NetWare network.

print spooler Tracks where print jobs should be sent and which ports are connected to which print device. Routes print jobs to the correct ports and printer pools, and controls priority assignments for print jobs.

process When a program runs, a Windows NT process is created. A process is an object type which consists of an executable program, a set of virtual memory addresses, and one or more threads.

profile A directory structure and portions of the Registry that provide configuration information to a user when logging on a computer or network.

protocol suite This suite is a set of rules and conventions for sending information over a network. These rules govern the content, format, timing, sequencing, and error control of messages exchanged among network devices.

public switched telephone network (PSTN) This is the communications medium typically used by telephones and modems for remote communication.

R

RAID *See* redundant array of inexpensive disks.

RAID 0 (striping) This is a non-fault-tolerant configuration of disks where two or more disk drives contain data that is logically represented as a single partition. Windows NT supports up to 32 disk drives in a stripe set of disks.

RAID 1 (mirror sets) A fully redundant or shadow copy of data, mirror sets provide an identical twin for a selected disk; all data written to the primary disk is also written to the shadow or mirror disk.

RAID 5 (stripe sets with parity) This term represents a method of data protection in which data is striped in large blocks across all of the disks in an array. Data redundancy is provided by the parity information contained in all disks in the stripe set. Windows NT Server supports stripe sets with parity configured on a minimum of 3 disks and a maximum of 32 disks in the set.

RAID 10 This term represents a method of data protection in which data is mirrored and striped across multiple disks. Striping (RAID 0) increases disk I/O performance while mirroring (RAID 1) provides fault tolerance for this configuration. *See* RAID 0 and RAID 1.

Read right This right allows a user to read and copy the contents of a directory and its subdirectories, run programs, and view the attributes of files.

redirector A network software component that allows a client to locate, open, read, write, and delete files and submit print jobs to the network. It also makes available application services such as named pipes and mailslots.

Reduced Instruction Set Computing (RISC) processor The RISC CPU is used in Alpha, MIPS, and PPC computers.

redundant array of inexpensive disks (RAID) A method used to standardize and categorize fault-tolerant disk systems. Six levels gauge various mixes of performance, reliability, and cost. Windows NT includes three of the RAID levels: Level 0, Level 1, and Level 5.

Registry The Registry is a database where Windows NT internal configuration information and machine and user-specific settings are stored.

Remote Access Service (RAS) Software that provides the ability to establish a remote node connection with a Microsoft Windows network. Users running the dial-out portion of this software can remotely access networks for services such as file and printer sharing, electronic mail, scheduling, and SQL database access

Remote Access Service Administrator (RAS Admin) A utility that allows for the administration of the remote access service running on a Windows NT Server.

Remoteboot service (RPL) The Remoteboot service allows a workstation to connect to a server using software on the server's hard disk instead of the workstation's hard disk. The workstation's network adapter card must have a Remote Program Load (RPL) ROM chip installed.

Remoteboot Service Manager Allows for the configuration of the Remoteboot service running on a Windows NT Server.

remote node A connection to a remote access server that functions similarly to a connection made over a local area network. RAS uses this connection method to provide remote services to clients.

remote printing device A printing device that is accessed over the network.

remote server administration The process of managing a Windows NT Server from a remote location, usually a Windows 9*x* or Windows NT Workstation client.

remote UPS shutdown If power is not restored before the battery reaches a critical low power state, a DTR voltage signal is sent to the UPS Service so that it can initiate an orderly server shutdown.

REPL$ An administrative share created by a Windows NT Server when the directory Replicator service is started. By default, this share points to the *winnt_root*\SYSTEM32\REPL\EXPORT directory.

report view One of four ways to analyze data provided by Performance Monitor. This view allows you to analyze data of current activity or logged data through a text-only display.

Reset Count After The maximum number of minutes that can occur between any two bad logon attempts. For example, if Lockout After is set to 10 bad logon attempts, and Reset Count After is set to 30 minutes, then 10 bad logon attempts, each 29 minutes apart, will cause account lockout.. If an incorrect password is attempted every 31 minutes, the Reset Count After value of 30 minutes would reset the bad logons attempts to 0 and the account would never lock.

RFC1542 A specification for relaying DHCP (modified BOOTP) requests from one network to another.

roaming profile A user's configuration information that is made network accessible when an administrator enters a user profile path into a user's account through User Manager for Domains. The first time the user logs off, the user's local configuration information is copied to the user profile path. Thereafter, the server copy of the user's configuration is downloaded each time the user logs on (if it is more current than the local copy) and is updated each time the user logs off. Note that a profile is only valid on the platform for which it was created. For example, a Windows NT 4.0 profile cannot be used on a Windows 95 computer.

router In the Windows NT environment, a router helps LANs and WANs achieve interoperability and connectivity and can link LANs with different network topologies (such as Ethernet and Token Ring). Routers match packet headers to a LAN segment and choose the best path for the packet, optimizing network performance.

routing This is the process of forwarding packets to other routers until the packet is eventually delivered to a router connected to the specified destination. *See* packet router.

Routing Information Protocol (RIP) RIP enables a router to dynamically exchange routing information with a neighboring router. Windows NT supports Reduced Instruction Set Computing. The RISC CPU is used in Alpha, MIPS both RIP over IPX/SPX and TCP/IP.

RSA MD5 A hashing algorithm developed by RSA Data Security, Inc. This algorithm generates a 128-bit hash value which is used in RAS for encrypted authentication.

RSA RC4 A data encryption method developed by RSA Data Security, Inc. This encryption technology can be used to encrypt data transmitted over a RAS connection.

S

SCSI A standard high-speed parallel interface defined by the American National Standards Institute (ANSI). A SCSI interface is used for connecting microcomputers to peripheral devices such as hard disks, CD-ROMs, and tape drives, and to other computers and local area networks.

Security Accounts Manager (SAM) database A collection of security information, such as user account names and passwords, and the security policy settings. For Windows NT Workstation, this information is managed through User Manager. For a Windows NT Server domain, it is managed through User Manager for Domains. Other Windows NT documents may refer to the SAM database as the "directory database."

security ID (SID) A unique name that identifies a logged-on user to the security system. SIDs also identify computers and domains to the Windows NT network.

Serial Line Internet Protocol (SLIP) An older industry standard that is part of Windows NT RAS client software used to ensure interoperability with third-party remote access servers.

server: bytes total/sec This is the number of bytes the Server service has sent and received over the network. It indicates how busy the server is for transmission and reception of data. A poorly performing network adapter is indicated by a low number and a long user wait time for service requests. These values could also suggest an over-utilized processor in the server, congestion from other network devices, or slow disk I/O in the server. To identify the actual bottleneck, monitor all primary objects in Performance Monitor

server: logon total This is the number of logon attempts for local authentication, over-the-network authentication, and service account authentication since the computer was last started. This counter is helpful on a domain controller for determining the amount of logon validation occurring over a designated period.

server work queues: queue length This is the number of requests in the queue for the selected processor. A consistent queue of over two indicates processor congestion.

Server Message Block (SMB) Protocol used by many servers, including Windows NT and LanManager servers to service all incoming requests. Used by Microsoft clients and servers, this set of rules defines how workstations request services from the server and how servers interpret and respond to those requests. Requests are typically for file, print, or account manipulation.

Service Advertising Protocol (SAP) In a Windows environment SAP is a service that broadcasts shared files, directories, and printers categorized first by domain or workgroup and then by server name.

In the context of routing and IPX, SAP is also used by servers to advertise their services and addresses on a network. Clients use SAP to determine what network resources are available.

In NetBEUI, SAP is an acronym for Service Access Point, in which each link-layer program identifies itself by registering a unique service access point.

Session Manager A Windows NT software component that is involved in the Windows NT startup process. It loads services, drivers and Windows NT subsystems during the startup process.

setup switches Text that follows a forward slash (/) while running the Windows NT installation command (winnt or winnt32). The text instructs the Windows NT installation program to perform specific functions such as automating the installation process.

share level permissions Used to restrict a shared resource's availability over the network to only certain users or groups.

share rights Used to restrict a shared resource's availability over the network to certain users.

shares In Windows NT, this refers to directories, printers, or named pipes made available to network users through the Server and Browser services.

Shiva Password Authentication Protocol (SPAP) A two-way (reversible) encryption mechanism employed by Shiva. Windows 9x and Windows NT RAS clients, when connecting to a Shiva LAN Rover, use SPAP, as does a Shiva client connecting to a Windows NT RAS Server.

software level RAID The Windows NT implementation of disk fault tolerance. This feature is enabled through the Windows NT Disk Administrator utility. *See also* RAID 1 and RAID 5.

source directory The directory containing the Windows NT distribution files. This directory is used to complete an over-the-network installation of Windows NT.

spooler Software that accepts documents sent by a user to be printed, and then stores those documents and sends them, one by one, to available printer(s).

startup process When a computer containing Windows NT is powered on, the computer and various Windows NT software components initiate a routine which loads Windows NT.

STOP message A character-mode message that occurs when the kernel detects an inconsistent condition from which it cannot recover. STOP messages are uniquely identified by a hexadecimal number and a symbolic string.

stripe set Refers to the process of saving data across identical partitions on different drives. A stripe set does not provide fault tolerance.

subnet mask The subnet mask resolves what portion of an IP address defines the network ID and what portion of the address defines the host ID. All computers on a network segment must use the same subnet mask. A computer using a different subnet mask will not be able to communicate with other hosts on the network. Consider a computer configured with IP address of 127.80.30.1 and a class C subnet mask of 255.255.255.0. This means that the network ID is 127.80.30.0 while the host ID is 1. Another host on the same network with an IP address of 127.80.30.2 and a class B subnet mask of 255.255.0.0 will not be able to communicate with the other host because its network ID is 127.80.0.0 and its host id is 30.0.

supervisor An account on a NetWare server used to administer a Novell network. This account is similar to the Windows NT Server administrator account.

System Network Architecture (SNA) A communications framework developed by IBM. Microsoft SNA is an optional solution that provides a gateway connection between personal computer LANs or WANs and IBM mainframe and AS/400 hosts.

system policy A collection of Registry settings that together define the computer resources available to a user. System policies are created with the System Policy Editor. System policies allow an administrator to control user work environments and actions, and to enforce system configurations.

System Policy Editor The utility used to create system policies. When this tool is run on a Windows NT computer, a system policy is created for Windows NT clients. When this tool is run on a Windows 95 computer, a system policy is created for Windows 95 clients. On a Windows NT computer, this tool is accessed from the Administrative Tools (Common) group.

system: processor queue length This is the number of requests the processor has in its queue. It indicates the number of threads that are ready to be executed and are waiting for processor time. Generally, a processor queue length that is consistently higher than two indicates congestion. Further analysis of the individual processes making requests on the processor is required to determine what is causing the congestion.

T

Tape Devices applet The Control Panel application used to add, remove, and configure tape device drivers.

thread Objects within processes that run program instructions. They allow concurrent operations within a process and enable one process to run different parts of its program on different processors simultaneously.

Transmission Control Protocol/Internet Protocol (TCP/IP) TCP/IP is a set of networking protocols that provides communications across interconnected networks made up of computers with diverse hardware architectures and various operating systems. TCP/IP includes standards for how computers communicate and conventions for connecting networks and routing traffic.

trusted domain A relationship formed between two domains. The trusted domain can access resources in the trusting domain.

trustee assignments Rights to directories and files on a Novell NetWare server. These rights to directories and files are similar to Windows NT Server local permissions.

trust relationship A link between domains that enables pass-through authentication where a trusting domain honors the logon authentications of a trusted domain. With this link, a user with only one user account in one domain can potentially access the entire network. User accounts and global groups defined in a trusted domain can be given rights and resource permissions in a trusting domain, even though those accounts do not exist in the trusting domain's directory database.

U

uninterruptible power supply (UPS) A battery-operated power supply connected to a computer to maintain system power during an alternating current power failure. Some UPS systems provide an orderly, automated shutdown procedure if alternating current does not return before battery power is depleted.

uninterruptible power supply (UPS) low battery signal at least two minutes from shutdown If the UPS can detect when it is running low on battery power, it will send a DCD Low battery voltage signal to the UPS Service. If the UPS does not support DCD, then the UPS Characteristics box should be used to specify the estimated length of time before a low battery condition has been reached.

uninterruptible power supply (UPS) power failure When AC power is lost and the UPS is providing AC through the battery the UPS sends a CTS voltage signal to the UPS Service indicating a power failure.

Uninterruptible Power Supply (UPS) Service The software component in Windows NT that interacts with a battery and provides an orderly system shutdown when necessary.

Uniqueness Database File (UDF) The UDF specifies workstation-specific settings that further automate an installation of Windows NT.

UPS applet The Control Panel application used to configure the UPS Service.

User Manager A Windows NT Workstation tool used to manage security for a workstation. This tool administers user accounts, groups, and security policies.

User Manager for Domains A Windows NT Server tool used to manage security for a domain or an individual computer. This tool administers user accounts, groups, and security policies.

user profile Configuration information that can be retained on a user-by-user basis, and is saved in a file for each user or multiple users. This information includes all of the per-user settings in the Windows NT environment, such as the desktop arrangement, personal start menu options, screen colors, screen savers, network connections, printer connections, mouse settings, window size and position. When a user logs on, the user's profile is loaded and the user's Windows NT environment is configured according to that profile.

user rights Defines a user's access to a computer or domain, and the actions that a user can perform on the computer or domain. User rights permit actions, such as computer or network logon, or permit administrative tasks, such as adding and deleting users in a workstation or domain.

V

VGA mode A Windows NT troubleshooting feature which allows you to load a standard VGA compatible driver running at 640-x-480 resolution and 16 colors. This function is implemented in the boot.ini file using the /basevideo switch.

views The ways in which data is presented in Performance Monitor. Data is represented as a chart, report, log, and alert in Performance Monitor.

virtual memory A symbolic representation of memory that Windows NT displays to running processes. The virtual memory manager (VMM) manages virtual memory through page tables, page files on disk, and pages in RAM.

Virtual Private Network (VPN) In the context of RAS, it is a remote LAN accessed through the Internet by using the new Point-to-Point Tunneling Protocol.

volume set A combination of partitions on a physical disk that appear as one logical drive.

W

wide area network (WAN) A communications network that connects geographically separated areas.

Win32 subsystem A software component in the Windows NT operating system that has exclusive responsibility for producing graphical output and collecting user input. Win32 manages all of the windows on the screen.

Windows Internet Naming Server (WINS) A name resolution service that resolves queries of NetBIOS computer names to IP addresses in a routed environment. It also handles NetBIOS name registrations, and releases.

Windows Internet Naming Server (WINS) Administrator Allows for the management of the Windows Internet Naming Service running on Windows NT Server.

Windows NT Backup A fault-tolerance utility used to back up files from a Windows NT computer to a tape drive and to restore files from a tape drive to a Windows NT computer.

Windows NT directory services A Windows NT protected subsystem that maintains the directory database and provides an application programming interface (API) for accessing the database.

Windows NT domain A collection of computers, defined by the administrator of a Windows NT Server network, that share a common directory database. A domain provides access to the centralized user accounts and group accounts maintained within the domain. Each domain has a unique name.

Windows NT domain controller Refers to the computer running Windows NT Server that manages all aspects of user-domain interactions, and uses information in the directory database to authenticate users logging on to domain accounts. One shared directory database is used to store security and user account information for the entire domain. A domain contains one primary domain controller (PDC) and one or more backup domain controllers (BDCs).

Windows NT fault-tolerance boot disk A diskette used to start the Windows NT operating system when the system partition on a Windows NT computer is not available or is damaged.

Windows NT Hardware Detection Tool (NTHQ) A utility on the Windows NT used to identify hardware installed in your computer.

Windows NT Server BDC A computer running Windows NT Server that receives a copy of the domain's directory database, which contains all account and security policy information for the domain. The copy is synchronized periodically and automatically with the master copy on the primary domain controller (PDC). BDCs also authenticate user logons and can be promoted to function as PDCs as needed. Multiple BDCs can exist on a domain.

Windows NT Server member server A computer that runs Windows NT Server but is not a primary domain controller (PDC) or backup domain controller (BDC) of a Windows NT domain. Member servers do not receive copies of the directory database. Also called a stand-alone server.

Windows NT Server PDC The computer running Windows NT Server that authenticates domain logons and maintains the directory database for a domain. The PDC tracks changes made to accounts of all computers on a domain. It is the only computer to receive these changes directly. A domain has only one PDC.

Windows NT workgroup A collection of computers that are grouped for viewing purposes. Each workgroup is identified by a unique name.

Windows Sockets A Microsoft Windows implementation of the widely used UC Berkeley sockets API. Microsoft TCP/IP, NWLink, and AppleTalk protocols can use this interface. This software provides the interface between programs and the transport protocol and works as a bidirectional pipe for incoming and outgoing data.

Winnt.exe The 16-bit Windows NT installation program used for installing or upgrading to Windows NT on computers running MS-DOS, Windows 3.*x*, WFW or Windows 95.

Winnt32.exe The 32-bit Windows NT installation program used for installing or upgrading Windows NT on computers running Windows NT.

workspace A method of saving all views of data in Performance Monitor. Data saved in this way is given an *.PMW extension.

Workstation service Provides network connections and communications. *See* redirector.

X

X.25 A recommendation published by the International Telecommunications Union (ITU), a communications standards organization that defines the connection between a terminal and a packet-switching network. This is a type of packet-switching network that routes units of information (packets) and is used in public data communications networks.

X.25 PAD A hardware device that provides a connection to an X.25 network. X.25 is a type of switching network that routes packets as specified by X.25 and is used in public data communications networks.

Index

MICROSOFT LICENSE AGREEMENT

(Book Companion CD)

IMPORTANT—READ CAREFULLY: This Microsoft End-User License Agreement ("EULA") is a legal agreement between you (either an individual or an entity) and Microsoft Corporation for the Microsoft product identified above, which includes computer software and may include associated media, printed materials, and "on-line" or electronic documentation ("SOFTWARE PRODUCT"). Any component included within the SOFTWARE PRODUCT that is accompanied by a separate End-User License Agreement shall be governed by such agreement and not the terms set forth below. By installing, copying, or otherwise using the SOFTWARE PRODUCT, you agree to be bound by the terms of this EULA. If you do not agree to the terms of this EULA, you are not authorized to install, copy, or otherwise use the SOFTWARE PRODUCT; you may, however, return the SOFTWARE PRODUCT, along with all printed materials and other items that form a part of the Microsoft product that includes the SOFTWARE PRODUCT, to the place you obtained them for a full refund.

SOFTWARE PRODUCT LICENSE

The SOFTWARE PRODUCT is protected by United States copyright laws and international copyright treaties, as well as other intellectual property laws and treaties. The SOFTWARE PRODUCT is licensed, not sold.

1. GRANT OF LICENSE. This EULA grants you the following rights:

   a. Software Product. You may install and use one copy of the SOFTWARE PRODUCT on a single computer. The primary user of the computer on which the SOFTWARE PRODUCT is installed may make a second copy for his or her exclusive use on a portable computer.

   b. Storage/Network Use. You may also store or install a copy of the SOFTWARE PRODUCT on a storage device, such as a network server, used only to install or run the SOFTWARE PRODUCT on your other computers over an internal network; however, you must acquire and dedicate a license for each separate computer on which the SOFTWARE PRODUCT is installed or run from the storage device. A license for the SOFTWARE PRODUCT may not be shared or used concurrently on different computers.

   c. License Pak. If you have acquired this EULA in a Microsoft License Pak, you may make the number of additional copies of the computer software portion of the SOFTWARE PRODUCT authorized on the printed copy of this EULA, and you may use each copy in the manner specified above. You are also entitled to make a corresponding number of secondary copies for portable computer use as specified above.

   d. Sample Code. Solely with respect to portions, if any, of the SOFTWARE PRODUCT that are identified within the SOFTWARE PRODUCT as sample code (the "SAMPLE CODE"):

      i. Use and Modification. Microsoft grants you the right to use and modify the source code version of the SAMPLE CODE, *provided* you comply with subsection (d)(iii) below. You may not distribute the SAMPLE CODE, or any modified version of the SAMPLE CODE, in source code form.

      ii. Redistributable Files. Provided you comply with subsection (d)(iii) below, Microsoft grants you a nonexclusive, royalty-free right to reproduce and distribute the object code version of the SAMPLE CODE and of any modified SAMPLE CODE, other than SAMPLE CODE (or any modified version thereof) designated as not redistributable in the Readme file that forms a part of the SOFTWARE PRODUCT (the "Non-Redistributable Sample Code"). All SAMPLE CODE other than the Non-Redistributable Sample Code is collectively referred to as the "REDISTRIBUTABLES."

      iii. Redistribution Requirements. If you redistribute the REDISTRIBUTABLES, you agree to: (i) distribute the REDISTRIBUTABLES in object code form only in conjunction with and as a part of your software application product; (ii) not use Microsoft's name, logo, or trademarks to market your software application product; (iii) include a valid copyright notice on your software application product; (iv) indemnify, hold harmless, and defend Microsoft from and against any claims or lawsuits, including attorney's fees, that arise or result from the use or distribution of your software application product; and (v) not permit further distribution of the REDISTRIBUTABLES by your end user. Contact Microsoft for the applicable royalties due and other licensing terms for all other uses and/or distribution of the REDISTRIBUTABLES.

2. DESCRIPTION OF OTHER RIGHTS AND LIMITATIONS.

- **Limitations on Reverse Engineering, Decompilation, and Disassembly.** You may not reverse engineer, decompile, or disassemble the SOFTWARE PRODUCT, except and only to the extent that such activity is expressly permitted by applicable law notwithstanding this limitation.

- **Separation of Components.** The SOFTWARE PRODUCT is licensed as a single product. Its component parts may not be separated for use on more than one computer.

- **Rental.** You may not rent, lease, or lend the SOFTWARE PRODUCT.

- **Support Services.** Microsoft may, but is not obligated to, provide you with support services related to the SOFTWARE PRODUCT ("Support Services"). Use of Support Services is governed by the Microsoft policies and programs described in the user manual, in "on-line" documentation, and/or in other Microsoft-provided materials. Any supplemental software code provided to you as part of the

Support Services shall be considered part of the SOFTWARE PRODUCT and subject to the terms and conditions of this EULA. With respect to technical information you provide to Microsoft as part of the Support Services, Microsoft may use such information for its business purposes, including for product support and development. Microsoft will not utilize such technical information in a form that personally identifies you.

- **Software Transfer.** You may permanently transfer all of your rights under this EULA, provided you retain no copies, you transfer all of the SOFTWARE PRODUCT (including all component parts, the media and printed materials, any upgrades, this EULA, and, if applicable, the Certificate of Authenticity), **and** the recipient agrees to the terms of this EULA.

- **Termination.** Without prejudice to any other rights, Microsoft may terminate this EULA if you fail to comply with the terms and conditions of this EULA. In such event, you must destroy all copies of the SOFTWARE PRODUCT and all of its component parts.

3. **COPYRIGHT.** All title and copyrights in and to the SOFTWARE PRODUCT (including but not limited to any images, photographs, animations, video, audio, music, text, SAMPLE CODE, REDISTRIBUTABLES, and "applets" incorporated into the SOFTWARE PRODUCT) and any copies of the SOFTWARE PRODUCT are owned by Microsoft or its suppliers. The SOFTWARE PRODUCT is protected by copyright laws and international treaty provisions. Therefore, you must treat the SOFTWARE PRODUCT like any other copyrighted material **except** that you may install the SOFTWARE PRODUCT on a single computer provided you keep the original solely for backup or archival purposes. You may not copy the printed materials accompanying the SOFTWARE PRODUCT.

4. **U.S. GOVERNMENT RESTRICTED RIGHTS.** The SOFTWARE PRODUCT and documentation are provided with RESTRICTED RIGHTS. Use, duplication, or disclosure by the Government is subject to restrictions as set forth in subparagraph (c)(1)(ii) of the Rights in Technical Data and Computer Software clause at DFARS 252.227-7013 or subparagraphs (c)(1) and (2) of the Commercial Computer Software—Restricted Rights at 48 CFR 52.227-19, as applicable. Manufacturer is Microsoft Corporation/One Microsoft Way/Redmond, WA 98052-6399.

5. **EXPORT RESTRICTIONS.** You agree that you will not export or re-export the SOFTWARE PRODUCT, any part thereof, or any process or service that is the direct product of the SOFTWARE PRODUCT (the foregoing collectively referred to as the "Restricted Components"), to any country, person, entity, or end user subject to U.S. export restrictions. You specifically agree not to export or re-export any of the Restricted Components (i) to any country to which the U.S. has embargoed or restricted the export of goods or services, which currently include, but are not necessarily limited to, Cuba, Iran, Iraq, Libya, North Korea, Sudan, and Syria, or to any national of any such country, wherever located, who intends to transmit or transport the Restricted Components back to such country; (ii) to any end user who you know or have reason to know will utilize the Restricted Components in the design, development, or production of nuclear, chemical, or biological weapons; or (iii) to any end user who has been prohibited from participating in U.S. export transactions by any federal agency of the U.S. government. You warrant and represent that neither the BXA nor any other U.S. federal agency has suspended, revoked, or denied your export privileges.

DISCLAIMER OF WARRANTY

NO WARRANTIES OR CONDITIONS. MICROSOFT EXPRESSLY DISCLAIMS ANY WARRANTY OR CONDITION FOR THE SOFTWARE PRODUCT. THE SOFTWARE PRODUCT AND ANY RELATED DOCUMENTATION IS PROVIDED "AS IS" WITHOUT WARRANTY OR CONDITION OF ANY KIND, EITHER EXPRESS OR IMPLIED, INCLUDING, WITHOUT LIMITATION, THE IMPLIED WARRANTIES OF MERCHANTABILITY, FITNESS FOR A PARTICULAR PURPOSE, OR NONINFRINGEMENT. THE ENTIRE RISK ARISING OUT OF USE OR PERFORMANCE OF THE SOFTWARE PRODUCT REMAINS WITH YOU.

LIMITATION OF LIABILITY. TO THE MAXIMUM EXTENT PERMITTED BY APPLICABLE LAW, IN NO EVENT SHALL MICROSOFT OR ITS SUPPLIERS BE LIABLE FOR ANY SPECIAL, INCIDENTAL, INDIRECT, OR CONSEQUEN-TIAL DAMAGES WHATSOEVER (INCLUDING, WITHOUT LIMITATION, DAMAGES FOR LOSS OF BUSINESS PROFITS, BUSINESS INTERRUPTION, LOSS OF BUSINESS INFORMATION, OR ANY OTHER PECUNIARY LOSS) ARISING OUT OF THE USE OF OR INABILITY TO USE THE SOFTWARE PRODUCT OR THE PROVISION OF OR FAILURE TO PROVIDE SUPPORT SERVICES, EVEN IF MICROSOFT HAS BEEN ADVISED OF THE POSSIBILITY OF SUCH DAMAGES. IN ANY CASE, MICROSOFT'S ENTIRE LIABILITY UNDER ANY PROVISION OF THIS EULA SHALL BE LIMITED TO THE GREATER OF THE AMOUNT ACTUALLY PAID BY YOU FOR THE SOFTWARE PRODUCT OR US$5.00; PROVIDED, HOWEVER, IF YOU HAVE ENTERED INTO A MICROSOFT SUPPORT SERVICES AGREEMENT, MICROSOFT'S ENTIRE LIABILITY REGARDING SUPPORT SERVICES SHALL BE GOVERNED BY THE TERMS OF THAT AGREEMENT. BECAUSE SOME STATES AND JURISDICTIONS DO NOT ALLOW THE EXCLUSION OR LIMITA-TION OF LIABILITY, THE ABOVE LIMITATION MAY NOT APPLY TO YOU.

MISCELLANEOUS

This EULA is governed by the laws of the State of Washington USA, except and only to the extent that applicable law mandates governing law of a different jurisdiction.

Should you have any questions concerning this EULA, or if you desire to contact Microsoft for any reason, please contact the Microsoft subsidiary serving your country, or write: Microsoft Sales Information Center/One Microsoft Way/Redmond, WA 98052-6399.

Register Today!

Return this
MCSE Readiness Review—Exam 70-067:
Microsoft® Windows NT® Server 4.0
registration card today

Microsoft® Press
mspress.microsoft.com

0-7356-0538-6

MCSE READINESS REVIEW—EXAM 70-067: MICROSOFT® WINDOWS NT® SERVER 4.0

FIRST NAME   MIDDLE INITIAL   LAST NAME

INSTITUTION OR COMPANY NAME

ADDRESS

CITY   STATE   ZIP

(   )

E-MAIL ADDRESS   PHONE NUMBER

U.S. and Canada addresses only. Fill in information above and mail postage-free.
Please mail only the bottom half of this page.

*For information about Microsoft Press®
products, visit our Web site at*
mspress.microsoft.com

Microsoft®*Press*